THE GERMAN LANGUAGE IN AMERICA

THE GERMAN LANGUAGE
IN AMERICA ❧ *A Symposium*

Edited with an Introduction by

GLENN G. GILBERT

Published for the Department of Germanic Languages
of The University of Texas at Austin by the
University of Texas Press, Austin and London

66616

International Standard Book Number 0–292–70149–7
Library of Congress Catalog Card Number 72–165919
© 1971 by the University of Texas Press

Printed by The University of Texas Printing Division, Austin
Bound by Universal Bookbindery, Inc., San Antonio

"The language of the German elements in the United States, the largest non-English group in colonial as well as in more recent times, has received surprisingly little attention from competent scholars. In the Middle West, in the Far West, and in Texas, investigators will find practically virgin soil. . . . However, the history of these German settlements [is] already well known, so that well-directed sampling operations preparatory to more systematic researches can be undertaken by any scholar trained in field work. It is to be hoped that some of the numerous Germanists in colleges and universities will recognize this unsurpassed opportunity to make a contribution to our understanding of the linguistic and the general cultural history of these German communities that constitute such an important part of the American people."

From the preface to the Conference on Non-English Speech in the United States (1942: 586), signed by Hans Kurath, Einar Haugen, Hayward Keniston, Taylor Starck, and Walther von Wartburg

CONTENTS

Introduction ix
GLENN G. GILBERT

1. The Dialectology of American Colonial German . . . 3
CARROLL E. REED

2. The Word Geography of Pennsylvania German:
Extent and Causes 14
LESTER W. J. SEIFERT

3. German in Wisconsin 43
JÜRGEN EICHHOFF

4. German in Virginia and West Virginia 58
WILLIAM J. PULTE, JR.

5. Pennsylvania German Folklore Research:
A Historical Analysis 70
DON YODER

6. German as an Immigrant, Indigenous, Foreign, and
Second Language in the United States 106
HEINZ KLOSS

7. A Unified Proposal for the Study of the German Language
in the United States: Discussion 128
PROPOSAL PRESENTED BY GLENN G. GILBERT
CHAIRMAN OF THE DISCUSSION: CARROLL E. REED

8. German Folklore in America: Discussion 148
CHAIRMAN OF THE DISCUSSION: DON YODER

9. German Pedagogy and the Survival of German in
   America: Discussion   164
   CHAIRMAN OF THE DISCUSSION: HEINZ KLOSS

References   179

Index   199

MAPS

1. Pennsylvania German Language Area   .   .   .   facing p. 18
2. Percentage of Persons in Wisconsin Who Were
   Born in Germany or Whose Parents Were
   Born in Germany, 1910   44
3. Distribution of Germans in Wisconsin, 1890   .   .   .   48

INTRODUCTION

This book presents the texts of the papers and discussions of the Tenth Germanic Languages Symposium held at The University of Texas at Austin on November 18–20, 1968. The essays by Carroll E. Reed and Lester W. J. Seifert are reproduced here in the form of their first presentation at the symposium; those of Jürgen Eichhoff, Don Yoder, and Heinz Kloss have been substantially revised and enlarged. The essay by William Pulte, Jr., has been added to those of the original contributors because of its timeliness and theoretical interest. We feel fortunate in being able to include it here.

The authors discuss a variety of topics, ranging from general bibliographical and areal studies (Reed, Eichhoff), and a more specialized, geographical-linguistic project (Seifert), to problems of phonological change (Pulte), the sociolinguistic role of German in American society (Kloss), and the history and bibliography of research on Pennsylvania German folklore (Yoder).

In addition to the papers read at the symposium, there were three formal discussions where the ideas brought out in the papers were further developed and offered for discussion by all who cared to express an opinion. This material was tape recorded, transcribed, and considerably shortened. We tried to retain all significant passages; footnotes were provided in places where better documentation of the arguments was called for. Especially important are those portions of the discussions that show basic disagreements regarding goals or methods. These passages seem to reflect the discomfort (helplessness, dismay) of teachers of German in this country who realize that the language, which was once so widespread as to render the United States the third largest German-speaking country in the world,[1] is slowly disappearing before their eyes.

These discussions constitute some of the most challenging observations and ideas ever formulated on the German language in America. They should not be regarded as an endless debate of no practical consequence. Much that has been proposed here could be undertaken if the time and money were available.

The discussion chairmen were Reed (with a paper presented by Gilbert), Yoder, and Kloss, respectively. Other active participants were Roger Abrahams (University of Texas at Austin), Roy A. Boggs (Pennsylvania State University), Robert King (University of Texas at Austin), Heinrich Meyer (Vanderbilt University), Marian Michael (University of Texas at Austin), Wolfgang W. Moelleken (University of California at Davis), Carol Phillips (University of Texas at Austin), William Pulte, Jr. (University of Texas at Austin), Barbara Reeves (University of Texas at Austin), Herfried Scheer (Moorhead State College), George Schulz-Behrend (University of Texas at Austin), Stanley N. Werbow (University of Texas at Austin), and Joseph B. Wilson (Rice University). In a few cases, speakers could not be identified.

Because of the vast geographic area involved, the term "American German" is limited here to the German of speakers born in the United States.[2] Specifically *excluded* are the sizeable American urban populations of German immigrants in which the language tends to fall into disuse in one generation. Also excluded are temporary German residents: tourists, students, businessmen, writers, and political refugees.

---

[1] Here, "German-speaking" means the number of speakers included within the borders of a sovereign country, irrespective of the official language(s) of the country. Germany and Austria occupied first and second place, respectively.

[2] The language of the German speakers in Canada certainly deserves to be studied in its own right. Whether it should be artificially divided from the German of the United States is debatable. Without competent studies of Canadian German, our knowledge of the extent and diversity of German from colonial times, as well as of the German brought by nineteenth-century immigrants to the tier of northern Middle-West states adjacent to Canada, will remain fragmentary.

Emphatically *included* are rural and urban German enclaves in which successive generations have retained German as the preferred language in at least one social function. Since the great majority of German/English bilinguals in the United States either cannot or prefer not to speak the standard language, a study of casual speech almost always involves intricate problems of German dialectology, both spatial and social. Often, dialects continue to be spoken in the United States that either no longer exist in the Old World or are difficult to reach; for example, the dialects of the former German speech islands in Eastern Europe (including European Russia), of the area east of the Oder-Neisse line, and of East Germany. The German dialects on this side of the Atlantic have followed divergent paths, incorporating a myriad of innovations unknown or unusual in the Old World. At the same time, though, they preserve archaic features that have fallen into disuse elsewhere. From what is known about the colonial German dialects in the New World, it can be positively stated that they are neither uniformly innovating nor uniformly archaic; they are simply *different*. It is clear that descriptions of American German are not merely objects of curiosity for Old World scholars, but constitute an important addition to our knowledge of the full social and geographic repertoire of the language.

If we follow the views of Whorf (1941), Sapir (1921),[3] and their European predecessors, and regard speakers of different languages as possessing divergent world-views, we should then inquire whether the German/English bilinguals switch world-views as easily as they change languages.[4] The corollary may also be posed: just how may the "American" world-view be defined? And does it always presuppose English monolingualism?

The formation of new, compromise German dialects is significant for both German linguistics and for studies of linguistic change. Un-

[3] See also Einar Haugen's comments on Dell Hymes' paper (Hymes 1966:164–165). In Germany, such ideas have long been entertained, at least since the time of Wilhelm von Humboldt (see Humboldt 1836; Robins 1967: 174–178).

[4] See in this regard Doroszewski (1938), which is often quoted but difficult of access; Thomas and Znaniecki (1918–1920); and especially Einar Haugen's monumental study (1953). Many unsolved linguistic problems are formulated and discussed by Haugen (1956 and elsewhere).

fortunately, the evidence of the rapidly changing dialects has rarely been used either to support or disprove competing diachronic models that claim to form a part of "universal grammar." Pulte's essay touches on the heart of this problem. He examines two clearly defined explanations of phonological change[5] and presents evidence from the centuries-old German dialect of Dayton, Virginia, that clearly supports one of them.

A linguistic atlas of the German language in the United States, as it was suggested more than thirty years ago by both Eduard Prokosch and Heinz Kloss, may still be possible.[6] Even after German has disappeared, it will leave behind loan-word isoglosses in American English that can be traced by geographical linguistic methods. Aside from such linguistic borrowings, we have well-documented evidence of significant German cultural influences surviving in parts of the United States. German folklore, for example, is still collectible even where most of the inhabitants of a particular region have become English monolinguals.

The strict separation of linguistic phenomena from other aspects of culture is, in many respects, artificial. On the other hand, an overly "universal" approach, coupled with deficient academic preparation, has been responsible for many of the ill-conceived descriptive and analytical efforts of the past. Perhaps a fresh point of view, using methods developed within anthropology, folklore, sociology, and/or descriptive linguistics, would blunt many of the criticisms that have been leveled at students of the areal and social structure of language.

We should bear in mind that the ultimate goal is not a mere cata-

---

[5] The Neogrammarian position as restated by Hockett (1958:439–445), and the generative formulation of Postal (1968:286–307).

[6] Kloss, in typical fashion, has followed up this suggestion with a large-scale cartographic study of the *locations* of American-born German speakers in the United States (Kloss, forthcoming). His presentation supplements, and in several important respects, supersedes both the raw data (and maps) of the United States Censuses of Population and the maps found in historical atlases such as Paullin (1932). Because of the technical difficulties involved in its production, this work, to be entitled "Atlas of Nineteenth-Century German Settlements in the United States," remains unpublished.

loguing of data, but rather its organization into meaningful structures, coherent in themselves and comparable to those of kindred disciplines. Through the diverse points of view presented here, the symposium represents a step toward this goal.

GLENN G. GILBERT
Southern Illinois University

THE GERMAN LANGUAGE IN AMERICA

1. THE DIALECTOLOGY OF AMERICAN COLONIAL GERMAN

CARROLL E. REED

University of Massachusetts, Amherst

DESCRIPTIONS OF American German range from enlightened summaries, such as Samuel Haldeman's treatment of Pennsylvania Dutch (1872), to highly sophisticated structural analyses, such as Glenn Gilbert's dissertation on Texas German (1963). The various directions taken by these studies have been predetermined frequently by the nature and distribution of the linguistic specimen treated, but certain methodological traditions have also exerted a dominant influence. Today it would seem desirable and even theoretically possible for us to establish a coherent dialectology of American colonial German. In order to make at least a tentative beginning in this direction, however, it is reasonable that we pause to examine the factors that have conditioned both the data and the discipline.

Modern dialectology may be said to have its origins in the age of Romanticism, with its evolutionary viewpoint and its fascination for the primitive as well as individualistic sources of human culture. Johannes Schmeller's works, *Die Mundarten Bayerns* (1821) and *Bayrisches Wörterbuch* (1827) have been considered as pioneer achievements in the recording of folk speech. With respect to their observations of diversity, of historical relevance and phonetic discrimination, they mark the beginning of a trend that has become both admirable and pernicious. J. Winteler's book, *Die Kerenzer Mundart des Kantons Glarus* (1876), represents a more rigorous phonetic viewpoint and a much more thorough analysis of structure. The Neogrammarian movement of which it was a part, however, continued to stress historical connections, so much so, in fact, that the subsequent development of purely descriptive techniques was almost neglected.

Neogrammarian doctrine, with its emphasis on linguistic laws akin to those of the natural sciences, initiated a kind of "search and discover" technique that led directly to the rise of linguistic geography. The theory that "sound laws have no exception" contained the corollary that apparent exceptions were only the results of further laws. Such assumptions had been strikingly confirmed in Karl Verner's treatment of the exceptions to Grimm's "law." Although the early insights of dialect geography seemed to put the whole theory in doubt, judicious refinement of the corollary still permits us to be guided by the basic principles involved. Modern structural linguistics has taken its cues from the insights of Ferdinand de Saussure, one of the chief contributors to Neogrammarian efforts, and our connections with nineteenth-century methodology have by no means been severed.

Georg Wenker's application of dialect geography to linguistic research was originally intended to confirm the proposition that sound laws have no exception. While his results seemed, at first, to have refuted that notion, his technique gradually assumed the roll of a "research tool," *Forschungsmittel*, and is proudly hailed as such even to the present day. As a result, linguistic geography has been respectfully endowed with a kind of humanistic Joseph's-coat, characterized by its motley aspects. Instead of developing its own self-contained methodology, this otherwise data-oriented science became a subordinate discipline, supporting the historical and anthropological research through which it should have been supported. In his lectures on general linguistics from 1906 to 1911, de Saussure classified dialect geography under diachronic linguistics, and some more recent scholars have even regarded it as peripheral to the realm of linguistics itself. In Germany, which was slow to concern itself with structural analysis or strictly synchronic linguistics, the initial historical bias has been perpetuated in the venerable monograph series *Deutsche Dialektgeographie*, which maintains a more or less standard format, beginning typically with a long historical account of a speech community, tracing the ultimate fate of Middle High (or Low) German in the dialect or dialects of that community, and ending with a discussion of isoglosses appearing on a series of maps. The fact that neither the historical base nor the dialects concerned are treated with any structural-analytical rigor is indication enough that the data assembled has an extradisciplinary purpose.

In the further study of dialects, moreover, so much attention has been paid to geographical distribution that the word *dialectology* has often been taken as synonymous with *dialect geography*. In his book *Historical Linguistics* (1962:117–118), Winfred Lehmann, for example, states that the "study of the varying forms of speech in one language is known as *dialect geography* or *dialectology*." And Sever Pop's two-volume compendium (1950), dealing almost exclusively with linguistic geography, bears the innocent title *La dialectologie*.

To be sure, linguistic geography has proved to be not merely a method for selecting, collecting, and presenting data; it has also developed its own rules of interpretation, and these have been modified gradually as the manner of gathering the data changed. While structural differentiations, for example, were virtually impossible in the transcriptions of Wenker's forty sentences, the Linguistic Atlas of the United States is much more helpful in this respect. As early as 1931, Trubetzkoy outlined a new structural approach to the type of data assembled by linguistic geographers. Uriel Weinreich's rediscovery of that essay was first reflected in his article, "Is a Structural Dialectology Possible?" (1954), which began with the stinging pronouncement, "In linguistics today the abyss between structural and dialectological studies appears greater than it ever was." Weinreich not only answered his own question affirmatively then, but in a series of subsequent articles he effectively supported his answer with appropriate examples from Yiddish.

Even before the geographical aspects of dialect study had become dominant, there was tacit recognition that dialect differences were apt to be based on social contours and, as is so often the case today, certain social distinctions were seen to be marked by dialectal criteria. In the questionnaires of linguistic geographers, therefore, efforts were made from the beginning to keep these contours in view. Only in the last fifteen years, however, have linguists begun to focus their attention on the sociological structures within which dialect behavior is so deeply embedded. In this country, Raven McDavid, Jr., and William Labov have recently made important contributions to what might now be called "sociolinguistic dialectology." A laudable effort has also been made by Gerhard Baur (1967), although here as in other representatives of the *Deutsche Dialektgeographie* series a rigorous structural approach is seriously lacking. It should be stated emphatically, then, that the realm of dialectology extends far beyond the geographical distribution of speech variation. It may deal with either simultaneous or successive aspects of a given language. It may concern itself with speech levels and their motivation between, among, or within social entities. It may also analyze various structural levels, or even the basic characteristics of usage, since both *langue* and *parole* exhibit certain predictable properties and are fair subjects for dialect analysis.

When adequate synchronic details are lacking, of course no satisfactory concept of diachronic development is possible. For this reason it follows that structural histories of specific dialects are exceedingly rare. With all of the rich resources we now have at our disposal, it is remarkable that Germanists have made so little effort to exploit them on behalf of linguistic theory. Notable bright spots, however, are William Moulton's highly productive articles on the German dialects of northern Switzerland (1960, 1963), Eberhard Kranzmeyer's chapters on the greater Bavarian speech area (1956), and Jean Fourquet's notes on Alsatian vocalism (1952).

Establishment of linguistic history in reasonably stable areas, such as western Germany, Switzerland, and Austria, can offer the best guide to derivative areas in which varieties of dialect mixture are involved. Colonial German, from its medieval development in Upper Saxony to its more recent specimens in North America or Australia, now furnishes us with ideal laboratories for the study of linguistic behavior, particularly linguistic change. American German represents various time-spans, ranging from 250 years among the Pennsylvania Germans to less than 100 among the Prussian Mennonites. Indeed, it is possible even to find large urban groups of German speakers whose stay in America encompasses but a single generation. The structural varieties represented, both synchronically and diachronically, are manifest and challenging. Pennsylvania Germans, for example, constitute a primary settlement from a more or less compact area of western Germany. Secondary offshoots or resettlements, such as those of Kitchener, Ontario, and Rockingham County, Virginia, clearly show divergent features that were once more pronounced in the primary settlement area than they are today. The Prussian Mennonites represent groups of speakers who had already migrated twice before coming to America, and whose fractional peregrination extends from the western reaches of Canada to the plains of northern Mexico.

Scarcely any such group is without some traces of dialect differentiation. In Pennsylvania the cleavage is geographically observable, and there are even slight structural deviations to be marked. The same situation seems to hold true, but to a lesser degree, in the Amana German of Iowa, in the Texas German studied by Gilbert (1963, 1964, 1965*a*, 1965*b*, 1970*a*), and the Mennonite German investigated by Moelleken (1966, 1967). Despite their size (or perhaps because of their size—and mutual outlook), these have remained relatively compact areas, with social, religious, or occupational continuity. They are typical examples of so-called speech islands, transplanted with their speakers from similar islands elsewhere or from portions of the mother country. Like all language colonies recorded in history, they have had in their inception the seeds of change, experienced as divergence or convergence during the subsequent periods of adjustment, and notably characterized by creative innovation.

Most of these German speech islands have been surrounded or penetrated by English, both early and late, and often enough the inroads of English have been introduced by force. Colloquial differences in English itself have sometimes developed opposing lines within or around the Pennsylvania German area, for example, and enabled us to trace a meaningful dialinguistic correspondence among bilinguals. The value of the speech island as an experimental linguistic entity is thus enhanced by its contribution to the study of bilingualism.

In the English of Lunenburg County, Nova Scotia, Wilson (1958) has observed a widespread stratification of relic features from a former German speech community that has long since given up German in favor of English. Pennsylvania German still contains traces of archaic

English, some of which are identified by its speakers as more truly German to them than English. In American colonial German at least one dimension is thus added to linguistic studies. The secondary settlements from Europe are especially interesting because of their having brought with them the results of other bilingual contacts. The northern Palatine dialect near Regina, Saskatchewan (Canada), formerly located in northeastern Rumania, contains loan words from Hungarian, Rumanian, and Russian (Mang 1954). Low German Mennonite dialects from the Ukraine preserve not only Russian loan words, but purportedly also features of Frisian—with which their speakers sometimes prefer to be associated.

But even more significant than these faint flashes in the mirror of history are the levels of usage to be detected as statistical approximations of German to English. In monolingual speech communities, levels of usage are normal manifestations of style or social standards. Bilingual areas often develop standards based on the acceptance of loan features, which are gauged on the relative concern of the topic, the position of the speaker or his correspondent, the measure of abstraction involved, and the available inventory of both lexica. Moreover, the gradual anglicizing of German colonial dialects also follows levels of approximation that correspond to age groups, or generations, so that when the last fading stage of bilingualism is reached, only a few older speakers will remain, and they will speak English to each other. Still a long way from this stage is the speaker from Ontario, Canada, who said: "Wann er die righti qualifications hot, for der position occupye, und is generally en upstandinger Karl, dann sette mir ihn electe" (Graeff 1946:57). Here there is less replacement than supplementation of German, but the trend is clearly visible.

Whether or not the deterioration of any given speech island is immediately apparent, it is obvious to dialectologists that such an area furnishes ideal grist for their mills. They should be stimulated, therefore, to record both graphically and acoustically the linguistic data confronting them. Theories of grammar require corroboration; it follows, then, that immediate analysis, hypothesis, and confirmation are urgently required. If it is true, as has been claimed recently, that dialects are different surface structures reflecting a common deep structure,[1] then it seems important that each such reflection be explored exhaustively, in order that an accurate concept of the deep structure can be inferred. Thus, it is desirable to have rather lengthy tape recordings of high quality produced in some sort of natural environment. Graphic supplements, to be sure, may include standard phonetic impressions, drawings, and pictures. (The early use of phonemic symbols implies prejudgment of the data and may obscure the communication of such data to other scholars.) An effort should be made to sample fully the syntactic inventory and to aim toward those relationships that may conceivably be described as "transformations." In any case, the data should be reasonably complete, and a clear line should be drawn between information and interpretation. No dialectologist, however, can fail to concern himself with both.

The dialectology of American colonial German is supported by a good deal of extralinguistic information with respect to geographical disposition and historical provenience of its speakers. Numerous studies have been made of the effects of settlement German on the English with which it comes into contact. Popular accounts of local German dialects, particularly from older periods, have contributed valuable evidence to scholars interested in piecing together some idea of their diachronic structure. As examples, we may recall the works of Haldeman (1872), Horne (1875), Frey (1942), Hays (1908), Buffington and Barba (1954), and Holtzman (1961). A few monographs written from the historical point of view provide us with even more useful linguistic data. Among these are Learned (1888–1889), Bender (1929), Buffington (1937), Shoemaker (1940), Görzen (1952), Mang (1954), Gehman (1949), and Dyck (1964).

The question of loan-word adaptation has been treated on numerous occasions, and lexical studies in general have tended to predominate among the many special articles dealing with American German. More modern structural descriptions, though varying greatly in length and quality, are not inconsiderable, however. They include Frey (1941),

---

[1] Marvin Loflin, in remarks to the annual meeting of the American Dialect Society, Chicago, 1967.

Selzer (1941), Reed and Seifert (1941), Kehlenbeck (1948), Oswald (1949), Kratz and Milnes (1953), Gumperz (1954), Reed
and Wiese (1957), Lehn (1957), Baerg (1960), Gilbert (1963),
Mierau (1965), Miller (1966), and Eikel (1966–1967).

Most of the works in this last group are fairly comprehensive descriptive studies based on the distributional model. Few of them are
concerned to any extent with syntax. In this respect they are what has
been termed "taxonomic" in character. Some of them are related to
one another in the sense of having used a common basic questionnaire.
Furthermore, the variety of dialectical types represented in either descriptive or historical works is very small: eight are devoted to Pennsylvania German or its secondary offshoots, another eight deal with
the Low German Mennonites, two with the Nassau Germans in Texas,
one with a Swabian colony near Ann Arbor, Michigan, two with a
Franconian mixture known as Amana German, one with a Palatine
group in Saskatchewan, another with the Low Saxon German in Iowa,
and one with Swiss settlements in Indiana and Ohio. It would appear
that a great deal remains to be done. Hutterite German, for example,
has been largely neglected, and there are still many groups of Pennsylvania Germans and Low German Mennonites to be investigated. A
more extensive survey of Amana German is still needed, and a great
wealth of information on the Wisconsin Germans is in dire need of
public display. In addition to this there are now a few post–World
War II groups assembled in urban centers; these may not endure very
long, but the processes of leveling and disintegration will be instructive, and someone should collect the data while it is still available.

    For most of the work to be done, dialect mixture and differentiation
can be tested suitably by modifications of the Seifert-Reed questionnaire. It should be remembered that such questionnaires have their
particular value in that they preserve comparability between areas, including those of Germany itself, on the basis of which most of the
original questionnaire was designed. In many of our investigations we
will be actively concerned with the matter of comparability, whether
it is historical, social, or areal in nature, and especially where bilingual
relations are of interest. Moreover, we will want to keep in mind not
only the basic coordinates of linguistic structures, but also the inci-

dence of forms within them, so that, while preserving the essence of linguistic comparability, we may have flexibility in the handling of new types of data.

Because of the current revolution in some areas of linguistic analysis, purely descriptive arrays of the traditional sort may, quite justly, prove too limited for today's young scholars. An entirely new look at current questionnaires is, therefore, in order. A strategic approach to syntactic inventories, for example, is now urgently needed. Just as the testing of "sound laws" in Wenker's forty sentences could not properly serve the interests of comparative grammar or word geography, likewise our present questionnaires fail to satisfy the needs of research in syntax.

While there has been no effort thus far to undertake comparative studies of German dialects from the viewpoint of generative grammar, there is no reason why this too should not be in order. Halle (1962) offers one example of the way in which problems of historical linguistics may be treated according to the generative model. In his review of Kurath and McDavid's *Pronunciation of English in the Atlantic States,* Keyser (1963) juxtaposes a group of features from various dialects and attempts to "generate" divergent forms through sets of ordered rules. Further adumbration of this technique has been supplied by O'Neil (1968), where examples are taken from Faroese. While it is difficult to imagine how one is to decide on the exact point of departure for generative analysis, it is just possible that this kind of process grammar will afford us new insights in dialectology. In this instance we will require more data than is normally required for distributional analysis, and the judicious use of the native informant will become more crucial, since we will have to rely on his linguistic judgments more extensively now than ever before.

In sum, there is more work to be done. An adherence to continuity and comparability will keep individual studies meaningful in relation to the total effort. Experimentation with new viewpoints, furthermore, may well improve our techniques and broaden our knowledge of linguistic processes. Dialectology as a discipline, if methodically applied, stands to profit immeasurably from the further investigation of colonial American German along these lines.

DISCUSSION

WILSON: You seem to be using the term "colonial German" in its widest possible sense; that is, not in the sense of the German that was spoken in Pennsylvania in pre-Revolutionary times, but as you pointed out, in the sense of any kind of compromise language based upon an amalgam of German dialects spoken in an immigrant or colonial situation. Is that correct?

REED: That is correct. Unfortunately, there is hardly a proper term to describe the German that has been permanently transplanted to the New World. "American colonial German" seemed to be less misleading and less burdened with undesirable connotations than the more traditional designations.

MEYER: Would it be possible to make an analysis of the syntax of Preston Barba's Pennsylvania German using his "'S Pennsylfawnisch Deitsch Eck"?

REED: It would be more desirable to work orally with Barba as a linguistic informant. The model to be followed could be either that proposed by the transformational generative grammarians, or the more traditional descriptive systems.

MEYER: So you would depend on the spoken language for the . . .

REED: If we were to restrict ourselves solely to the "'S Pennsylfawnisch Deitsch Eck," the resultant grammar would pertain only to that particular written variety of Pennsylvania German.

———: You mentioned a publication in which it is stated that interdialect differences in Pennsylvania German belong to the surface structure instead of to the deep structure. Do you agree with this?

REED: I have not yet formed an opinion. It is a theory proposed by Marvin Loflin (summarized in remarks to the American Dialect Society, December 1967). In order to demonstrate its validity, we would have to show that this type of description can state the linguistic facts in a simpler way.

WERBOW: Do you have copies of the unpublished works you mentioned?

REED: I do not. However, almost all of them are available on microfilm.

WILSON: Acoustic phonetics, including automatic speech recognition and computer-aided spectographic analysis of speech sounds, could possibly provide us with much quicker sorting and classifying techniques in dealing with long stretches of tape-recorded speech.

REED: Although tape recording has proved of great value to the linguistic fieldworker, we should still be careful not to rely too heavily upon such permanent acoustic records per se.

2. THE WORD GEOGRAPHY OF PENNSYLVANIA GERMAN: EXTENT AND CAUSES

LESTER W. J. SEIFERT

University of Wisconsin, Madison

THE STUDY OF Pennsylvania German (PaG) now reaches back almost a century to 1872, when Samuel S. Haldeman's monograph appeared under the title *Pennsylvania Dutch: A dialect of South German with an Infusion of English*.[1] Since that date, this American German dialect has attracted the interest of a number of scholars, and the linguistic bibliography in this field alone is by no means inconsiderable. After Haldeman, the most important contributions to the study of PaG have been Horne (1875), Rauch (1879), Learned (1888–1889), Hoffman (1889a), Miller (1903, 1911), Barba, (1913, 1949, 1953, and other publications), Lambert (1924), Buffington (1939, 1948), Reed and Seifert (1941), Frey (1942), Reed (1942, and other publications), Springer (1943), Schach (1948, 1949, 1951, 1952, 1954), Kloss (1952), and Buffington and Barba (1954). It must, however, be pointed out that only Buffington and Reed have shared by interest in the investigation of geographically or regionally delimited linguistic phenomena.

Of all the non-indigenous, non-English languages and dialects that have been or still are spoken in the United States, PaG has held a special

[1] Published simultaneously in London and Philadelphia by the Philological Society and the Reformed Church Publication Board respectively. The monograph had actually been written in 1870 at the urging of the English scholar Alexander J. Ellis and had been read by him to the Philological Society of London on June 3, 1870.

position, since it has a history dating back to colonial times of unbroken use in a compact area. From the original settlement at Germantown in 1683, the Germans spread northward and westward; by the time of the Revolutionary War, they were concentrated in that area of Pennsylvania roughly bounded by the Blue Mountain in the north and the Susquehanna River in the west, but the Susquehanna had been crossed in the southern part of Pennsylvania so that there were numerous German settlers in present-day York, Adams, and Cumberland counties. In addition, the PaG settlements had spilled over into the northern and western counties of Maryland and into the Shenandoah Valley of Virginia. At that time, according to Dr. Benjamin Rush of Philadelphia (1789:54),[2] the Germans composed nearly one-third of the population of Pennsylvania, or approximately 150,000 of a total of 434,373.[3] Except for Philadelphia and the nearby countryside, Delaware and Chester counties for example, and except for the larger urban centers, the rural parts of southeastern Pennsylvania seem to have been occupied predominantly by Germans.

The Germans, of course, were not always the first to settle in a particular area or on a particular piece of land. Often the English and the Scotch-Irish were already there when the Germans arrived, but as the number of Germans grew, both by natural increase and by the addition of new arrivals from the homeland, they tended to buy up the properties previously held by the English and Scotch-Irish. After the Revolutionary War, settlers in large numbers moved into the many valleys north of the Blue Mountain and west of the Susquehanna River.[4] In these settlements the mixture of English-speaking and Ger-

[2] I have used the annotated edition by I. D. Rupp, published by Samuel P. Town, Philadelphia, 1875. In the footnote on p. 54, Rupp gives the figure 145,000; but in a footnote beginning on p. 51, he gives the figure of 200,000 as early as 1754, a number that is much too high for that date. Rush, although of English descent, held the German settlers in high regard; he believed that additional migration from Germany to Pennsylvania should be encouraged and that these settlers should also be encouraged to maintain their language. In these respects he was directly opposed to the views of his famous fellow-Philadelphian Benjamin Franklin.

[3] The latter figure is reported by the *First Census of the United States* (United States 1791:45).

[4] As Learned (1888–1889:13–15) pointed out, there was some movement into these valleys before the Revolutionary War, but he did not go on to say that these

man-speaking people seems to have been fairly even. It is true of at least the German component that it consisted largely of an overflow resulting from the natural increase in population in the older settlements to the south and the east. Again, the Germans tended to buy up those farms that they did not originally clear, but in the cities, towns, and even in many villages the English-speaking population was more than able to maintain itself.

If we consider the German element alone, we may speak of the post–Revolutionary War movement across the Blue Mountain and the Susquehanna River as a secondary settlement because of the origins of the settlers. For the primary settlement of southeastern Pennsylvania, which took place before the Revolutionary War, there were steady additions from the homeland; in the secondary settlement, growth resulted from internal increase with only sporadic additions from the primary settlement area. Moreover, in the secondary area, the German-speaking component was never able to reach the same high proportion of the total population as in the primary area.

For the purposes of this study, the secondary PaG settlements came to an end around 1830. Even earlier, groups had moved farther westward and had spilled over into Ohio. As the frontier moved on, smaller groups advanced into Indiana, Illinois, and Iowa. In all these later settlements, unless the Mennonites or the Amish were involved, the PaG dialect suffered the same fate—extinction.[5] The high point in the

---

sparse settlements were to a large extent ravaged by the Indian raids connected with the French and Indian War and the Revolution; as a result, the more remote settlements were for the most part completely abandoned.

[5] Of course, not all Mennonite settlements in the United States derive from Pennsylvania. There are also Low German, Ukrainian German, and Volga German Mennonites in this country. For information on Ohio see Schreiber (1962b); for Illinois see Shoemaker (1940). An early PaG settlement was also made in Canada centering on present-day Kitchener (first called Ebyville, then Berlin), Ontario. I have always held that this settlement was first made by PaG Tories at the beginning of the Revolutionary War, but Graeff (1946:11), gives 1786 as the earliest date; the dialect has not yet died out, perhaps again because there are many Mennonites in this group. A late secondary PaG settlement was made during World War II on the Eastern Shore of Maryland; these settlers are Amish from Lancaster County and are reclaiming worn-out, largely abandoned tobacco farms. Two small, tertiary settlements of Amish from Iowa have in recent years been established in Wisconsin.

use of this dialect must have come sometime between 1870 and 1890, when there may very well have been 750,000 speakers for whom PaG was the preferred and normal vehicle of communication. Of this number, perhaps 600,000 lived in Pennsylvania.[6] After this high point was reached, a gradual attrition set in that is still continuing. At the present time there may be 300,000 speakers of the dialect. Of this number, about 200,000 live in southeastern Pennsylvania in a roughly elliptical area stretching from Northampton and Bucks counties in the east to Centre and Mifflin counties in the west, from Lancaster and York counties in the south to Northumberland and Union counties in the north; the other 100,000 are scattered in smaller areas over the rest of Pennsylvania, in Maryland, Virginia, Ohio, Indiana, Illinois, Iowa, Wisconsin, and Ontario.[7] In the main area the greatest length along the east-west axis of the ellipse is approximately 125 miles, along the south-north axis approximately 75 miles. Only the northern and western sections of the ellipse include parts of the secondary PaG settlement area. On the other hand, some parts of the primary settlement area, such as southern Lancaster and York counties and all of Adams County, no longer lie within the ellipse.

Up to this point we have used such general terms as "German-speaking" population and "Pennsylvania German" speakers. These terms must now be given greater precision. The Germans who came to Pennsylvania in the years before the Revolutionary War, the period of prime importance, did not come in an even distribution from all parts of Europe where German was spoken. The vast majority of them actually came from a rather small southwestern section of the German language area. Although it would be desirable to have more detailed information than is available at present, the general outlines of the picture are clear enough. More people came to Pennsylvania from the Rhenish Palatinate than from any other region. However, the western

---

[6] These and the following figures are admittedly only estimates. The arithmetic used by Learned (1888–1889:17) is unclear to me, but surely the figure of 1,139,854 for Pennsylvania alone in 1870 is completely unrealistic if it is meant to refer to the number of speakers of PaG. The total population of Pennsylvania for that year is given as 3,521,975.

[7] Buffington and Barba (1954:1) give the figure of 300,000 for Pennsylvania. I do not think it is possible to carry on a profitable argument about the exact number.

German cantons of Switzerland, the part of Hesse south of the Main River, and the western part of Württemberg also furnished large contingents of settlers. Smaller numbers came from Alsace, Baden, Lorraine, the part of Hesse just north of the Main, and from the Rhineland lying north of the Palatinate.

With a few exceptions that will be treated later, the details of how the groups from these various regions dispersed in Pennsylvania are unknown, and very likely such details are by now lost forever. Nevertheless, the exceptions support our common-sense conclusion that such groups did not settle in an even mix, or to put it positively, that the Swiss, for example, tended to settle together in smaller or larger enclaves; likewise the Württembergers, and so on. However, if such a group as the Swiss did not already find some Palatines present in the area they had chosen, Palatines soon joined them. This method of settlement had important linguistic consequences. It meant that the groups from each region could continue using their native dialects in most everyday situations. However, there must have been times when a Franconian-speaking Palatine either wished or had to communicate with an Alemannic-speaking Swiss or a Swabian-speaking Württemberger. The use of English was ruled out if one of the partners in such a situation was a new arrival, and it is very likely that many of the early settlers never really learned English in their lifetime. Another possibility immediately occurs to us: they could use Standard German. Certainly, Standard German was not unknown to these settlers. Although it was often strongly colored by dialect, they heard it in their churches, they read it in their Bibles, they sang it in their hymns and songs, and it was even the vehicle of instruction in their schools. Yet it is doubtful that many of these pre–Revolutionary War settlers could speak Standard German with any degree of facility. In all likelihood, it was simpler for each partner to use his dialect; with a little practice, accompanied by patience and good will, communication was quite possible.

Conditions such as these inevitably led to dialect leveling, a process in which each dialect group gradually eliminated those features that made a particular dialect distinct and different from all other dialects. As it turned out, the Palatines, of all the groups, had to accommodate themselves least to this game of give and take, very likely because of their numerical superiority, but social and economic factors may also have been involved. We can never know the precise details of dialect leveling, for this process is not open to direct observation. We can only see the results, and in Pennsylvania it resulted in the development of a Franconian, Palatine dialect with some Alemannic features.[8] Of course, with increasing exposure to, and command of, the official language of the United States, English has had a considerable, but not an overwhelming influence. The fact that the Revolutionary War caused a break of almost fifteen years' duration in the stream of immigration undoubtedly helped the leveling process. There was perhaps a distinctive PaG dialect as early as 1800.

As mentioned previously, only Buffington, Reed, and I have systematically studied the regional differences in PaG. All other investigators have treated PaG as a single, uniform dialect. Two quotations on this point may be cited here to show the different views. The first is from Lambert (1924:viii): "The constant intermingling of those speaking different dialects has had a smoothing-out and leveling effect, so that the Pennsylvania-German dialect is quite homogeneous." Accordingly, if Lambert was aware of regional variations, they find no mention in the *Dictionary* proper. The second citation is from Buffington (1948:251), "It should be pointed out here, that even though the form used by a speaker in one area may differ from that used by a native of another area, the variant forms, nevertheless, will generally have been heard at some time or other by each speaker. . . . Thus speakers from all areas are easily mutually intelligible, and in spite of the array of differences which we have noted above, we can still say that the Pennsylvania German dialect is fairly homogeneous." Of the two statements, Buffington's is, of course, the more precise and accurate.

It is then permissible, at times even desirable, to speak of a single

---

[8] I must agree with Buffington (1939) that PaG is closer to the eastern Palatine dialect than to the western. In connection with the development of PaG, it is possible that Standard German, rudimentary as the knowledge of it must have been, could have provided certain norms for the elimination of dialectal features. This is a difficult problem, and a method of analysis has yet to be developed. The only statement in writing concerning this was made by Lambert (1924:viii).

PaG dialect, if we bear in mind that the processes of dialect leveling were not carried to their complete and ultimate conclusion. In the linguistic data collected by Reed and Seifert (1954)[9], the lexical differences fall into eight main categories of regional distribution, the eighth category being really a group of distributional types that do not fit into the other seven. Types V, VI, and VII are much less important than the others, because the numbers of examples are relatively small; nevertheless the distributions are so striking and informative that they deserve separate categorization. In the following sections the lemmata and the numbers in parentheses refer to the "Wordatlas of Pennsylvania German" (Reed and Seifert, forthcoming) containing 144 linguistic maps.[10]

TYPE I
The eastern region versus the rest of the PaG area

Of the 144 maps in the "Wordatlas," 29 fall into this type.[11] As a rule, the eastern region includes the speakers we recorded in Bucks,

[9] Most of the material, in phonetic transcription, was collected by us in the summers of 1940 and 1941. Reed, using a shortened version of our questionnaire, made eleven additional records shortly after World War II. The distribution of the 87 informants by county is as follows: Berks, 24; Bucks, 3; Carbon, 1; Dauphin, 4; Lancaster, 15; Lebanon, 2; Lehigh, 21; Montgomery, 1; Northumberland, 4; Schuylkill, 6; Snyder, 6. Two short visits to the PaG area that I made in the early 1960's gave evidence that any differences from our collection are very minor. When our materials differ from Buffington (1948), such divergences are noted; nevertheless, the analysis given here is based strictly upon our own collections. There are copies of our recordings at the University of California at Riverside, the University of Michigan (in the collections of the "Linguistic Atlas of the United States and Canada"), and the University of Wisconsin. I assume that Buffington's collection is now at Arizona State University.

[10] The maps lie ready for duplication at the Forschungsinstitut für deutsche Sprache (Deutscher Sprachatlas) of the University of Marburg. The introduction to the atlas will be completed in 1970.

This paper extends and partly replaces Seifert (1946*b*) in three important ways. First, it draws upon the eleven additional records made by Reed (see footnote 9, above). Second, it is based upon a much more thorough analysis of our records than was possible for me to undertake twenty years ago. Finally, in 1946 it was not yet possible to connect certain distributional types with settlement history.

[11] Map numbers: 1, 2, 15, 20, 21, 22, 23, 24, 27, 33, 35, 38, 39, 40, 46, 47, 50, 64, 66, 80, 88, 96, 98, 105, 110, 125, 131, 134, 141.

Carbon, Lehigh, and Montgomery counties. With certain items, however, an eastern strip of Berks County that varies in width as far west as the Schuylkill River agrees with the usage of the eastern region. For three items, virtually all of Berks has the same terms as the eastern region, though we otherwise classify Berks as belonging to the central region. Some typical examples are the following:

1. *Stone house* (1). Three terms were recorded: es ˈʃdeːnix ˈhaus/, /es ˈʃdeː: (n)₁haus/,/ es ˈʃdeːne₁haus/. The last of these is the eastern term, for it was recorded twelve times in Lehigh and only once in Schuylkill. In Lehigh the second term is in competition with the third; in the rest of our records the first two terms show no clear regional distribution and numerous speakers seem to use them interchangeably.[12]

2. *Cradle* [for a baby] (15). In Carbon and Lehigh the usual designation is /di ˈʃogel/, but elsewhere, including Bucks, southern Lehigh, Montgomery, it is /di ˈwiːg/. Oddly, /di ˈʃogel/ was recorded once in western Lancaster.[13]

3. *Mower* [for cutting hay] (20). In the eastern region, this time including all of Berks and one Lebanon informant, the implement is called either /di ˈgraːsme₁ʃiːn/ or /di ˈmeːme₁ʃiːn/ in rather haphazard variation. The second designation was also recorded once in Lancaster and once in Schuylkill. Elsewhere the common terms are /der ˈriːber/,/der ˈgraːs₁riːber/,/der ˈmoːr/,/der ˈgraːs₁moːr/. The simplex forms predominate in Lancaster, the compounds in Dauphin, Northumberland, Schuylkill, and Snyder. One informant in Dauphin and one in Snyder used /der ˈgraːs₁meːer/; one informant in Snyder gave this as the correct word after first saying /der ˈmoːr/, and another in Snyder gave it as an alternate after saying /der ˈriːber/.

4. *Lantern* (23). The eastern counties, including an eastern strip of Berks, are solid in the use of /di (occasionally /der/) ˈludser/. The rest of the area is just as solid in the use of /di laˈdarn/.[14]

---

[12] A somewhat different distribution is indicated by Buffington (1948:230).
[13] Ibid., p. 241.
[14] Ibid., p. 242.

5. *To bark* (27). The eastern counties, again including an eastern strip of Berks, are solid in using /ˈblafe/. One informant in Northumberland used this verb and one in western Berks first said /ˈblafe/ but then corrected his response to /ˈgaudse/, the term used in the rest of our area. One informant in southern Lehigh who responded with /ˈblafe/ volunteered the information that other speakers use /ˈgaudse/ and one informant in Northumberland who responded with /ˈgaudse/ said that he also used /ˈblafe/.[15]

TYPE II

The southern region versus the rest of the PaG area

There are forty-nine maps in the "Wordatlas" that fall into this type of distribution,[16] the largest number for any one type. As far as our records are concerned, the southern region is chiefly represented by the fifteen informants from Lancaster County. For a number of items the two informants in Lebanon County agree with the usage of Lancaster. With still other items, though fewer in number, the southern region embraces parts or all of southern and western Berks County. Five typical examples are again given.

1. *Sink* [in the kitchen] (7). In the southern region a new term /di ˈʃbiːlbaŋg/ (the phonological equivalent of a hypothetical *die Spülbank*), was coined. One Lancaster informant expanded the compound to /di ˈufˌʃbiːlˌbaŋg/. Another informant in Lancaster said /di ˈsiŋg/, the usual designation in the rest of the PaG area. Two Berks informants responded with di ˈsiŋg/, but one then said he also called it /di ˈweʃˌbang/ and the other said that the term /di ˈwaserˌbang/ had died out. Three informants, two in Dauphin and one in Northumberland called it /der ˈʃang/, but one of those in Dauphin gave the secondary response /di ˈsiŋg/. It is interesting that two people in northwestern Lehigh, after first saying /der ˈsiŋg/, gave the secondary response /der ˈʃang/.[17]

---

[15] Ibid.

[16] Map numbers: 4, 5, 7, 12, 17, 18, 19, 29, 32, 36, 37, 51, 54, 57, 58, 59, 60, 61, 67, 68, 69, 72, 73, 74, 77, 83, 89, 90, 94, 95, 97, 102, 104, 106, 107, 109, 112, 116, 121, 122, 123, 132, 135, 136, 137, 138, 139, 140, 142.

[17] The loan word shows an interesting regional split in grammatical gender. In

2. *Pail* [for water] (12). All informants in Lancaster, the two in Lebanon, and one in western Berks called this utensil /der ˈkiwel/. Outside the southern region, one informant in Dauphin and one in Snyder used this term; one in Northumberland gave it as his second response. The other, more common designation is /der ˈe:mer/.[18]

3. *Bundle* [of grain] (19). In this instance the southern region includes Lancaster, Lebanon, all of Berks west of the Schuylkill River, and one of the informants in Dauphin. Here we find the dialectal equivalent of Standard German *die Garbe*, in Lancaster usually as a diminutive, /es ˈgarewli/, elsewhere as /di (occasionally /der/) ˈgareb/. Three speakers in southwestern Lehigh called it /der ˈbindel/, although one of these gave the secondary response /der ˈʃe:b/, the word recorded in the rest of the area. Two informants in Schuylkill said that /ˈgareb/ was used by others.[19]

4. *Autumn* (102). By the speakers in Lancaster and Lebanon, by four in western Berks, and one in Dauphin this season is called /der ˈharebʃd/, but in the rest of the area we recorded /es ˈʃbo:dˌja:r/. The four informants in western Berks who first responded with /ˈharebʃd said that they also used /ˈʃbo:dˌja:r/. One person in Lancaster reversed this situation. One speaker in Dauphin, in Northumberland, and in Snyder used /ˈʃbo:dˌja:r/ but said that others called it /ˈharebʃd/. One person in northwestern Lehigh expresed the opinion that /ˈharebʃd/ was dying out.[20]

5. *Midnight* (106). In Lancaster, usage is evenly divided between /di ˈmidˌnaxd/ and /di ˈmiderˌnaxd/. The first term was also recorded twice in western Berks, twice in Snyder, once in southwestern Lehigh. One other Lehigh informant used the phrase /di ˈmide in derˌnaxd/. Otherwise the term is /di ˈhalbˌnaxd/.[21]

---

the eastern region—Berks east of the Schuylkill River, Bucks, Carbon, Lehigh, Montgomery—it is almost always /der ˈsiŋg/; in the rest of Berks and in Lebanon it is always /di ˈsiŋg/. In Dauphin, Northumberland, Schuylkill, and Snyder the genders are in haphazard variation.

[18] Buffington (1948:242).

[19] Buffington (1948: 242) gives the gender of both /ˈgareb/ and /ˈʃe:b/ as being neuter, a usage we did not record. The first word is listed in Lambert (1924:60, s.v. *garb*) only as feminine; the second word is not listed in this dictionary.

[20] Buffington (1948:242).   [21] Ibid., p. 248.

TYPE III

The northwestern region versus the rest of the PaG area

There are eighteen examples of this type of distribution in the "Wordatlas."[22] For this region we made twenty recordings in Schuylkill, Dauphin, Northumberland, and Snyder Counties, but three of these are incomplete because the informants were not willing to continue. Moreover, the dialect is not as commonly used in this region as in those regions to the south and east; for many items, some speakers could not think of or did not know the dialect expression, and then they often preferred pleading ignorance to using English. Accordingly, on the maps there are often fewer than twenty entries for this region.

1. *Forenoon lunch* (30). In the northwest this dying institution is called /es ₁dse:ᶅu:r₁ʃdig/, but one informant in Snyder said /es ₁nainᶅu:r₁ʃdig/, the only term recorded in the rest of the PaG area. Moreover, one person in Northumberland, after considerable cogitation called it /es(?) kaidel/.[23]

2. *Car* (48). Except for the easternmost informant in Schuylkill, all in the northwest region used /di ᶅkar/. This term is also used in the rest of the PaG area but in competition with another loan word /di meᶅʃi:n/. In northern Lehigh the latter has almost replaced the former, but in this subregion a third loan word was recorded three times, /es ᶅa:deme₁b:l/. The exception in Schuylkill used /di meᶅʃi:n/. Another person in Schuylkill gave /esᶅa:deme₁bi:l/ as his second response.[24]

3. *Pneumonia* (71). Two designations were recorded in the northwest region that occurred nowhere else. The majority of persons used /es ᶅluŋe₁fi:wer/, but three in Snyder said /es ₁kald uf der ᶅluŋ/. The easternmost informant in Schuylkill used /es ᶅbruʃd₁fi:wer/,

---

[22] Map numbers: 9, 30, 48, 52, 70, 71, 76, 79, 91, 92, 93, 100, 103, 108, 111, 119, 126, 127.

[23] The word is listed in several German dialect dictionaries, but the meaning is always given as a large, thick slice or piece of bread. Moreover, the gender is always masculine.

[24] Buffington (1948:225,236).

the term recorded elsewhere. Only in western Berks three informants used the loan word /es ˌnu:ˈmo:nja/; two of these said that
/es ˈluŋeˌfi:wer/ was dying out. One Snyder informant who used
/es ˈluŋeˌfi:wer/ gave the opinion that /es ˌnu:ˈmo:nja/ was the
new and spreading designation. One person in Schuylkill who himself used /es ˈluŋeˌfi:wer/ said that other speakers used /es ˈbruʃd-
ˌfi:wer/.

4. *To do arithmetic* (76). In the northwest three different verbs are
used: the loan word /ˈfig(e)re/ (nine informants), /ˈrexle/ six informants),/ˈdsif(e)re/ (two informants). The first response of one
person in Dauphin was /ˈrexle/, but he then gave the opinion that
/ˈfig(e)re/ was the incoming verb. Another person in Northumberland who used /ˈfig(e)re/ said that other speakers used /ˈrexle/.
Still another person in Snyder who gave /ˈdsif(e)re/ as his first
response added that he also used /ˈrexle/. The rest of the PaG area,
again including the easternmost informant in Schuylkill, was almost
solid in the use of /ˈrexle/. Only one informant in northwestern
Berks and one in southwestern Lehigh used /ˈdsif(e)re/. One person in Lancaster, after some hesitation, said /ˈdse:le/, but this is
most likely to be considered an error.

5. *Satisfied* (79). Usage seems about evenly split in the northwest,
since eight persons responded with the loan word /ˈgsedisˌfaid/ and
eight with the native German word /ˌdsuˈfri(:)de/. One informant
each in Northumberland and Schuylkill corrected the loan word to
the German word, and another in Northumberland said that the
German word had died out. Elsewhere (and again this includes the
easternmost speaker in Schuylkill) only the German word was recorded.

TYPE IV
The central region versus the rest of the PaG area

In the "Wordatlas" there are ten examples of this distribution.[25] It
is clear, as far as the lexicon is concerned, that the central region is not
as sharply delineated as the three regions already discussed. Berks

[25] Map numbers: 3, 11, 31, 43, 56, 99, 101, 118, 120, 130.

County west of the Schuylkill River is really the core of the central region, but as we have already seen, at times even this core agrees in usage with the eastern region, at other times with the southern region. In a wider sense, the central region includes eastern Berks and Lebanon, but for some items it embraces Schuylkill and even part of Northumberland. Moreover, our records indicate that a term used in the central region is almost sure to occur sporadically in the rest of the PaG area.

1. *Lawn* (3). The responses were elicited by the sentence: 'He is mowing/cutting the lawn.' In the central region the usual response for the item in question was /es ˈgra:s/, a term that occurred sporadically elsewhere instead of the usual /der ˈho:f/. The latter term was used by four speakers in western Berks and Lebanon, but one corrected it to /es ˈgra:s/ and two said that they also used /es ˈgra:s/. One speaker in western Berks and one in Lebanon corrected the first response /es ˈgra:s/ to /der ˈho:f/. Two speakers (one in Berks and one in Dauphin) were explicit to the point of saying /es ˈgra:s im ˈho:f/.[26]

2. [Woman's] *dress* (56). For this item the central region includes eastern Berks, Lebanon, Schuylkill, and southeastern Northumberland, where this type of woman's apparel is designated as /der/ or /di ˈgaund/, a word recorded once in Lancaster and once as the first response in Lehigh. Elsewhere the designation is /der/ or /di ˈfrag/, except that /es ˈdres/ was used by one speaker in Lehigh (who said that /ˈfrag/ was the old word) and by two in Schuylkill (who said the same thing about /ˈgaund/). A number of others either gave /ˈgaund/ as their secondary response or said that the word was dying out.[27]

3. *Spree* (99). In the core of the central region /der ˈsuf/ competes with /di/ or /der ˈʃbri:/, with one occurrence of the first word in Schuylkill (again the easternmost informant) and one in Dauphin. The second word predominates elsewhere, but seven other terms

[26] Buffington (1948:230).
[27] Ibid., p. 244.

were also recorded: /di ˌsaufeˈrai/, /di ˈarig ˈdsaid/, /di (ˈsauf)
ˌpardi/, /der ˈrib/, der ˈaufˌruːr/, /ˈʃgeːd/(gender?), /ˈkediˌgoː/
(gender?).

4. *Weekday* (101). We are dealing here, it seems, with a relic term.
The word /der ˈwarˌdaːg/ was recorded only five times in the central region, once in each of the three other regions, and it was the secondary response of one other speaker in the northwest (Dauphin).
The most common word in the PaG area as a whole is /der
ˈʃafˌdaːg/, but in the eastern and especially in the northwestern
regions we also recorded /der ˈwox(e)ˌdaːg/, /der ˌdaːg in der
ˈwox/, and /der ˌdaːg ˌdarix der ˈwox/.

5. *Ever* (120). Elicited by the sentence: 'We didn't know if he would
ever get back.' In the central region we recorded /ˌsai[n] ˈleːwes/,
/ˌsai[n] ˈleːwe/, and once/ in ˌsaim ˈleːwe/; but the adverbial genitive occurred about 50 percent more often than the adverbial accusative. The genitive also occurred once in Lehigh. The rest of the PaG
area is solid in the use of the accusative /ˌsai[n] ˈleːwe/, although
one Lehigh informant used the definite article /es ˈleːwe/ and one
Dauphin informant gave the prepositional phrase /in ˌsaim ˈleːwe/
as a secondary response.

TYPE V

*The southern and eastern regions versus the central and northwestern
regions*

This is the least common type of distribution to be found in our
records, for there are only four examples. Nevertheless, it is so striking that it deserves separate classification, because the eastern and
southern regions are not contiguous.

1. *Washboiler* (13). This household utensil is hardly in use today,
but at the time our records were made, everyone knew what it was
called. In the southern region, exclusively, and in the eastern region, predominantly, we recorded /der ˈweʃˌkesel/; in the other
two regions it was exclusively /der ˈweʃˌbailer/ or its phonological
variant /der ˈweʃˌboiler/. The latter word, in both variants, does
occur in the eastern region, especially in northern Lehigh. It is in-

teresting that the phonological variant /der ˡweʃˌbailer/ predominates by far in the central region.[28]

2. *Market basket* (14). In the south and east this type of basket is called /der ˡʃdo:rˌkareb/, but the majority of speakers in Lehigh said that the item was no longer used and gave no term for it. The other term is /der ˡmarigˌkareb/, which clearly predominates in the central region. In the northwest a third term, /der ˡheŋgeˌkareb/, was recorded twice. In Lancaster /der ˡmarigˌkareb/ was the only response of one informant, the secondary response of another.

3. *Hawk* (44). In the south and east only /der ˡwoi/ was recorded, except for one instance of /der ˡha:g/ in Lehigh. In the central and northwestern areas /der ˡhabix/ was also recorded. In western Berks, Dauphin, Northumberland, and Schuylkill /der ˡhabix/ was clearly predominant over /der ˡwoi/, but, oddly enough, across the Susquehanna River in Snyder only /der ˡwoi/ was recorded.[29]

4. *Stubborn* (82). The southern and eastern regions call this trait /ˡʃdarˌkebix/ or, four times in northern Lehigh, /ˡdigˌkebix/. For the other two regions usage is split between /ˡʃdowerix/ and /ˡʃdarˌkebix/. One informant in the south (Lancaster County) and one in the east (Carbon County) used /ˡʃdowerix/.[30]

TYPE VI

The eastern and (part of) the northwestern regions versus the rest of the PaG area

There are only five examples of this type in the "Wordatlas." The size of the eastern region varies considerably from item to item; the same is true of the part of the northwestern region that agrees with eastern usage in these items.

1. *Doorknob* (6). The basic dichotomy for this item is between the native German word /der ˡgnob/ (and its compounds /ˡdi:rˌgnob/, /ˡdi:reˌgnob/) and the English loan word /der ˡnab/ (and its compounds /ˡdi:rˌnab/, /ˡdi:reˌnab/), but in addition there is a phono-

[28] Ibid., pp. 223, 242.
[29] Ibid., p. 244.
[30] Ibid., p. 254.

logical hybrid /der ˈgnab/, which was recorded only in the compound /ˈdi:reˌgnab/. The native word was used in a large eastern region including all of Berks and, for the northwestern region, in Schuylkill and southeastern Northumberland. The loan word was recorded in Lancaster and Lebanon, for the south, and in Dauphin, southwestern Northumberland, and Snyder, for the northwest. The hybrid was recorded four times in Lancaster and once in Dauphin. Where the loan word or hybrid were used, there were also scattered instances of the native word. Moreover, one Snyder informant used only /der ˈledʃ/ and a compound /der ˈdi:rˌledʃ/ was the only response of one Lancaster informant. Another Lancaster speaker used only /der ˈdi:rˌhendel/, and still another only /di ˈdi:reˌfal/. The compounded form /ˈdi:reˌgnob/ was the only response given in Lehigh and by those speakers in the northwest who used the native word.[31]

2. *Meadow* (16). In the eastern region, including the easternmost informant in Schuylkill, in southeastern Northumberland, and in most of Snyder such a piece of land is /der ˈʃwam/. Elsewhere it is /di ˈwi(:)s/, although two speakers in Lancaster called it /der ˈʃwam/, one of whom said he also used the other word. Still another person in Lancaster gave /der ˈʃwam/ as his secondary response. Conversely, one of the Snyder speakers gave /di ˈwi(:)s/ as his secondary response.[32]

3. *Lard* (34). Only two terms are involved: / es ˈʃmals/ and /es ˈfed/. The former is used in a large eastern region, again including all of Berks, and, for the north, in Schuylkill, in part of Dauphin, part of Northumberland, and part of Snyder. In Berks one person said that he also used /es ˈfed/ and one Schuylkill informant said that /es ˈfed/ was used by others. Two Dauphin informants corrected their first response of /es ˈfed/ to /es ˈʃmals/ and one North-

---

[31] For Mifflin County, adjacent to Snyder on the west, Buffington (1948:222) lists the other possible hybrid in the compound /ˈdi:rˌnob/.

[32] Buffington (1948:242). Only one informant, in Lebanon, said that the two words differed in meaning, in that /der ˈʃwam/ referred to a swamp. Lambert (1924:147, s.v. *schwamm*) gives the meanings mushroom, toadstool, meadow, swamp, sponge, punk; for the other word (s.v. *wiss, wies*, p. 179) he gives only meadow.

umberland informant who used /es ǀfed/ said that others used /es ǀʃmals/.

4. [Man's] *suit* (55). In the east and northwest this was predominantly recorded as /der/ or /es ǀsu:d/ with a sprinkling of /der/ or /es ₁su:d ǀgle:der/. Both of these occur in the central and southern regions together with /di ǀmans₁gle:der/.

5. *To deny* (113). Two terms are about equally common in the east and the northwest: /ǀle:gle/ and /ferǀle:gle/. Twice /ǀab₁le:gle/ was recorded in Lehigh, but one of the two speakers said that he also used the other two words. In the central and southern regions only /ferǀle:gle/ was recorded. One informant in Schuylkill who used /ferǀle:gle/ gave /ǀweg₁le:gle/ as his secondary response.

TYPE VII
The eastern region versus the southern region versus the rest of the PaG area

Again, there are only five examples of this distributional type and unfortunately all of them are rather complicated. Nevertheless this is a distinct type because of the clear differences in every case between eastern and southern usage.

1. *Bald* (53). The simplex /ǀblod/ or the compound /ǀblod₁kebix/ designate this unfortunate condition in the east. In the south it is usually /ǀba:l₁kebix/, but the variant /ǀba:le₁kebix/ occurred twice. In the central region we recorded /ǀblod/, /ǀblod₁kebix/, /ǀba:le/, /ǀba:l₁kebix/, and /ǀba:le₁kebix/. In the northwest we found /ǀblod/ (once the phonological variant /ǀblud/), /ǀblod₁kebix/, and /ǀba:l₁kebix/. Under these conditions it is not surprising that six informants gave a secondary response.[33]

2. *To shivaree* (87). Because this institution is dying out, a number of informants could give no response. In a large eastern region, including Berks, a phrase was used, /di ǀbul(s)₁bend (ǀbul(s)₁gaid, ǀsai₁gaig) ǀʃbi:le/. In the northwest the verb was usually /ǀbele/ or /ǀaus₁bele/; but the southern verb and the eastern phrase were also recorded.

[33] Buffington (1948:245).

3. *To* (114). This item was recorded in two sentences widely separated in the questionnaire: 'We walked to the red barn' and 'I went to the station.' The three prepositions /ˈan/, /ˈno(:)x/, and /ˈdsu(:)/ were recorded. The eastern region used /ˈno(:)x/ overwhelmingly, but three informants in Lehigh used /ˈno(:)x/ in one sentence, /ˈan/ in the other. Only one informant (Carbon) used /ˈan/ in both, and one (Lehigh) used /ˈdsu(:)/ in both. In the southern region, including Lebanon, all informants used /ˈan/, but three in Lancaster used /ˈan/ in one sentence, /ˈdsu(:)/ in the other. There is no clear preponderance of either /ˈan/ or /ˈno(:)x/ in the central and northwestern regions, but in both regions more speakers used different prepositions in the two sentences. Seven informants in the central region (Berks) used both /ˈan/ and /ˈno(:)x/, two used /ˈan/ and /ˈdsu(:)/, one used /ˈno(:)x/ and /ˈdsu(:)/. In the northwest four speakers used both /ˈan/ and /ˈno(:)x/, one used /ˈan/ and /ˈdsu(:)/ and another /ˈno(:)x/ and /ˈdsu(:)/. The small number of occurrences of /ˈdsu(:)/—it was used by only nine informants, of which eight also used another preposition in either one or the other of the two sentences—indicates that the prepositional function of this word has undergone marked attrition. On the other hand, one of the prepositional functions of /ˈno(:)x/ has been greatly extended.

4. *Several* (124). Elicited by the sentence: 'There are several villages around here.' For the eastern region this was most often recorded as /(en) ˈde:l/, but three informants in Lehigh said /(en) ˈpa:r/, which was virtually the only word recorded in a large southern region including Lebanon, Berks, and even the eastern part of Schuylkill; the only exceptions were one informant in Lancaster and one in eastern Berks just across the county line from Lehigh who used /ˈedlixe/. In the northwest /(en) ˈpa:r/ and /ˈedlixe/ were in haphazard variation.

5. *Since* (129). Recorded in the sentence: 'It's a long time since it snowed.' The eastern region stands apart in the two distinctive ways in which this concept was expressed. About half the informants used the conjunction /ˈdas/, in which case the subordinate clause could be either positive or negative: /es is ʃun ˈlaŋ | ˌdas es (ned)

ˈgʃne:d ˌhodↆ/. An equal number of people used the more basic structure /es ˌhod ʃun ˈlaŋ ˌnimi ˈgʃne:d/. One person in Lehigh used /ˈas/ instead of /ˈdas/ and another said /ˈdsider ˌas/. The use of /ˈas/ was solid in the south, again either with or without the negative. The other two regions are characterized by the use of /ˈdsider ˌas/ in haphazard variation with one or more other terms. Thus, in the central region /ˈas/ was recorded somewhat more frequently than /ˈdsider ˌas/, but of three informants who first used /ˈas/, one said that he also used /ˈdsider ˌas/ and two said the same about /ˈdsider/. One other central informant used only /ˈdsider/. In the northwest /ˈdsider ˌas/ was recorded twice as often as /ˈas/, but two persons gave /ˈdsider/ as their only response and one used the eastern phrase /ʃun ˈlaŋ ˌnimi/. The clause introduced by /ˈdsider (ˌas)/was rarely negated.[34]

TYPE VIII
Complex distributions

Of the 144 maps in the "Wordatlas," 24 fall into this type.[35] Actually, they constitute a type only insofar as the regional distributions shown by these maps do not fall into any one of the seven types already discussed. Moreover, no two of these 24 maps exhibit the same geographic distribution. It will therefore be necessary to proceed map by map in delineating the region or regions in which the words on a map were current.

1. [Water] faucet (8). Only two words were recorded: /der ˈʃbiged/ and /der ˈgra:ne/. The regional distribution is, at first glance, very simple. The native German word was recorded predominantly in Lehigh and then, contrary to all the types of distribution already given, in southwestern Berks and eastern Lancaster. There were also two occurrences in northwestern Berks and another informant corrected /der ˈʃbiged/ to /der ˈgra:ne/. In Lehigh two of the five

---

[34] Buffington and Barba (1954:91) and Frey (1942:44) do not mention this particular conjunctional function of /ˈas/ and /ˈdas/; Lambert (1924:37, s.v. *dass, ass*) uses a negative in his example.

[35] Map numbers: 8, 10, 25, 26, 28, 41, 42, 45, 49, 62, 63, 65, 75, 78, 81, 84, 85, 86, 115, 117, 128, 133, 143, 144.

persons who first responded with the English loan word said that they also used the native word. The same holds for one speaker in Dauphin, and one in Schuylkill informed us that others used the German word. One person in Lancaster said that /der ˈgra:ne/ was the "old" word. A number who gave the native word as their response said that they also used the loan word or that others used it. Two speakers, one in Lehigh and one in southwestern Berks, even gave the opinion that /der ˈʃbiged/ was the "old" word.

2. *Handle* [of a pan] (10). The most common term recorded in the PaG area as a whole was /der ˈhendel/ and in the northwest region it was by far predominant. The next most common designation was /der ˈʃdi:l/; in northwestern Berks and northwestern Lehigh it was predominant; it was given only once in the northwestern region, and that was by the easternmost informant in Schuylkill. In central Lancaster there was a pocket of informants who called it /di ˈhand‚he:b/, and this also occurred once each in western Berks, in Carbon, and in Dauphin. The fourth designation was /der/ or /di ˈheŋg/. This word usually refers to the arched handle across the top of a kettle or pail, called 'the bail' in the English of many areas, and so we might consider this an erroneous response. However, in that case seven informants (three in Bucks, one in Lehigh, two in western Berks, and one in southern Snyder) made the same mistake, something which does not seem very likely. It is more probable that the German word has been extended in meaning after the pattern of the English word 'handle,' which is often used for both types of devices for carrying or handling a utensil.

3. *Squirrel* (41). There is a threefold distribution of words for this animal, but not of the kind discussed under Types V, VI, VII. In most of Lehigh and in the central region we recorded /der ˈe:x‚ha:s/, which also occurred once in eastern Lancaster and once in southern Snyder; one other Lancaster informant and one in Northumberland said that others used this word; one in Schuylkill gave it as his secondary response, and two in Dauphin said that it was obsolete. In Lancaster three speakers called the little animal /der ˈe:xer/, but ten used the diminutive /es ˈe:xerli/. We recorded the English loan word in three phonological shapes: /der ˈʃgwarl/,

/gǀʃwarl/, /ǀgʃgwarl/. With one exception already noted, this was the word used in the northwest and again in a solid region in Bucks, southern Lehigh, and Montgomery. Finally, one informant in eastern Berks just across the county line from Lehigh, who gave /der ǀe:xᵢha:s/ as his first response, said that he also used /es ǀe:xᵢharnxe/; and a nearby informant in southwestern Lehigh, whose first response was /der ǀʃgwarl/, said that others called it /es ǀe:xᵢharnxe/; perhaps there was (still is?) a small region in which this was the usual designation.[36]

4. *Sparrow* (42). In the PaG area as a whole, the most common term is /der/ or /di ǀʃbads/ and the diminutives /es ǀʃbedsel/ (northern Lehigh, Berks) or /es ǀʃbedsli/ (Lancaster, Berks). The diminutives /es ǀʃbadsi/ and the odd /es ǀʃbadi/ were recorded in the northwest, the former once in western Schuylkill, the latter twice (Dauphin, western Schuylkill). Two informants in northern Lehigh gave /di ǀʃbads/ as their secondary response, but one in Berks and two in Schuylkill, for whom /der ǀʃbads/ was the first response, said that they also used /es ǀʃbedsel/. The other native German word /der ǀʃbarliŋ/ was recorded only six times, all of them in Berks, and one of them corrected it to /der ǀʃbads/. There is also the English loan word /der ǀʃbere/ in the western part of the northwestern region, in southwestern Berks, and in western Lancaster.

5. *Corncrib* (143). Here we are dealing with the distribution of four compounds made up of native German elements and one compound consisting of German and English elements. The basic /es ǀwelʃkarnᵢhaus/ was commonly recorded in the central region and the eastern half of the northwestern region. In the same regions it was less frequently designated by the diminutive /es ǀwelʃkarnᵢhaisel/, the most common term in the east. Another diminutive, /es ǀwesʃkarnᵢhaisli/, was found in the south. Still another diminutive,

---

[36] Buffington (1948:251). The initial consonant sequence in /ǀgʃgwarl/ is, as far as I know, the only one of its kind in PaG and is hard to explain. The sequence in /ǀgʃwarl/ (we recorded it only a few times) is a case of metathesis yielding a sequence that was fairly common in the dialect, especially in such past participles as /ǀgʃwuŋe/ (*geschwungen*). Perhaps, after the metathesized shape had become established, the second /g/ was reintroduced from the basic but unusual shape /ǀʃgwarl/.

/es ˈwelʃkarnˌhaiselxe/ was the secondary response of one person in Schuylkill (primary /es ˈwelʃkarnˌhaus/). The first response of one informant in Lancaster was /diˈwelʃkarnˌʃaier/; he added that he also said /ˈwelʃkarnˌgrib/. Two other persons in Lancaster also gave /di ˈwelʃkarnʃaier/ as their secondary response, one of whom had first said /ˈwelʃkarnˌhaisli/, the other /ˈwelʃkarnˌgrib/. Finally, this hybrid compound /es/ or /di ˈwelʃkarnˌgrib/ was used in three distinct subregions; the western half of the northwest, the western part of the south, and the southern part of the east.[37]

In the last section of this paper the possible causes of some of the types of regional distribution will be presented. Our knowledge is simply not extensive enough to make more than some fairly general remarks. Perhaps it is even impossible to find causes for some of the eight types.

We begin with the discussion of Type IV because a basic assumption is involved. In this type, the lexical usage of the central region differs from that of the rest of the PaG area, and there were relatively few examples, only ten, of this type. Thus, the central region is much less distinctively marked as a separate region than the east, the south, and the northwest. This could well mean that the central region, Berks County in particular, played a key role in the processes of dialect leveling whereby the PaG dialect came into being.

There are certain reasons for making this assumption. The earlier settlements in Germantown and those fanning out from there in Bucks and Montgomery Counties could not play this role. They were too close to Philadelphia for them to escape from the city's sphere of influence, where the dominant language was from the beginning English. Today, even in northern Bucks and northern Montgomery, dialect speakers make up only a small percentage of the population. Consider the case of Lehigh County, which is today one of the strongholds of PaG.[38] It was mainly settled by Germans in the two decades between

---

[37] Buffington (1948: 222, 241). There are ten maps in the "Wordatlas," 135–142 and 144, where additional examples of the diminutive suffixes are to be found. A comprehensive treatment of this interesting feature of word formation is given in Seifert (1947).

[38] As late as 1940 many Poles and Slovaks working in the large cement plant near

1740 and 1760, although some English-speaking settlers were there at least two decades earlier. Thus the German settlements of Lehigh were too late to become dominant in the development of the dialect. There were early German-speaking settlements in Lancaster County dating back to 1712, when a group of Swiss settled along Pequea Creek. However, Lancaster from the beginning attracted an unusually high percentage of Mennonites and Amish. These groups as a matter of principle formed closed societies and refrained as much as possible from contacts with outsiders, including the Germans of other religious groups. Since this is hardly the kind of population that will take an active part in the social give and take that must be involved in dialect leveling, we are left with Berks County. As early as 1705 there were German settlements in southeastern Berks, but they were part of the northward expansion already mentioned for Bucks and Montgomery; accordingly, their orientation was toward Philadelphia. Then, in 1723, a large group of at least two hundred families, mostly Palatines, settled in west-central Berks along Tulpehocken Creek and established the present-day borough of Womelsdorf. This settlement had an unusually fast growth and soon attained a position of great influence, especially after 1729 under the energetic leadership of Conrad Weiser.[39] After 1748, when Reading was founded on the Schuylkill River by Württembergers and Palatines, Berks possessed a second focal point of influence, but virtually until the Revolutionary War, Womelsdorf and the Tulpehocken remained more influential.

If we accept this basic assumption as correct, and I think it is about as well supported as any assumption can be, some of the types of regional distribution become easily understandable. Let us take a concrete example. Dialect equivalents of Standard German *Eimer* and *Kübel* occur throughout the southwestern German language area, sometimes with a differentiation in meaning. Both words must at one

---

Fogelsville found it useful to learn PaG. Fogelsville is a village in the center of Lehigh, lying about fifteen miles west of the important twin cities of Allentown and Bethlehem.

[39] Weiser, perhaps more than any other person, was responsible for the peaceful relations between the Indians and whites of Pennsylvania up to the outbreak of the French and Indian War.

time have been used throughout the PaG area, but the dialect term /ˡeːmer/ became established in Berks and gradually spread eastward, northward, and westward. However, this particular word could not penetrate the separatistic southern region with its relatively large numbers of Swiss, and especially of Mennonites and Amish; thus in the south /ˡkiwel/ was generalized. Because many items underwent the same process, we find the relatively large number of examples (49) in distributional Type II. Less frequently, as in the case of /ˡwiːg/ versus /ˡʃogel/ the eastern region was closed to the leveling influence emanating from Berks and this gave rise to distributional Type I, with 29 examples. In Type V, with only four examples, both south and east were closed to the Berks influence. The development of the north-western region, with 18 examples in Type III, is very likely connected with the fact that this was a secondary settlement with settlers coming from the central and eastern regions, and in smaller numbers from the south. It was undoubtedly also important that the dialect in this region never gained the same preponderance over English as elsewhere. After all, when the northwest stands apart, there is almost always at least one English loan word involved. For Types VI and VII, and especially for the complex distributions gathered together under Type VIII, lack of information prevents us from attempting an explanation at the present time.

DISCUSSION

MOELLEKEN: Would you call the settlements in West Virginia primary or secondary, considering that they were founded as early as the 1760's, and in many instances by settlers coming directly from Germany, that is, not via Pennsylvania?[1]

SEIFERT: The West Virginia area would have to be considered secondary, because it was separated from the beginning from the original settlements.

[1] See Wust (1965).

MEYER: I lived in the Lehigh Valley of Pennsylvania for about fifteen years. The Pennsylvania German intonation from Lancaster County or from west of Reading seemed to be similar to that of the Swabian dialects in Germany. Speakers in the remainder of the Pennsylvania German area seemed to have an intonation similar to that of the Palatinate or Upper Franconia. Did you study features of stress, pitch, or terminal contours in the course of your work?

SEIFERT: Unfortunately we did not. A separate study or a supplement to our work would have to be prepared.

MEYER: Are the *Eimer* and *Kiwel,* 'pail, bucket,' made of the same material, or is the one perhaps wooden and the other metal?

SEIFERT: Most people make no distinction between the two. Those who say [ˀẽ:mɒ] use it in all contexts; the same thing holds for [kʰɪβḷ].

KLOSS: At the beginning of your paper you mentioned Germantown, now a suburb of Philadelphia. It may be appropriate to point out that Germantown never belonged to the Pennsylvania German dialect area. Probably Low German instead of a South German dialect was spoken there. William Hull in his book on the early Quakers in Pennsylvania[2] even calls them, with some exaggeration, "simple Dutch" (i.e., Netherlanders). Most of the followers of Pastorius came from a part of Germany where a Low Franconian dialect was spoken. This dialect is of course much more closely related to Standard Dutch than to the speech of the Palatinate.

SEIFERT: It is important to note that this settlement was influential in attracting additional settlers. Pastorius, who actively recruited new settlers, concentrated not so much on the northern part of the Rhine, but rather on the region farther south extending to the Palatinate. Despite the varied composition of the early settlers, I think we must regard Germantown as the beginning point of the Pennsylvania German culture.

KLOSS: I did not mean to minimize the historical importance of Germantown, but it should be clear that from the point of view of dialectology, it stands apart from the rest of Pennsylvania German.

[2] Hull (1935); see also Lohr (1933:95–96).

SEIFERT: Surely. But it was never influential in the development of Pennsylvania German as a separate, New World dialect.

KLOSS: You stated that it is difficult to gain an insight into the processes of linguistic leveling that must have taken place in southeastern Pennsylvania in the latter part of the eighteenth century. In this regard, the process of leveling occurring at the present time among the older and middle generations in the German rural settlements founded in the last decades of the nineteenth century could be profitably studied with a view toward constructing a model for the leveling which we know must have taken place in Pennsylvania German. In 1937, I traveled through parts of North Dakota where Russian-German settlers from the Ukraine formed one large, compact area of predominately German speech. In the Ukraine the Germans had lived in compact linguistic enclaves speaking predominately Swabian, Franconian, or Hessian dialects. The enclaves were separated from each other by large numbers of Ukrainian speakers so that the opportunities for dialect leveling were very small. When the settlers arrived in North Dakota, however, a process of social mixing, intermarriage, and linguistic leveling began almost at once. My initial impression was supported by the local linguistic folklore: the Swabian dialect was in the process of giving way to the Franconian dialect. A thorough linguistic investigation is urgently needed, since English is doubtless replacing all these dialects at a fast pace.

SEIFERT: When I said that the processes of dialect leveling are not open to direct observation, I meant that we can only see its results. In synchronic field work, it is possible to describe the clash of two or more dialects occurring in the speech of the same informant. From our point of view we describe the varying usages as being free variants. We cannot predict which of the competing forms is going to win out. Only at the end of the process can we observe that this or that variant is being used exclusively and that its competitors have fallen into disuse.

KLOSS: In North Dakota I remember having met people who called themselves Swabians. Although they said, "We speak *Schwäbisch*," they actually spoke Franconian. Only in old-fashioned language, such as that of proverbs, were many Swabian forms retained. Although in formalized, archaic speech, Swabian elements were still very much in evidence, everyday language was strictly Franconian.

SEIFERT: There is a similar situation in parts of the German-settled Banat. The inhabitants call themselves Swabians, but their dialect is Palatine.

GILBERT: What if we were to study the lexical characteristics of Pennsylvania German outside of Pennsylvania, say among the few speakers of the dialect in the Shenandoah Valley of Virginia, in Ohio, Ontario, the Midwest, and on through the tier of states adjoining the "Great American Desert?" Could research into the geographical origins in Pennsylvania of these migrant speakers shed light on clear lexical distributions that are no longer amenable to study in Pennsylvania itself? We might thereby be able to illuminate a portion of the puzzling history that you said may be gone forever.

SEIFERT: It might be possible.

PULTE: In working with dialects of the Pennsylvania German type spoken in Virginia, West Virginia, Kansas, and Oklahoma, it seems that English *picture* has been uniformly borrowed by all informants as [ˈpɪktʊ] Has the German *Bild* completely disappeared in Pennsylvania also?

SEIFERT: No. [ˈpɪktʊ] is more common than [b̥ɪlt̥], but the latter is still widely used.

YODER: Your emphasis on the study of the settlement history of the eighteenth century is well taken. In order to study the settlement patterns of persons with certain Swiss-German surnames in Pennsylvania, I have been working extensively with German-Swiss archival sources dealing with the eighteenth-century emigration across the Atlantic. The evidence from the surnames coincides exactly with your linguistic mappings. The central area, Berks County, is of course the place where the Swiss, Swabians, and Palatines settled together. There, they became the "church people," as opposed to the sectarians in Lancaster County and the Skippack area, which stood somewhat apart from the central region. Berks County adopted the institution of the Union Church, where Lutheran and Reformed congregations shared one church building. Normally the Reformed were of Swiss and Palatine background; the Lutherans were from Württemberg and other Lutheran areas of southwest Germany. The two ethnic groups settled together because they were the representatives of church-type Christianity who could cooperate with each other in the formation of a common church. In the process, they must have adjusted their dialects as well as their religions. The sectarians—Mennonites and other sects which insisted on nonconformity to the world—formed close-knit settlements that enabled them to preserve more Swiss linguistic elements in their subdialect.

SEIFERT: Much remains to be done in combining the evidence of history and linguistics in Pennsylvania.

MOELLEKEN: I should like to offer a few examples solicited from speakers in West Virginia showing dialect leveling: [gaʊtsə] 'to bark' and [kʰɪβl] 'bucket' are used consistently, and instead of the terms [rɔk] or [drɛs] for 'dress' which you have mentioned, only [ˈhɛbɪt], probably from English *habit*, is used as a dialect term.

SEIFERT: I have heard [ˈhɛbɪt] in conversation; however, none of our informants used the word during the actual interviews so that it did not appear on our map at all.

————: You mentioned the word *Spielbank*. Is there a corresponding verb *spielen*?

SEIFERT: Yes, Pennsylvania German [ˈʃb̥i:lə]. It means both 'to wash' and 'to play.'

SCHEER: The use of a questionnaire will be a source of considerable bias, particularly if the interview language is English rather than Standard German, Pennsylvania German, or another German dialect.

SEIFERT: You are quite right. The use of a questionnaire written in a language other than Standard German admittedly introduces a certain bias into the results. However, when Dr. Reed and I began our field work, neither of us could speak Pennsylvania German. On the other hand, both we and all of our informants (with one exception) knew English well. The one exception was the oldest informant that I recorded. Although I posed each question first in English, I was then often forced to expand on the question in Standard German. He was an intelligent man, and I have no doubt that his record was a good example of Pennsylvania German usage.

Regarding the geographical qualifications of our informants, we attempted to find people who not only themselves had lived all of their lives in the same area but whose parents also had been born and lived there. It is true that the Pennsylvania German population has been considerably more mobile for many years than its Old World counterpart in the Palatinate and Switzerland. Especially in the northwestern part of the Pennsylvania German area, a peripheral region, it was necessary to exercise much caution. Our maps embody a geographical tolerance that would be most unusual in European linguistic geography.

WILSON: Is Pennsylvania German still actively used by people of all ages?

SEIFERT: Only in a sharply decreasing number of families. In isolated areas such as the northwestern corner of Lehigh County, many children still use the dialect. As late as the 1940's it was still so firmly entrenched that popular songs were sung in Pennsylvania German translation. Although urban speakers are becoming rare, I would conservatively estimate the total number of speakers in southeastern Pennsylvania as exceeding 200,000, not to mention additional speakers in western Pennsylvania and elsewhere.

In recent times, Pennsylvania German has been taught as an academic subject at Muhlenberg College, Franklin and Marshall College, and Pennsylvania State University. Although a considerable amount of writing is done in the dialect, much of it has not yet been published. Once or twice a year, Lutheran and Reformed ministers will use Pennsylvania German as a kind of novelty for their congregations. The Amish, who conduct their informal services in private homes rather than in church buildings, use what they call *Hochdeutsch*. Only in the case of the Amish has the role of High German as the language of religion been maintained.

3. GERMAN IN WISCONSIN

JÜRGEN EICHHOFF
University of Wisconsin, Madison

THE NUMBER OF non-English languages brought to America by immigrants can only be estimated, but there is no doubt that German was spoken by more immigrants than any other non-English language. For this reason it is surprising—or maybe not surprising at all—that no attempt has been made to create a German equivalent to Einar Haugen's exemplary study of the Norwegian language in the United States (1953). There are, to be sure, a number of studies of German in the various parts of the nation. Wolfgang Viereck (1967, 1968) lists more than 150 books and articles on Pennsylvania German alone, followed by Texas German with less than a dozen and Wisconsin, Iowa, Kansas, and Illinois with three studies each. Some of these are valuable contributions toward a comprehensive description of the German language in the United States, but such a description has yet to be written.

This undertaking would probably go beyond the capacity of a single scholar. A carefully coordinated team of linguists seems to be the most promising solution. Besides the task of linguistic analysis, special emphasis will have to be placed on problems of language development, contact, and change, as well as on psychological and social implications for the speakers. The different conditions and developments in Pennsylvania, Texas, Wisconsin, and other states demand separate treat-

44

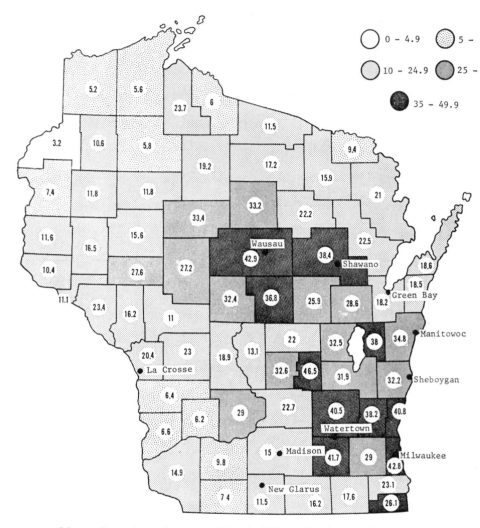

Map 2. Percentage of persons living in Wisconsin who were born in Germany or whose parents were born in Germany, according to the U.S. Census of 1910. From *Deutsches Archive für Landes- und Volksforschung* 3(1939), map 10 (corrected).

ment, and so probably do the dialects of the various religious groups, especially the Mennonites.

Certainly Wisconsin is one of the states that cannot be bypassed when the history of the German language in America is written. The statistics on German settlement in Wisconsin will support this statement. In addition to pertinent statistics, this paper presents the results of a preliminary survey of the actual situation of German in the state, concluding with a survey of what has been done and what will have to be done in the investigation of the German language in Wisconsin.

1. *German Settlement in Wisconsin.* During the latter two-thirds of the nineteenth century, Wisconsin was a favorite destination of immigrants whose native tongue was German. Table 1, adapted from the official census reports,[1] shows the number of persons living in Wisconsin in 1880 through 1910 who were born in Germany. In order to facilitate comparison, the figures for New York, Illinois, Ohio, and Pennsylvania are also listed. These were the states with the highest numbers of German immigrants in those years. The figures in parentheses show the percentage of those who were born in Germany in the total population of each state.

Table 1 indicates that in the time span 1880–1910, Wisconsin had a larger percentage of German-born inhabitants than any other state.

TABLE I. Number and Percentage of Persons Born in Germany in the Five States with the Highest Numbers of German Immigrants, 1880–1910

	1880	1890	1900	1910
Wisconsin	184,328(14.0%)	259,819(15.3%)	242,777(11.7%)	233,384(10.0%)
New York	355,913(7.0%)	498,602(8.3%)	480,026(6.6%)	436,911(4.8%)
Illinois	235,786(7.8%)	338,382(8.8%)	332,169(6.9%)	319,199(5.7%)
Ohio	192,597(6.0%)	235,668(6.4%)	204,160(4.9%)	175,095(3.7%)
Pennsylvania	168,426(3.9%)	230,516(4.4%)	212,453(3.4%)	195,202(2.5%)

[1] The census reports used here are United States (1853, 1864, 1872, 1883, 1895, 1901, 1913).

TABLE 2. Number of Wisconsin Residents Born outside Wisconsin, 1850–1910

Born in	1850	1860	1870	1880	1890	1900	1910
U.S. except Wisconsin	139,620	251,777	239,899	221,634	214,407	248,053	262,540
Foreign countries except Germany	72,413	153,048	202,184	221,097	259,380	273,194	279,481
Germany	38,064	123,879	162,314	184,328	259,819	242,777	233,384

TABLE 3. Percentage of Wisconsin Residents Born outside Wisconsin, 1850–1910

Born in	1850	1860	1870	1880	1890	1900	1910
U.S. except Wisconsin	55.8	47.6	39.6	35.4	29.2	32.4	33.9
Foreign countries except Germany	28.9	29.0	33.5	35.2	35.4	35.8	36.0
Germany	15.3	23.4	26.9	29.4	35.4	31.8	30.1

In the total number of immigrants from Germany it stood fourth in the nation in 1880 and third from 1890 through 1910.

The German element in the Wisconsin population during the nineteenth and early twentieth centuries may be fairly accurately apprised by comparing the countries of birth of those persons who moved into Wisconsin from beyond its borders. The figures may again be computed from the census reports, as shown in Tables 2 and 3.

Table 3 gives the population figures in percentages. In 1850, sixteen years after the Wisconsin territory had been established, only about 15 percent of Wisconsin residents had been born in Germany. At the same time, more than half of the population had come from other parts of the United States. During the following years the German element increased steadily, reaching a peak in 1890 of more than 35 percent of those born outside Wisconsin. In this year the number of persons born in Germany slightly exceeded the total number of those born in all other foreign countries. The next census, taken ten years later, shows a marked decrease in the number of German-born.

German in Wisconsin 47

TABLE 4. Wisconsin Residents Born in Germany or with Parents Born in Germany, 1880–1910

	German-born	Born in U.S., Both Parents Born in Germany	Born in U.S., One Parent Born in Germany, One in U.S.*	Total "German Stock"†	Percentage of German Stock in Total Wisconsin Population
1880	184,328	226,325	25,136	435,789	33.1
1890	259,819	293,039	73,536	626,394	37.0
1900	268,384‡	333,759	132,972	735,115	35.5
1910	233,384	561,559		794,943	34.0

* These persons are included in order to arrive at the "German stock" as defined by the census office. There were frequent marriages between immigrants and natives with German-born parents. Thirteen of the sixty-two informants mentioned in part 2 fall into this category. It is likely that some of the persons listed under this column no longer spoke German. However, their number is more than offset by those who *did* speak German but are *not* included in these figures; see below.

† These figures, as defined by the Bureau of the Census, include "the combined total of three classes, namely, the foreign-born whites themselves, the native whites of foreign parentage (those having both parents born abroad), and the native whites of mixed parentage (those having one parent native and the other foreign born)" (United States 1913:875).

‡ The figures quoted here for the year 1900 are those given in United States 1913. They differ from those given in United States 1901 for same year.

Actually, German immigration reached its peak in 1882 (Everest 1892)[2] and tapered off in the years thereafter, leaving the German element at slightly over 30 percent during the first decade of the twentieth century.

The census records for the same years also give information on the number of persons of German parentage. This is summarized in Table 4.

Table 4 does not include the third-generation residents of German descent, nor are the German-speaking immigrants from Switzerland, Austria, Poland, Hungary, other Eastern European countries, and their descendants taken into account. Together with the evidence previously

[2] The Wisconsin census for 1885 gives the number of German-born residents as 265,756, which was 53.8 percent of the foreign-born population and 17 percent of the population in the state (Wisconsin 1886: table between pp. 36 and 37).

48

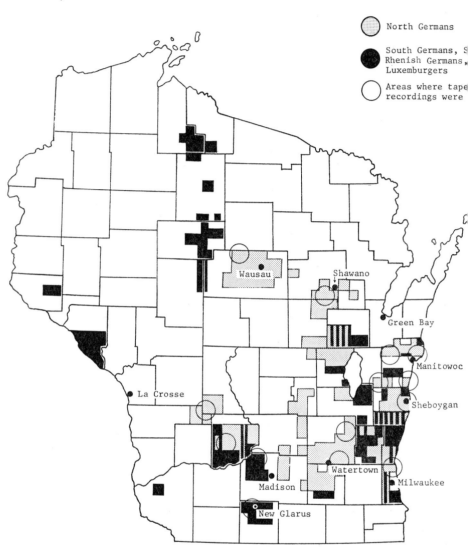

Map 3. Distribution of Germans in Wisconsin according to the U.S. Census of 1890. From *Collections of the State Historical Society of Wisconsin* 14(1898), opposite p. 341. Areas of recordings added by the author.

obtained, the figures leave no doubt that around the turn of the century about one-third of the Wisconsin population could at least passively understand if not actively speak German.

The majority of the German immigrants established their homes in the southeastern counties of the state. It is in these areas that we find the eleven out of Wisconsin's (then) seventy counties in which, according to the census of 1910, there was a German-stock population of 35 percent or more, with 46.5 percent in Green Lake County as the maximum. A number of Wisconsin townships were inhabited chiefly or exclusively by settlers from Germany.

The strong position of German in Wisconsin is reflected by the powerful and vociferous German-language press (Arndt and Olson 1961:647–709). The first German newspaper, the weekly *Wiskonsin Banner*, was founded in Milwaukee as early as 1844. Soon a great number of other newspapers, magazines, religious and professional publications appeared in that city and in dozens of places elsewhere in the state. The peak was reached in 1900, when there were approximately one hundred newspapers of general interest printed in German in more than fifty places in Wisconsin. Of the four daily newspapers in 1900, two were printed in Milwaukee, one in La Crosse, and one in Sheboygan. Seven newspapers appeared two or three times a week; the others were weeklies. In addition to the one hundred German-language newspapers of general interest there were at least thirty-four of special interest for teachers, housewives, poultry breeders, freethinkers, and religious communities. (This number, however, includes supplements to other newspapers.) Most of these publications appeared weekly or less often. In 1884 the three German newspapers in Milwaukee, the *Germania*, the *Herold*, and the *Seebote*, claimed a combined circulation of 92,000 copies. It is remarkable that this was about twice the number of copies printed by the three English newspapers in that city (Wittke 1957:204).

2. *The German Language in Wisconsin Today*. Considering the strong and relatively recent German immigration to Wisconsin, one might expect that the German language would be well preserved in the state. However, a survey conducted during the summer of 1968 indicates that the decline which began about 1900 has continued at an

ever-accelerating pace.[3] While in some areas German is still spoken, especially among older relatives or good friends, almost all speakers switch to English in the presence of persons whom they do not know well or who do not understand German well, a situation that is becoming increasingly frequent. According to what could be ascertained, German is best preserved in Marathon County west of Wausau. In the townships of Hamburg, Berlin, and parts of the surrounding townships, virtually everyone over thirty years of age at least understands the local Low German (Pomeranian) dialect. Knowledge of Pomeranian Low German and also of Standard German is widespread among older persons in some townships north of Milwaukee in parts of Ozaukee and Washington Counties, where the first settlement of German Lutherans was founded in 1839, and in the Watertown area. Out of a sample of sixty-two informants whose German was tape recorded, not one had spoken English before he went to school. However only eight claimed greater fluency in German than in English at the time of the recording—a very small number if one takes into consideration that an investigator inquiring about suitable speakers is normally referred to the best informants in a community. Seven informants reported that, when talking to relatives, they could speak German more easily than English. Thirteen informants told the investigator that they still speak German with their children (three of them "sometimes" or "rarely"), but only five of these informants were born in this century (1901, 1908, 1912 [2], 1923). The youngest informant brought up speaking German was born in 1937; he is a farmer in Manitowoc County and speaks an excellent Pomeranian dialect, but his wife does not speak German, nor do his children. Children of American-born parents who are still brought up with German as their first language have not come to the attention of the investigator. It is safe to predict that the German brought to Wisconsin by nineteenth-century settlers will have all but died out within a few years.

Most of the informants from rural areas were able to speak two kinds

[3] The survey was supported by grants from the Research Committee of the University of Wisconsin Graduate School and the American Philosophical Society (Penrose Fund). A detailed report has been published in the 1969 yearbook of the American Philosophical Society.

of German—a dialect and a language close to Standard German. In addition, they all have a good or very good command of English, thus making a number of them trilingual. The dialects are almost identical to those still spoken in Germany. They may differ considerably from the standard language, especially in the case of the Low German dialects from northern Germany. The informants who speak only Standard German learned it from their parents. Some of those who were brought up with Standard German nevertheless learned the local dialect through contact with friends and neighbors. Where dialects were spoken in the homes, Standard German was often learned from instruction in parochial schools and from the pulpit. In some areas instruction in Lutheran parochial schools was conducted partly in German as recently as in the 1930's. Lutheran church services in German are being held to this day.

The relationship of the dialects to Standard German in Wisconsin closely reflects the situation in mid-nineteenth-century Germany. In rural areas of Germany the dialects reigned almost exclusively, while in the cities the standard language was gaining predominance, especially among the educated. Accordingly, the Wisconsin descendants of immigrants who had been farmers and day-laborers still speak the dialect, whereas the descendants of immigrants who were professional men are more likely to speak Standard German. Among the latter were the so-called Forty-Eighters—students, professors, journalists, and others of high social standing—most of whom settled in such urban areas as Milwaukee, Sheboygan, Manitowoc, and Watertown during the 1850's. It is to them that these cities, during the second half of the nineteenth century, owed their fame as centers of German-American culture. And it is to them that we can trace back a few frail and short-lived approaches toward a fairly uniform Wisconsin German on the basis of Standard German. The rudiments of such a development can still be found in the urban and semi-urban areas along Lake Michigan.

According to Kate Everest Levi's surprisingly thorough study (1898), the Wisconsin German settlers came from practically all major German dialect areas: from Mecklenburg, Pomerania, Prussia, Posen, and Brandenburg in northeastern Germany; Holstein, Province of Hanover, Westphalia, and Lippe-Detmold in northwestern Germany; Rhenish Prusia, Luxemburg, and Saxony in middle Germany; and Baden and Bavaria in southern Germany. German-speaking settlers also came from Switzerland and Austria. The German provinces contributed very unequally to the strong influx of immigrants. There were more arrivals from Pomerania than from any other dialect area of Germany. Many of the Pomeranians had left the Old World for religious reasons, and it is only natural that they should have remained together and have joined around their churches after they disembarked. This accounts for the tenacity of the Pomeranian Low German dialect in many of the areas that are known to have been settled by immigrants from northern Germany. Group settlement of immigrants from narrowly circumscribed German localities resulted in the preservation of, for example, an Eastphalian dialect in Sauk County, a Holstein dialect in Calumet County, and a Swiss dialect in Green County. There was a settlement made up of immigrants from the Rhineland in northwestern Dane County, but their dialect has all but disappeared. As a rule, group settlement was not extensively practiced in Wisconsin. There are reports that newcomers preferred to settle close to their countrymen, but the availability of suitable land often proved to be more decisive. A number of speakers of Bavarian dialects have been found in different areas. No systematic search has been made for speakers of the dialects of Prussia, Posen, Brandenburg, Lippe-Detmold, Luxemburg, Saxony, Baden, and Austria. Most probably many of these can still be found. On the whole it can be said that German (both standard and dialectal) is better preserved in Protestant than in Roman Catholic areas. This is due to the fact that German has been maintained for a long time as the language of Protestant church services and was taught in Protestant (especially Lutheran) parochial schools much longer than in Roman Catholic schools (Hense-Jensen and Bruncken 1900–1902: II, 153–154).

Wherever dialects are found, they faithfully continue the language of nineteenth-century Germany. Practically no inter-German influence could be identified.[4] Speakers of different dialects did not divest their language of its primary characteristics in order to develop a new dialect

[4] The same observation was made by Einar Haugen (1942:627) in his study of the Norwegian language in the United States.

mutually intelligible to all. Such a development, which might have paralleled the development of Pennsylvania German, was obviously prevented by the availability of another common language. This was Standard German in the beginning, but English later became increasingly important. It is for this reason that different German dialects in Wisconsin are often found to occupy small, compact areas. Occasionally, a dialect may be restricted to a single family or a group of related families. English would then be used for all practical purposes outside the smaller or larger family.

As has often been observed, in cases where a dialect and a standard language come into contact, the dialect, although not losing its primary characteristics, will nevertheless be subject to strong influence from the standard (prestige) language. It is difficult to assess the influence Standard German had on the German dialects during their period of geographical contiguity in the United States. There are loans from Standard German in the dialects, such as the words beginning with *ge-* in Low German. However, most of these loans were present prior to emigration. The influence of English, which has been considerable, can be more easily ascertained. Not only are there numerous English loan words in all Wisconsin German dialects (and in "Standard German" as spoken in Wisconsin), but also the phonology, morphology, and syntax of the dialects show the effect of contact. In Sauk County Low German, a Hanoverian dialect, the auxiliary *sein* was completely replaced by *haben*, resulting in such sentences as *Hast du gewesen?* instead of German *Bist du gewesen?* Sentences like *Tust du ihn sehen?* instead of *Siehst du ihn?* can be heard in northern Germany, to be sure; but their frequency of usage has increased considerably in Wisconsin under the influence of English.

The variety of Standard German spoken by descendants of nineteenth-century German settlers in Wisconsin normally does not differ significantly from the regional High German *Umgangssprache* in Germany. In some of the areas where informants spoke Standard German in addition to their dialect, Standard German tended to show the influence of professional instruction, for example in the careful pronunciation of unstressed syllables and the "correct" usage of *brauchen* with *zu*. In small, isolated settlements some informants did not know Standard German at all, even though they possessed a firm knowledge of both Low German and English.

Both the dialects and the Standard German spoken in Wisconsin have undergone a considerable impoverishment in vocabulary and reduction of versatility due to illiteracy in German and general acculturation. Informants often found it difficult to converse in German if they were asked questions not related to house and farm, family and community life.

The English of the informants was generally very good, although some older speakers substituted [s] for [θ] since the apico-dental or interdental slit fricative does not occur in German. The speakers also use German lexical items and fixed expressions in an otherwise English context; these are fairly well integrated into Wisconsin English, e.g., *wie geht's, macht nichts, ach du lieber*.

3. *Outline of a Future Study of German in Wisconsin.* In his exposition "Problems of Linguistic Research Among Scandinavian Immigrants in America," Einar Haugen (1942) elaborated the ultimate goals of linguistic research for this group as well as the methods of approaching these goals. These apply *mutatis mutandis* to the other immigrant languages, including German. The goal is "nothing less than *a total delineation of the immigrant as a communicating individual* . . . from the moment he steps ashore in America to the time when he or his descendants are completely assimilated to the English-speaking community" (Haugen 1942:630). This includes a detailed study of the foreign-language community, the technical analysis of the spoken language, and a study of the written language, as well as the names used in such a community. The scholar will first have to compile the relevant historical and statistical material, then, with the help of individual studies, prepare a questionnaire. The next and most laborious step is the field work, with the object of recording linguistic material from numerous carefully selected speakers. Excerption and analysis of written literature is a final though no less important task.

In the almost thirty years since Haugen outlined his goals and methods, much evidence has been lost forever. Immigrant culture and immigrant languages have tended to disappear in the broad stream of

American life. It is becoming increasingly difficult to find suitable informants for the cultural and social history of immigration and post-immigration times. On the other hand, the linguist can now take advantage of modern technical apparatus. The tape recorder, sound spectrograph, and computer allow a preservation and retrieval of data facilitating collation and analysis.

One special problem to be dealt with is the study of German in urban areas. Milwaukee had a German-stock population of almost one-third in the nineteenth century, but Milwaukee German suffered an early and rapid breakdown. The reasons for this breakdown and the processes by which it occurred have not been investigated.

In Wisconsin, as in the other midwestern states, those persons who spoke a language other than English have at times been considered suspect by their fellow-citizens. At the same time, the bilinguals themselves were often ashamed of their nonconformity. Having German as one's mother tongue, even if balanced by the knowledge of English as a second language, could be socially and economically disadvantageous. In this respect, Wisconsin is unlike Texas, where Spanish was (and is) widely spoken and where there was somewhat less pressure to conform. The situation in Wisconsin is also different from that in Pennsylvania, where longtime settlement has leveled out many of the dialect differences. Detailed comparisons have yet to be carried out.

A considerable amount of historical and statistical material dealing with the Germans in Wisconsin has been collected by historians (see Pochmann and Schultz 1953), but much remains to be done. In some cases, the 100th or 125th anniversary of settlement inspired members of a community to research their own past and write about the history of the place.

A linguistic questionnaire for the investigation of German in Wisconsin has been compiled by Seifert (1946a), who was brought up in a German community in Dodge County, Wisconsin. The effective combination of linguistic and folk-cultural materials has made this questionnaire an excellent tool used in numerous recordings. Professor Seifert has gathered about one hundred written interviews in field work done since 1945. I have obtained more than sixty tape recordings of conversation and twenty-eight using the Wisconsin German

Questionnaire (mostly of Low German dialects). Within the Department of German at the University of Wisconsin, dissertations have been completed on a Swiss German and a Low German (Hanoverian) dialect (Lewis 1968, Donnelly 1969). A linguistic analysis of the Pomeranian dialect of the Freistadt Lutherans is in progress for the *Lautbibliothek der europäischen Sprachen und Mundarten*. Because of the fragmentation of German in Wisconsin, many more studies of this kind would be desirable. Certainly a native speaker, or even better still, a student raised in a Wisconsin German community would be the most qualified person to undertake such a study. However, we can now no longer wait for such persons to take up this task. Careful guidance of students who are non-native speakers will nevertheless result in adequate descriptive studies.

Little has been achieved in the field of excerpting the written language. Although this task is less urgent, it should be carried out in conjunction with the other projects. A student of Professor Seifert is preparing a dissertation on the language of one of the most long-lived Wisconsin newspapers printed in German, the *Dodge County Pionier* (see Arndt and Olson 1961:665), which went out of print in 1946 after seventy years of continuous publication.

Also worthy of study is the influence of German on the English language in regions with extensive German settlements. In addition to the German loans mentioned above, there are dozens of additional German words and phrases found in such areas. In and around Manitowoc, *by* is used in a way that may or may not have been influenced by Low German: *I am going by Prange's store* or *I am going by grandma's*. But these influences are rapidly disappearing. School, radio, and television have brought into even the remotest places an awareness of Standard English, resulting in the abandonment of foreign elements. For this reason an investigation of such non-standard features should be begun without delay, preferably by a person raised in the area to be studied.

The heyday of every dialectologist's career is the preparation of a linguistic atlas. Large-scale atlases dealing with Pennsylvania and Texas German will soon be published (Reed and Seifert, forthcoming; Gilbert, 1971). But for the dialectologist gathering data on the German language in Wisconsin, such an undertaking is out of the question. Although dialects come into frequent and intimate contact, there has been almost no mutual leveling of the differences. Therefore it is futile to search for such a thing as "Wisconsin German," a misleading expression that should be avoided. By contrast, Wisconsin is an unusually good place to study the contact of German and English, and it is this topic that should receive prime attention in the future.

4. GERMAN IN VIRGINIA
AND WEST VIRGINIA

WILLIAM J. PULTE, JR.
University of Texas at Austin

THOSE FORMS OF Pennsylvania German still spoken today in Virginia and West Virginia are among the most interesting, and at the same time the least well known, of all American German dialects. In this paper an outline sketch of the history of the Virginia dialects will be presented, and it will be suggested that their study can shed light upon the historical development of the German language in Pennsylvania itself. In addition, a strikingly conservative feature of one of the Virginia dialects, the retention of front-rounded vowels, is felt to be of interest for linguistic theory and will be discussed at some length.

Although German has been spoken continuously for two centuries in the Shenandoah Valley of Virginia and in West Virginia, this fact has been almost totally ignored by students of American German. The few who were aware of the influx of Germans from Pennsylvania into the Virginias during the eighteenth century probably tended to assume that Virginia German had long been extinct, a supposition supported by early twentieth-century sources that reported German as having fallen into disuse throughout most of the Shenandoah Valley. John Walter Wayland, for example, had stated as early as 1907: "The older order has changed; and has very generally given place to the new. As one generation has succeeded another, the circles in which the German language and customs are preserved have steadily narrowed, until at the present time it is not probable that over five per cent of the German families in the Valley still use the German language. Most of these are to be found in the western sections of the counties of Rockingham and Shenandoah" (Wayland 1907:102).

Field trips by this writer to the old Virginia German area in the fall of 1967 revealed, however, that the language is still spoken in both the Shenandoah Valley and in isolated areas of the nearby West Virginia Alleghenies.[1] At that time tape recordings were made and field notes taken on the dialects spoken near Dayton, Rockingham County, Virginia, and at Sugar Grove, Pendleton County, West Virginia; it is upon these notes that the present study is based.

The migration of Germans from Pennsylvania across the Potomac southward into the Valley of Virginia began around 1740 and was more or less complete by 1790. By that time, most of the area extending from the northernmost rim of the Valley south to Staunton and Waynesboro was German-speaking, with the southwestern German dialects of the settlers used in daily life and a form of Standard German employed in church, school, and printing. In the eastern half of the Valley, which had a large admixture of Scotch-Irish settlers, spoken German began to recede during the first decades of the nineteenth century. Standard German had been completely replaced by English in public functions by 1850, although it remained in use in religious services in western areas of the Valley, as well as in West Virginia, for several decades longer. By 1900 the Virginia German dialects were virtually extinct, as noted above; since that time almost nothing has been published on the fate of German in Virginia.[2]

It should be pointed out that the German dialects spoken in Virginia are, from one point of view, not merely the result of secondary settle-

---

[1] On one occasion I was accompanied by Wolfgang W. Moelleken, who has since informed me that he has continued the study of the Sugar Grove dialect and hopes to publish a study of its phonology. At the time this field investigation was undertaken, I was unaware that a survey of the remaining speakers of German in the area had recently been completed by Smith, Stewart, and Kyger (1962).

[2] Since the study by Hays (1908), the first publication to appear on the subject was a series of articles by Ernest G. Gehman (1963).

ments of Pennsylvania Germans. They represent, rather, independent dialects almost as old as Pennsylvania German itself. While the Pennsylvania German speech islands existing today in Amish and Mennonite communities in Ohio, Indiana, and elsewhere are the result of secondary settlements that took place during the nineteenth century, the origin of Virginia German is quite different. The first Germans who moved into the Shenandoah, and from there spilled over in small groups across the Shenandoah range into West Virginia, were in almost all instances either themselves natives of Germany who had spent only a few years in Pennsylvania before moving on, or they were the children of German natives. The leveling process, which has molded the language of Pennsylvania into what it is today, had little or no time to influence the dialects spoken by the first Virginia Germans. Since Virginia German has had its own more or less independent development together with that of Pennsylvania German, we might expect to find many features shared by the two, while others might be divergent; still other features might be present in both but arranged in different patterns.

This is, in fact, exactly what an examination of Virginia German reveals. Both Dayton German and Sugar Grove German differ in a number of respects from Pennsylvania German as described by Reed and Seifert (1954).[3] They also differ rather widely from each other, the expected result in view of the lack of communication between the isolated mountain communities. The available data indicate that Virginia German was actually not a homogeneous dialect, but rather a cluster of small groups of dialect speakers living together in isolated communities, in each of which separate leveling processes were active.

A comparison of lexical items from the two Virginia dialects with Pennsylvania German illustrates how leveling has produced different results in each instance. In the *Linguistic Atlas of Pennsylvania German* Reed and Seifert (1954) mapped the geographical distribution of a number of words exhibiting interesting phonological and morphological variation. Various distinct dialect subareas are indicated by their maps. Lancaster and Lehigh counties, in particular, often stand

[3] See also Reed (1948*b*). Pennsylvania German forms in this paper are given in the Reed-Seifert orthography.

out, since variants present in their dialects are frequently found nowhere else in the Pennsylvania German area surveyed by Reed and
Seifert. Berks County is occasionally also distinguished by a unique feature, and it is frequently the case that a form present in both the Lehigh
and Berks dialects will contrast with a form found only in Lancaster
County. Bucks County seems to be a less important dialect area; a form
will occasionally be found there only, or in Bucks County and in adjacent areas of Lehigh and Berks counties.

A cursory examination of the Sugar Grove dialect at first makes it
appear that there is much agreement between it and the dialect of
Berks County, since the forms Reed and Seifert show to be predominant there are frequently recorded for Sugar Grove German. Closer
study, however, shows that there are many items present in the Sugar
Grove dialect that were not recorded at all for Berks County. What
is most interesting is that the variants found in Sugar Grove German
are, at times, Lancaster County forms not found anywhere else in the
Pennsylvania area, while at other times Sugar Grove German agrees
with the Lehigh or Bucks dialects and disagrees with the dialects of
Berks and Lancaster counties. There is also a large class of items in
Sugar Grove German not recorded at all by Reed and Seifert in Pennsylvania. Lancaster forms recorded in Sugar Grove include *finef* 'five,'
kiwel 'bucket,' and *fett* 'lard'; Sugar Grove items present in Pennsylvania only in Lehigh County include *grumbēre* 'potatoes,' *wōnd* 'he
lives,' and *hen* 'to have'; while the Sugar Grove forms not recorded
in Pennsylvania are illustrated by *besen* 'broom' (contrasting with the
Pennsylvania German *bēsem* and *bēse*), *nunner* 'down' in 'to sit down.'
and *hāwet* 'dress.' The lack of a consistent agreement between Sugar
Grove German and any particular Pennsylvania subdialect clearly indicates that the leveling process which must have taken place at Sugar
Grove has been an independent process resulting in a dialect distinct
from any spoken today in Pennsylvania.

If we are interested, however, in reconstructing the leveling process
for Pennsylvania German itself, and if we wish to know at how early
a date it was completed, the above data do not enable us to say anything definite, since it is conceivable that the subdialects in Pennsylvania had already taken shape when the Sugar Grove community was

founded. We might suppose, then, that the first speakers of the dialect at Sugar Grove came together from various areas of Pennsylvania and spoke their own already distinct dialects, which eventually became leveled; or it could be the case that the first settlers came directly from Germany without remaining long enough in Pennsylvania to have their dialects much influenced by the linguistic situation there. When data from the Dayton dialect is examined, however, it becomes possible to say something rather definite about the history of the leveling process in Pennsylvania, Lancaster County in particular. This is because we do know the area from which the earliest speakers of Dayton German came, since they were members of the plain sects: they moved to Virginia via Lancaster County, which was always the Mennonite stronghold; and if they were natives of Germany or Switzerland, they came from the same towns as did the Mennonites who established themselves permanently in Lancaster County.

We might accordingly expect Dayton German to be closer to the Lancaster subdialect than to any other, a fact subsequently borne out by the data. A great many of the forms found by Reed and Seifert only, or predominantly, in Lancaster County, agree with the Dayton forms, just as Sugar Grove was found to agree most often with the Berks dialect. There are a large number of exceptions, however, and Dayton German often agrees with the Lehigh dialect, which is the most different from the Lancaster dialect of all the Pennsylvania areas. Dayton German agrees with Lehigh as opposed to Lancaster in such instances as *grumbēre* 'potatoes,' *mūndǫg* 'Monday,' *der* 'door,' and *kǐch* 'kitchen.' Variants peculiar to the Dayton dialect also appear occasionally, for example, *härschd* 'autumn.'

It is likely, then, that the present-day Dayton forms which agree with the Lehigh dialect must have been present at one time in the Lancaster dialect also, since the settlement history of the Mennonite group at Dayton parallels that of the Mennonites in Lancaster County so closely. We may conclude that considerable leveling took place at one time in Lancaster County to produce the dialect spoken there today. The same is true for Dayton German, but with different combinations of features finally selected in each case.

Dayton German also differs from the German spoken in Lancaster

County in one striking phonological feature: it retains front-rounded vowels, which are phonemic in the dialect. We may suppose that front-rounding was present at one time also in the German of Lancaster County, but that it has been leveled out, while it is only now in the process of being leveled in Dayton German.

It also seems possible to determine with some degree of accuracy approximately how long it took for the subdialects spoken in Pennsylvania to emerge from the leveling process in what is essentially their present-day form. This can be done by taking into consideration data from additional Pennsylvania German speech islands, those of the Middle West. Data available on two such dialects spoken today in Kansas and Oklahoma,[4] indicate that there is much less difference between these dialects and Pennsylvania German proper than is the case when the Virginia dialects are compared with Pennsylvania speech. Furthermore, these Middle Western dialects are virtually identical to each other, which is not found to be the case when the Dayton and Sugar Grove dialects are compared. The Kansas and Oklahoma dialects reveal almost no instances of forms not recorded at all in Pennsylvania by Reed and Seifert. There is no trace of front-rounded vowels, even though the speakers are descended from the same group of Mennonites who settled in Lancaster County and who gave rise to the Dayton dialect. The explanation for the deviance of the Virginia dialects as compared to those of the Middle West is not difficult to find. Informants in the latter group can trace their history back to small groups of Mennonites who had left the Lancaster area in the 1840's to move westward into Ohio.[5] Later, some of the families continued farther west to make their homes in Kansas and Oklahoma in the last quarter of the nineteenth century. The close similarities of these dialects to

---

[4] Near Hutchinson, Reno County, Kansas, and at Thomas, Custer County, Oklahoma. The Oklahoma data was gathered in 1966 and 1967, while the Hutchinson dialect was studied during August 1968 as a part of Glenn G. Gilbert's Kansas German project.

[5] Informants in Kansas and Oklahoma, as well as at Dayton, Virginia, all of which are Mennonite communities, are conscious of their Lancaster County origins and can verify it by reference to old family Bibles. The German speakers at Sugar Grove, West Virginia, on the other hand, are not as certain of their family histories; they are members of the Lutheran Church.

each other and to the Pennsylvania dialects of today can only be accounted for by assuming that the leveling process which must have occurred in Lancaster County had operated quite effectively to produce a homogeneous dialect, essentially the dialect spoken in Lancaster County today, prior to the time of divergence in the second quarter of the nineteenth century. Many of the competing features present at the time of the founding of the German settlements in Virginia and West Virginia must, accordingly, have been eliminated by the time of the later westward migration.

The time required for the leveling process to move toward completion in Lancaster County was a relatively short one. It is interesting to note that the front-rounded vowels of Dayton German are only now being lost, indicating a much slower process of leveling with regard to at least this one feature of the phonology. This can be expected, however, since it seems reasonable to suppose that, other things being equal, leveling will occur the more rapidly the greater the number of the speakers in contact with each other and the less self-contained the speech community involved. Speakers of Dayton German have not been able to converse with speakers of German from the next county for many decades, while the opposite is true in Pennsylvania.

Any discussion of Virginia German would be incomplete without examining the problem of front-rounded vowels in the Dayton dialect, since an attempt to account for their gradual loss is of interest when considered in the light of the recent debate within linguistics concerning the nature of sound change.[6]

Dayton German retains the high-front rounded /ü/ and mid-front rounded /ö/, which have never been reported previously in descriptions of Pennsylvania German and which are generally absent in the southwestern German dialects that gave rise to Pennsylvania German. It seems likely that a minority of the early German and Swiss immigrants to Pennsylvania spoke dialects preserving the front-rounded vowels, and that at least some of the first German speakers to settle at Dayton were members of this group. This seems particularly likely

---

[6] The traditional neo-grammarian position on sound change is termed, in this paper, the gradualist hypothesis; it is set forth in Hockett (1958:439–445). This view is challenged by Postal (1968:286–307).

since Swiss settlers were probably well represented among the founders of the Dayton community. The Swiss dialects have been more conservative in retaining the front-rounded vowels than have the neighboring German dialects.[7]

The most interesting aspect of the data obtained from informants at Dayton is, however, a purely phonetic one. Whenever front-rounded vowels occur in Dayton German, they are always found to have only a slight phonetic degree of rounding. The data also indicate that a process of on-going sound change is now taking place in the dialect, leading to the loss of the umlaut vowels altogether. The mid-front rounded /ö/ occurs only in the speech of the oldest generation; younger speakers have only the high-front rounded /ü/, and both these vowels only occur contiguous to bilabials. /ü/ and /ö/ are phonemic, since they are found only in forms where they would be expected historically and contrast with their unrounded counterparts /e/ and /i/, which also occur contiguous to bilabial consonants.[8]

The data seem interesting in the light of the recent discussion on the nature of sound change. Since the slight degree of rounding, noted in a dialect apparently losing its front-rounded vowels, might seem to point to a pre-terminal stage in a process of gradual change, an attempt to interpret the data in this way might prove enlightening.

The term "gradual sound change" is here taken to be a change resulting from innumerable, imperceptible shifts in the articulatory habits of native speakers, caused by factors of linguistic performance, and eventually culminating in the addition or deletion of a phonologically distinctive feature. If it could be shown that in the case of Dayton German a gradual decrease in the degree of rounding of /ü/ and /ö/ has actually caused, or is causing, the loss of distinctive front-rounding, it would then be possible to assert that gradual sound change has

---

[7] Large numbers of the Mennonites who came to Pennsylvania, and to Lancaster County in particular, were from Switzerland. "Von den hochdeutschen Mundarten haben die gerundeten [Vorder]vokale bewahrt: im Norden das Ripuarische, in der Mitte das Ostfränkische einschließlich des südlichen Ausläufers des Thüringschen (Ruhle), im Süden das Oberalemannische (der größte Teil der Schweiz außer den südlichen Mundarten von Bern und dem Wallis); ferner Vorarlberg und Südbaden.... Die übrigen hochdeutschen Mundarten entrunden" (Schirmunski, 1962:205).

[8] Length was not found to be phonemic.

actually taken place in at least one documented instance. Examination of the data, however, immediately reveals certain problems in attempting to posit such a change. The occurrence of front-rounded vowels was observed in the speech of three informants, members of successive generations of the same family.[9] As mentioned above, only the oldest speaker has the mid-front rounded /ö/, while all the informants have the high-front rounded /ü/. In addition, the degree of rounding in particular occurrences of /ü/ seems to decrease slightly with each successive generation, with the youngest speaker having the least rounding.

If an attempt is made to account for all stages of the observed change by positing gradual drift, then at least three distinct shifts in habits of articulation, taking place in distinct environments, would have to be assumed. At least one process of gradual drift would be needed to account for the loss of front-rounding in all environments other than contiguous to bilabials. This would be followed by another gradual change deleting /ö/; a further process of shifts in the articulatory habits of the speakers would finally result in the disappearance of /ü/. Such a series of gradual changes would require the passage of a long period of time and would surely take place during many generations of speakers. It would be sufficient, however, to point to any one stage in the process of change; by showing that this stage is gradient, one could cite an actual instance of gradual change. Perhaps the potential loss of /ü/, articulated with progressively less rounding by members of the younger generations, could supply the evidence.

The question is whether the hypothesis of gradual change is compatible with the fact that younger speakers have the least rounding. Gradient change would not necessarily be incompatible with such observed differences in the speech of various generations. What is essential to the gradualist hypothesis is that shifts in habits of articulation take place within a group of speakers who imitate each other, and whose articulations drift along together. The relative rate of drift might well

[9] In Dayton, the informant from the oldest generation was 78 years of age. He is the uncle of the informant from the next oldest age group, who was 65 and the father of the third informant, a single woman of 32 living at home. Only one informant was interviewed at Sugar Grove. He was 86 years of age and represented the one generation that still speaks German.

proceed more rapidly among members of one generation than among members of another. If each generation is thought of as forming, in a sense, its own speech community, then, in the case of Dayton German, younger speakers could be considered as belonging to progressively more bilingual speech communities. The fact that the youngest speakers speak English, perhaps more often than German, might cause them to tend to articulate particular occurrences of the German front-rounded vowels with progressively less rounding as their habits of articulation slowly change under the influence of English.

If this were the case, then parallel developments would be expected in other dialects of American German; but the available evidence reveals the contrary to be true. In a recent study by this writer of the German spoken in two North Texas communities it was found that speakers who had ceased using German in 1916 nonetheless articulated front-rounded vowels with a phonetic degree of rounding approximating that of Standard German. There were no instances of very slight rounding as a result of the speakers' almost exclusive use of English over a period of nearly half a century (Pulte 1970).

Further evidence is supplied by Kehlenbeck (1948) in his description of a Low German dialect spoken in Iowa since 1840. Kehlenbeck finds five front-rounded vowels in the dialect and concludes that the vocalism has remained unchanged during a long period of German-English bilingualism.

This seems to indicate that the use of English is incapable of causing gradual loss of front-rounding in the dialects of American German that have been studied, and the data from Dayton German must be accounted for in some other way. No alternative solution for the slight phonetic degree of rounding readily suggests itself. In any case, what is really significant is the implication that this conclusion has for the entire hypothesis of gradual sound change. If gradient change were ever to occur, we might expect to find it in progress in language contact situations, which seem to provide an optimal environment for this sort of change. Such an optimal environment would consist of an immigrant language yielding to a national or standard language that is used increasingly by the bilingual speakers, particularly those of the younger generations. The receding language would have distinctive feature(s) not found in the predominant language. It might be supposed that any such features would tend to have their degree of phonetic realization gradually and imperceptibly reduced as the speakers' articulations shift in the direction of the second language. This would seem particularly likely when the feature in question is a relatively unstable, highly marked feature such as rounding of front vowels. We would then expect to be able to observe the gradual change in progress by noting that the more bilingual speakers would exhibit a lesser phonetic degree of the feature in question in their articulation than would less bilingual speakers. It should then be possible to find several degrees of, say, rounding, which could be correlated with the extent to which a speaker uses the prestige language.

But if no examples of this kind can be found in particular cases of languages-in-contact, then the entire gradualist hypothesis becomes untenable. If such a constant, ever-present factor of linguistic performance as the daily use of a second language, at times used exclusively over a period of decades, cannot be shown to bring about gradual sound change, then it would seem pointless to entertain the notion that such change occurs in a statistically random fashion.

This discussion of a method of testing for gradual sound change due to performance factors has led rather far afield from a rote description of German as it is still spoken in Virginia, but perhaps this is desirable. Writers on various aspects of dialectology are often reproached, and rightfully so, for not looking at the data they present in the light of linguistic theory, thus failing to contribute to an understanding of what language is and how it operates and changes through time. In this instance, an attempt to account for data from a little-known German dialect has led to a concrete and workable proposal for an empirical test of the hypothesis of gradual sound change, something that might have been done before had the theoreticians wrestled with enough real language data.[10]

In conclusion, it should be said that the six or seven German dialects remaining in Virginia and West Virginia can be fruitfully studied from

[10] Hockett (1958:445), for instance, states that his position on sound change is not accepted by many scholars, since "direct observation" of the process he posits "is impossible."

several points of view.[11] For those interested in the development of Pennsylvania German, they provide ample data for the reconstruction of much of the language as it was spoken in the eighteenth century. For those interested in the theory of linguistic change and for the effects of bilingualism upon this change, the Virginia dialects provide a living laboratory in which these processes can be observed. And finally, sociolinguists might wish to inquire why it is that the few communities in question have retained the German language for nearly a century longer than have the monolingual English-speaking areas that now surround them.

[11] In addition to Dayton, Virginia, and Sugar Grove, West Virginia, German dialect speakers may also be found at the following locations: Jerome, Shenandoah County, Virginia; at Bergton and Crider, Rockingham County, Virginia; and in Grant and Hardy Counties, West Virginia. This information is provided by Smith, Stewart, and Kyger (1962, map).

5. PENNSYLVANIA GERMAN FOLKLORE RESEARCH: A HISTORICAL ANALYSIS

DON YODER

University of Pennsylvania

Introduction

THE PENNSYLVANIA GERMANS are the most completely re-searched German-language group in the United States. Almost every folk-cultural phenomenon has been studied in its Pennsylvania German setting, from witchcraft to folk art, from barn architecture to dialect literature; the bibliography of Pennsylvania German folklore alone is immense. This paper will present a historical analysis of the rise and progress of folklore scholarship on the Pennsylvania Germans from the 1890's to the present. It is intended to provide a model for similar work on the other German ethnic cultures of the United States and Canada, and the conclusions and discussions following it are designed to promote further research in all the German-language areas of America.

The Pennsylvania Germans were "discovered" in the nineteenth century by the international travelers, especially those from Germany, who commented on their "bastard patois"—their "Busch-Deutsch," to use Kohl's word (1856:539)—and their antique manners and customs; by the American historians Bancroft and Parkman; and finally by such locals as Phebe Earle Gibbons, whose book *"Pennsylvania Dutch," and Other Essays* (1872) is the first objective analysis.

In the twentieth century they have been discovered by the Philadelphia press and the American tourist of the automobile era, who found them quaint, picturesque, superstitious, and all the other clichés of tourist journalism; and finally by the serious scholar. The comments of scholars have ranged from William Wells Newell's somewhat premature reference (1883) to the Pennsylvania Germans as "that strangely unimaginative race,"[1] to John Joseph Stoudt's reluctant claims (1955: xxxi–xxxii) that quantitatively there was more poetry (German of course) produced in colonial Pennsylvania than in Puritan New England. When they have not been skirmishing with each other over the terms "Pennsylvania Dutch" and "Pennsylvania German," the native scholars from within the culture have produced many monographs of scholarly value; and they have been joined increasingly by representatives from various academic disciplines who have contributed objective outside views of this geographically extensive and historically important American culture.

The Pennsylvania German cultural areas—where Pennsylvania German is still spoken—include southeastern Pennsylvania, the original locus of the culture, and parts of the Pennsylvania German diaspora.[2] The diaspora settlements include central and western Pennsylvania, parts of western Maryland, the Shenandoah Valley of Virginia, parts of Ontario, and the ethnic-sectarian enclaves of Pennsylvania Germans in the Midwest, from Ohio to Kansas.[3] The three areas of this ethnic-cultural map that have been most thoroughly researched with regard to German folklore are southeastern Pennsylvania, the Shenandoah area, and Ontario. From the 1890's to the present, work has been done by various institutions and private scholars and amateurs to gather

---

[1] Cited in B. A. Botkin (1944:807). The full statement is, "The game there is called 'Ring,' and has inspired certain verses of Harbach, the nearest approach to a poet which that unimaginative race has produced."

[2] The mapping of the diffusion of Pennsylvania German cultural influences in the United States began of course with the linguistic atlases. Recently the folklife scholars have begun to trace the diffusion of the material culture of the Pennsylvania Germans; see Henry Glassie (1965–1966, 1968).

[3] Colonial German settlements, independent of the Pennsylvania German migrations, existed in Maryland, Virginia, North Carolina, South Carolina, Georgia, and Louisiana, as well as in New Jersey, New York, Maine, and Nova Scotia.

what remains of the entire folk-culture as preserved in the matrix of the dialect.

We will begin with what has been done in the original Pennsylvania German territory, southeastern Pennsylvania. While there are several ways of organizing the analysis, one being to concentrate on the two periods in which Pennsylvania German studies moved rapidly ahead, the 1890's and the 1930's, I prefer in this paper to center upon the types of institutions that have developed to do the major work in this field, and which, at the same time, themselves reflect, in differing degrees, the culture they wish to study: (1) academic institutions, (2) the ethnic societies, and (3) the "new folklore" institutions of the twentieth century.

Academic Institutions

The University of Pennsylvania was the pioneer institution in the study of Pennsylvania German language and culture. Its many contributions extend from Rush's *An Account of the Manners of the German Inhabitants of Pennsylvania* (1789), through Samuel Stehman Haldeman's pioneer linguistic study of the dialect, *Pennsylvania Dutch: A Dialect of South German with an Infusion of English* (1872);[4] Oswald Seidensticker's *The First Century of German Printing in America, 1728–1830* (1893);[5] and Otto Springer's *A Working Bibliography for the Study of the Pennsylvania German Language and Its Sources* (1941); to the present Graduate Program in Folklore and Folklife that is looking in detail at Pennsylvania German culture. The high point in the earlier period was reached with the work of Marion Dexter Learned (1857–1917), who headed the German Department at Pennsylvania, 1895–1917.[6] Although his work had many facets, his major emphasis was on American-German cultural relations. His linguistic studies of Pennsylvania German, his publication of colonial German source materials, and his survey of German archival materials

---

[4] For Haldeman (1812–1880), see *Dictionary of American Biography* 8:94–95; also Charles Henry Hart (1881).

[5] For Seidensticker (1825–1894), see *Dictionary of American Biography* 16:561; also C. F. Huch (1909).

[6] *Dictionary of American Biography* 11:78–79; see also the recent appraisal of Learned's work in John J. Appel (1962).

relating to emigration to the United States all contributed to our understanding of Pennsylvania German culture. Learned also deserves the credit for setting up the first American ethnographic survey in the United States dealing with European rather than American Indian cultures—the American Ethnographical Survey of 1902. This concentrated on the Conestoga Valley, in particular on Strasburg Township, Lancaster County, which had at that time been settled for 175 years and was almost uniformly Pennsylvania German in its ethnic consistency (Learned 1911, 1915). The survey, which looked at a wide variety of folk-cultural phenomena, makes Learned one of the pioneers of the folklife studies movement in the United States. Learned's guidance and rigid academic standards were a help in spreading Pennsylvania German studies through the medium of students like Preston A. Barba, Edwin M. Fogel, and others.[7] Learned's biographer in the *Dictionary of American Biography* tells us that "he scorned the popular demand for readable books as something unworthy, tending to lower scientific standards." In typical German university fashion, he preferred to "let truth unadorned radiate from the documents."

Edwin Miller Fogel (1874–1949), a student and later a colleague of Learned's on the Pennsylvania faculty, contributed several of the best American regional treatments of superstitions and of proverbs and proverbial lore—the volumes entitled *Beliefs and Superstitions of the Pennsylvania Germans* (1915a) and *Proverbs of the Pennsylvania Germans* (1925). Fogel was also one of the principal founders of the Pennsylvania German Folklore Society in 1935.[8]

Cornelius Weygandt (1871–1957) of Pennsylvania's English faculty is remembered today for his reminiscent books on the life of the "Country Dutch" as viewed by a Philadelphian, from *The Red Hills: A Record of Good Days Outdoors and In, With Things Pennsylvania*

---

[7] For Learned's students and their bibliography, see *University of Pennsylvania Newsletter: Department of Germanic Languages* 2(1959):42–59.

[8] For Fogel's biography, see Barba (1949). His "pornographic" *Supplement to Beliefs and Superstitions of the Pennsylvania Germans* (1915b:345–357) was recently republished. It had been marked "For Private Distribution, Not for Public Perusal." See George Swetnam (1965).

Dutch (1929), dedicated to Oswald Seidensticker, to *The Dutch Country: Folks and Treasures in the Red Hills of Pennsylvania* (1939). With these books, Weygandt helped the nation to discover the charms of rural "Dutch" Pennsylvania; more than any other single writer of the twentieth century, he gave Pennsylvania tourism and Pennsylvania antiquery and folk-art studies their rationale.[9]

In the history of Pennsylvania German studies, the friendly rivalry between Muhlenberg College and Franklin and Marshall College is an important one to analyze. The colleges represented the two majority religious traditions of the Pennsylvania Germans (the Lutherans and the Reformed), and it was from these churches that the first interest in the dialect, dialect literature, and native folklore had sprung—in the work of Harbaugh, Keller, Schantz, Dubbs, and other pioneer writers. In the 1920's and 1930's the combination at Muhlenberg College of Preston A. Barba and Harry Hess Reichard[10] on the German faculty, and the addition for a time of Ralph C. Wood and Alfred L. Shoemaker, made it the center of Pennsylvania German studies. Preston Barba, a protegé of Learned, had perhaps the widest influence on younger scholars in the field in the second quarter of the twentieth century.[11] His interest in cultural history and thorough knowledge of the European folk-cultures which contributed to the eighteenth century emigration to Pennsylvania led him to set his work in a broad perspective. He will be remembered for two voluminous and important contributions to the bibliography in this field. His weekly column in the Allentown *Morning Call*, *'S Pennsylfawnisch Deitsch Eck* (known among the cognoscenti as simply the *Eck*), which ran regularly from 1935 until 1969, is available bound in long galley-like reprint form in many libraries. The contents of the *Eck* have ranged from dialect poetry and prose to Pennsylvania German history, biography, and folklore

[9] See Olive G. Zehner (1953) and Cornelius Weygandt (1953). The issue of *The Pennsylvania Dutchman* in which these articles appeared was dedicated to Weygandt, "whose writings first won national recognition for the Dutch Country and its culture."

[10] See the biography of Reichard (1878–1956) in *The Pennsylvania Dutchman* (May 19, 1949) 1(3):1; also Homer T. Rosenberger (1966, index).

[11] For an appraisal of Preston A. Barba's work, see *The Pennsylvania Dutchman* (June 15, 1950) 2(4):1, 4; also Rosenberger (1966:202–206).

per se. Particularly good have been his long series of word studies in the *Wörter und Sachen* tradition. His second large contribution has been the scholarly editing of the yearbooks of the Pennsylvania German Folklore Society (of which he was also one of the founders) from volume 1 (1935) to volume 28 (1966).

Franklin and Marshall College was for the decade of the 1950's the center of the most active movement to study Pennsylvania German culture, not only in its linguistic and folkloristic aspects, but—using the European *Volkskunde* and *Folklivsforskning* methodology—studying the entire folk-culture, historically and ethnographically, in its verbal, spiritual, social, and material aspects. The movement began in 1949 when three of the scholars who had worked widely in the area, Alfred L. Shoemaker, J. William Frey, and Don Yoder, converged at the college. The movement started on an ethnic note, calling itself the Pennsylvania Dutch Folklore Center and its periodical *The Pennsylvania Dutchman*. Increasingly, though, through Shoemaker's contacts with folk-cultural research in Europe immediately after World War II and my own contacts with European institutes and scholars beginning in 1950, the center was shaped into a folklife research institution. In the mid-1950's, long after we had come to the conclusion that the folklife approach was the more valid orientation, the name of the institution was formally changed to the Pennsylvania Folklife Society and the periodical, now in its eighteenth volume, to *Pennsylvania Folklife*.[12]

In a sense we went through the same "conversion"—pardon this word that reveals my religious thought connections—that younger scholars are now going through, the conversion from the narrow Anglo-American definition of "folklore" to "folklife," just as in the local and regional history field, scholars are beginning to see local history not only in the linear American history framework but also in the folk-cultural framework. The most recent general introduction to American folklore makes the statement, "A safe generalization is that

[12] For the background of the Pennsylvania Dutch Folklore Center and the Pennsylvania Folklife Society, see Don Yoder (1963).

76 DON YODER

American folklorists are gradually accepting the European concept of folklife as constituting their subject matter, and they are borrowing from ethnography and ethnology for new field methods and theories" (Brunvand 1968:198–199).

Several other Pennsylvania academic institutions deserve mention: (1) the Pennsylvania State University, where Albert F. Buffington for some years taught a course in Pennsylvania German culture and directed master's theses in Pennsylvania German linguistics and folklore;[13] (2) Susquehanna University, where Russell W. Gilbert, a graduate of the University of Pennsylvania, has written a series of analytical studies of Pennsylvania German dialect institutions such as the *Versammlinge*; and (3) Millersville State College, where the work of Henry J. Kauffman, Clyde S. Stine, and C. Richard Beam has been centered, and which is presently considering plans for a program in Pennsylvania German studies.

The Ethnic Societies

The second type of institution that has produced studies of Pennsylvania German folklore has been the ethnic society. These were organized from within the group to study its own culture and, originally, to minister to the feeling of group identity. The two examples are (1) the Pennsylvania German Society, founded in 1891, and (2) the Pennsylvania German Folklore Society, founded in 1935. After decades of rivalry the two have finally merged in this ecumenical age into a new Pennsylvania German Society.

In these days when ethnic identification and conflict are daily topics of discussion in the United States, it will be instructive to look at the ferment of ethnic feelings and frustrations that helped to produce the first native Pennsylvania German organizations. The Pennsylvania German Society (1891), which has had such a distinguished career of publishing not only Pennsylvania German folklore but history as well— sixty-three volumes up to the time of the merger with the sister society —reflects in its origins many of the cultural tensions undergone by all

---

[13] For example, the valuable work of Mary C. Kreider (1957); one chapter has been published in Kreider (1961).

minority ethnic groups struggling for acceptance. By the 1890's a certain group of eastern Pennsylvania ministers, teachers, and other leaders, tired of references to the "Dumb Dutch," conceived the idea of a Pennsylvania German Society. According to the Society's founders, the idea was far from new.

In fact, it was a favorite scheme with writers and thinkers of Pennsylvania German origin for generations. The "Sleeping Giant," as the Pennsylvania-German element had been aptly called, could not fail to impress them with his latent possibilities, and for almost a century there seems to have been a yearning among these people towards that fuller recognition, which, as the preponderating element of this great State, it was felt they deserved. But, with characteristic diffidence, they kept themselves in the background and permitted men of other nationalities to fill the places and exercise controlling influence where they themselves should have assumed direction.[14]

At the organization meeting "an animated discussion arose over the name to be given to the proposed organization, the names 'Pennsylvania-German Society' and 'Pennsylvania-Dutch Society' being warmly supported." At the first regular meeting, after listening to the Lancaster Maennerchor singing "characteristic [German-] German folksongs," the praise of the forefathers began. In many fields, in war and in peace, it was pointed out that "the Pennsylvania-German-Swiss element has equalled any other race."[15] Another speaker sounded the caution, however, that "we do not propose to organize a German society, to praise our ancestors as Germans, or to bother with foreign German problems, or customs. We have too many organizations in this land whose sole concern is with Old World conditions. We are

---

[14] The quotations in the present discussion in this and the following paragraph are from *The Pennsylvania-German Society: Sketch of Its Origin, with the Proceedings and Addresses at Its Organization* (1891) 1: v, vii, 9, 24.

[15] One common objection to the term "Pennsylvania German" is that it disguises the fact that a significant proportion of the Pennsylvania German population were of Swiss derivation. The Reformed, Mennonite, and Amish contingents among the emigrants bore for the most part Swiss names. Some of these families had emigrated directly from Switzerland in the eighteenth century; others had sojourned for a generation or more in Württemberg, Alsace, or the Palatinate before coming to the British Colonies.

Americans, and as such let us frown upon the insolence that seeks to exalt any other than the American flag." This interesting alternation between "Germanness" and flag-waving American nativism can be traced in detail in the fully reported speeches, addresses, and toasts given at the early meetings of the society. The nativist note was undoubtedly prompted by the "new immigration" that was making inroads in the Pennsylvania Dutch country. Since the national language was English, nativism even led some of the society's founders to an anti-dialect attitude. Nevertheless on the occasions when "Parre" Schantz told dialect stories, "laughter" and "applause" are noted in the minutes.

The membership rules involved three classes of membership: regular, associate, and honorary. "No one shall be eligible as a regular member unless he be of full age, of good moral character, and a direct descendant of early German or Swiss emigrants to Pennsylvania." Associate members had to be "of full age, good moral character, and of German descent not native in this State, or a foreign-born German naturalized and resident in this State not less than ten years." Finally, honorary membership was open to "persons who have made the history, genealogy, principles, etc., of the Pennsylvania Germans a special subject of study and research, and any other persons eminent in their profession or calling, to whatever nationality they may belong, who have shown themselves in sympathy with the Pennsylvania Germans."[16] Wavering thus between Pennsylvania-Germanism, American-Germanism, and American-nativism, the society's rules and regulations reflect the "identity crisis" that Pennsylvania Germans were going through at the turn of the century, a crisis reflected in school, church, and every other Pennsylvania German institution.

Preoccupation with ethnic identity, a necessary phase of ethnic group development, was to color Pennsylvania German scholarship for decades. So interested were the Pennsylvania Germans in proving who they were and in determining the boundaries of their ethnic consciousness that they occasionally fell into three serious distortions of Pennsylvania German culture: (1) a racial approach that defined "Pennsyl-

---

[16] This from the Constitution of the Society, adopted April 15, 1891.

vania German" on the basis of blood descent rather than cultural influence;[17] (2) a linear ethnic approach to culture that overemphasized solely "Germanic" influences on the Pennsylvania Germans to the neglect of the larger element of acculturation that every ethnic group has undergone in the American experience; and (3) a highly selective emphasis that focused only upon what one scholar used to call the "better elements" of the culture.[18] All these are of course examples of common defensive reactions of ethnic groups wrestling with the problem of their own identity in a larger society; the parallels to the present Negro identity crisis should be obvious. Unfortunately these biases were to affect Pennsylvania German scholarship for generations. In its early development the Pennsylvania German Society was the principal sounding board for these extreme ethnic positions from

[17] Some examples from vol. 1 of the *Proceedings of the Pennsylvania German Society*: One of the early members described himself as "a Pennsylvania German of five generations, of unbroken Pennsylvania descent and unmixed German blood." The insecurities revealed in such statements are also indicated by the constant habit of pointing to "great Pennsylvania Germans," or as the yearbook of the society expresses it, "citing bright examples of the men of mark of our State whose birth and lineage are Pennsylvania-German." This attitude continued into the 1930's; local newspaper columnists as well as some local scholars enlightened the world with the fact that Clark Gable, Herbert Hoover, John J. Pershing, and practically everyone but Franklin Delano Roosevelt were "Pennsylvania German" or had "Pennsylvania German blood," which made them into instant Pennsylvania Germans. The only time when this habit of overemphasizing Germanness became embarrassing was during the First World War. Several conspicuous Pennsylvania Germans suddenly became "Pennsylvania Frenchmen" and organized in 1918 the Huguenot Society of Pennsylvania. At the first meeting of the society in Reading, Pa., the members sang the Marseillaise (no doubt with Dutch accents), listened to addresses aimed at "fellow Huguenots," and made the "Huguenot" general, John J. Pershing, an honorary member.

[18] Arthur D. Graeff, columnist in the *Reading Times*, seems to have been responsible for this phrase. Emphasis on "better" elements implies that there are "worse" elements that someone must be ashamed of; it leaves out powwowing, *Hexerei*, and a great deal more. Determined to present to the public a dignified, stable, almost faultless middle-class Pennsylvania German, such approaches distort the truth and miss the great humanity and vitality in the earlier stages of Pennsylvania German culture. Recently, by contrast, a number of frank, no-holds-barred sociological studies, such as the model treatment of Amish tensions by John A. Hostetler, are providing us at last with an objective analysis of Pennsylvania German authoritarian fathers as well as Pennsylvania German adherence to "superstitious" folk-medical practices; see Hostetler (1961, 1963–1964, 1968).

within the culture. They are reflected principally in the addresses, toasts, and other communications reported in the minutes of the annual meetings. The monographs published by the society, however, represent for the most part a different level. They are scholarly and objective approaches to historical, folkloristic, and linguistic aspects of Pennsylvania German culture. For example, the society sponsored a series of important studies of the dialect and its literature. These include Marcus Bachman Lambert, *A Dictionary of the Non-English Words of the Pennsylvaia German Dialect* (vol. 30, 1924); Harry Hess Reichard, *Pennsylvania Dutch Dialect Writings and Their Writers* (vol. 26, 1918) and his anthology, *Pennsylvania German Verse* (vol. 48, 1940). Significant studies of religion have included Howard Wiegner Kriebel, *The Schwenkfelders in Pennsylvania* (vol. 13, 1904), and Calvin George Bachman, *The Old Order Amish of Lancaster County* (vols. 49, 1942, and 60, 1961). On the material culture there have been G. Edwin Brumbaugh's indispensable *Colonial Architecture of the Pennsylvania Germans* (vol. 41, 1930), and Henry Kinzer Landis, *Early Kitchens of the Pennsylvania Germans* (vol. 47, 1939). The pioneer volume on folklore as such is John Baer Stoudt, *The Folklore of the Pennsylvania Germans* (vol. 23, supplement, 1916). This was followed by a distinguished series of works by Thomas R. Brendle, who from the 1930's through the 1950's represented the acknowledged scholarly direction of the Society: (1) David E. Lick and Thomas R. Brendle, *Plant Names and Plant Lore among the Pennsylvania Germans* (vol. 33, 1923), which is perhaps the finest American study of regional herb lore and herbal medicine; (2) Thomas R. Brendle and Claude W. Unger, *Folk Medicine of the Pennsylvania Germans: The Non-Occult Cures* (vol. 45, 1935); and (3) Thomas R. Brendle and William S. Troxell, *Pennsylvania German Folk Tales, Legends, Once-upon-a-Time Stories, Maxims, and Sayings Spoken in the Dialect Popularly Known as Pennsylvania Dutch* (vol. 50, 1944). Similar to Brendle's work, and influenced by his approach, has been the scholarly contribution of William J. Rupp, *Bird Names and Bird Lore among the Pennsylvania Germans* (vol. 52, 1946). Folk art studies include Henry S. Borneman's *Pennsylvania German Illuminated Manuscripts* (vol. 46, 1937) and *Pennsylvania German Book-*

plates: A Study (vol. 54, 1953). One of the best regional approaches is George Korson, *Black Rock: Mining Folklore of the Pennsylvania Dutch* (vol. 59, 1960). And for folklore as well as dialect studies, there is the highly pleasing biography by Elizabeth Clarke Kieffer, *Henry Harbaugh, Pennsylvania Dutchman, 1817–1867* (vol. 51, 1945). These are a few examples of the most pertinent monographs issued by the Pennsylvania German Society in the sixty or more years of its existence.

By the 1930's, partially because of the continuing presence and publishing record of the Pennsylvania German Society, the Pennsylvania ethnic climate had changed. "Dutch" was now "beautiful," and what some writers have called a renaissance of Pennsylvania German studies was in full swing. A second generation of Pennsylvania Germans could now organize a new society dedicated specifically to folklore, the Pennsylvania German Folklore Society, founded May 4, 1935.

"Cognizant of the fact that with the passing of the years the Pennsylvania German dialect was slowly losing its hold in the life of the people, conscious of the necessity of preserving in scholarly fashion the culture of our people, and aware of the interest in the formation of an organization to carry out such a program, a group of interested individuals took the initiative and issued a call for a society."[19] The foreword to the first volume of the Society's publications announced that "the sphere of this Society is, of course, ethnological, seeking to record permanently the folk-mind of our own people. History, as such, is therefore to be subordinated, the main emphasis falling upon the cultural aspects of Pennsylvania German life." The phrase "our people" betrays a lingering ethnocentric emphasis, but the orientation is now folk-cultural and the defensive note is lacking.

The impressive and attractive series of yearbooks of the Pennsylvania German Folklore Society, bound in linen and stamped with traditional designs, represents an achievement in folk-cultural scholarship equally impressive to that of the older society. While some "history" was published, much of it is social history dealing with the Atlantic migration and the migrations to the South, to Canada, and to

---

[19] *The Pennsylvania German Folklore Society* 1 (1936, foreword).

the Midwest. The most pertinent of the migration studies is Elmer Lewis Smith, John G. Stewart, and M. Ellsworth Kyger, *The Pennsylvania Germans of the Shenandoah Valley* (vol. 26, 1962), based on extensive field recordings. Dialect studies have included the reprint of Charles Calvin Ziegler's *Drauss un Deheem* (vol. 1, 1936); John Birmelin's *Gezwitscher* (vol. 3, 1938), and his *Later Poems* (vol. 16, 1951); Clarence F. Iobst's play, *En Quart Millich un en Halb Beint Raahm* (vol. 4, 1939); and Lloyd A. Moll's prose collection, *Am Schwarze Baer* (vol. 12, 1947). There are also more formal dialect studies by Lester W. J. Seifert, *Lexical Differences between Four Pennsylvania German Regions* (vol. 11, 1946); and Albert F. Buffington, *Linguistic Variants in the Pennsylvania German Dialect* (vol. 13, 1948).

Craft studies are represented by Henry Kinzer Landis and George Diller Landis, *Lancaster Rifle Accessories* (vol. 9, 1944); Henry J. Kauffman, *Coppersmithing in Pennsylvania* (vol. 11, 1946); Guy F. Reinert, *Coverlets of the Pennsylvania Germans* (vol. 13, 1948); and Charles H. Dornbusch, *Pennsylvania German Barns* (vol. 21, 1956). Customs of the year have been treated in Edwin M. Fogel's later studies, *Of Months and Days* (vol. 5, 1940) and *Twelvetide* (vol. 6, 1941); George E. Nitzsche, *The Christmas Putz of the Pennsylvania Germans* (vol. 6, 1941); and William N. Schwarze, translator, *Transcriptions of Items from the Bethlehem Diary Relating to Early Celebrations of Christmas in Bethlehem, Pennsylvania* (vol. 6, 1941). Folk-art studies include John Joseph Stoudt, *Consider the Lilies How They Grow* (vol. 2, 1937), which is the best study of the religious and literary symbolism of Pennsylvania German folk art and is now in its third edition as *Pennsylvania German Folk Art: An Interpretation* (vol. 28, 1966); Preston Barba and Eleanor Barba, *Lewis Miller, Pennsylvania German Folk Artist* (vol. 4, 1939); Preston A. Barba, *Pennsylvania German Tombstones: A Study in Folk Art* (vol. 18, 1953); and Donald A. Shelley, *The Fraktur-Writings or Illuminated Manuscripts of the Pennsylvania Germans* (vol. 23, 1958–1959). Finally, there is an excellent categorization of Pennsylvania German folklore and the rationale of its study by John Joseph Stoudt, *Pennsylvania German Folklore: An Interpretation* (vol. 16, 1951).

It has been suggested that the two great waves of interest in Pennsylvania German culture, in the 1890's and 1930's, were reflex reactions among the Pennsylvania German intelligentsia to the political and cultural changes in continental German nationalism. This point will not be argued here, since the Pennsylvania German renaissance (complete with its own ethnic societies) can be more readily accounted for by fitting it against the background of ethnic patterns and problems within the United States. The ethnic societies were in a sense Pennsylvania German replicas of such national patriotic societies as the Daughters of the American Revolution. At least in its earliest stages the Pennsylvania German Society, like the Daughters of the American Revolution, was based on heredity and had a highly selective view of American history.[20] But there were also in the post–Civil War era similar ethnocentric movements among other American ethnic groups. A recent study by John J. Appel (1955) on the historical societies formed by American ethnic groups discusses the motivation of such organizations. Appel points out the difficulty of merging nineteenth-century emigrant-German interests with Pennsylvania German interests. By contrast, the Scotch-Irish Presbyterians were more fortunate. The "Scotch-Irish Congresses" of the 1880's could make an appeal, based on a highly ethnic, cultural nationalism, to both descendants of colonial Scotch-Irish Presbyterians and to nineteenth-century emigrants. The people involved were often successful businessmen and Presbyterian clergymen who upgraded their Scotch-Irishism by differentiating themselves from the Catholic or "mere" Irish (Appel 1955: Chapter 2).

Different in approach from the American ethnic societies was the American Folklore Society, which was founded in 1888 on the model of the (British) Folklore Society. Its national orientation and its concern for all ethnic groups foreshadowed the pluralistic approach of the social sciences today and stirred up interest in regional folklore, including that of the Pennsylvania Germans. In the first two decades of its existence, while the leaders of the Pennsylvania German Society

[20] For the background of the DAR and related "hereditary organizations," see Wallace E. Davies (1955), especially chapter 3, "Blue Blood Turns Red, White, and Blue."

were still wrestling with ethnic identity and had not yet really discovered folklore in the Anglo-American sense of the word, the American Folklore Society began to publish articles on Pennsylvania
German lore. These include W. J. Hoffman, "Folklore of the Pennsylvania Germans" (vols. 1–2, 1888–1889); J. G. Owens, "Folk-Lore
from Buffalo Valley, Central Pennsylvania" (vol. 4, 1891); Frederick
Starr, "Some Pennsylvania-German Lore" (vol. 4, 1891); "Pennsylvania Germans" (Moravians) (vol. 8, 1895); and John Baer Stoudt,
"Pennsylvania-German Riddles and Nursery Rhymes" (vol. 19,
1906). This work of Stoudt deserves mention as a link between the
two societies. It led to his later book, *The Folklore of the Pennsylvania
Germans*, which was the Pennsylvania German Society's first venture
into publishing folklore as such (vol. 23, supplement, 1916).[21] The
example of the American Folklore Society is reflected also in the work
of its regional daughter organization, the Pennsylvania Folklore Society
(organized in 1926). Through the years its publications have offered
many items on the Pennsylvania Germans.

From the earliest period of concentration on Pennsylvania German
culture, a number of distinguished contributions by American and
European scholars have been made independently of the ethnic societies. Especially worthy of mention are the important works of the
American ethnologist, Dr. Walter J. Hoffman (1846–1899), from
"Folk Medicine of the Pennsylvania Germans," *American Philosophical Society Proceedings* (vol. 26, 1889)[22] to *Folklore and Language of
the Pennsylvania Germans* (1899).

The works of Henry C. Mercer (1856–1930), one of the first Pennsylvania scholars to study the material folk-culture, are worthy of detailed note. He developed the Bucks County Historical Society and its
Mercer Museum into the finest collection in Pennsylvania (and one of
the finest in the United States) for the study of tools, crafts, and industries of early America. In the general American field his work was
an inspiration for the Early American Industries Association. In the

---

[21] John Baer Stoudt (1878–1944) was the leading spirit in the organization of the
Pennsylvania German Folklore Society in 1935. See Harry Hess Reichard (1944).

[22] For Hoffman's work, see his biography in *The Pennsylvania-German* (Dec.
1907: 583–585).

field of Pennsylvania German he ranks as the discoverer of *Fraktur,* Pennsylvania's most important folk-art tradition.[23]

Of the European scholars, the elusive Karl Knortz, who was one of the founders of both American and American-German folklore studies, began to publish articles on Pennsylvania German dialect and lore as early as 1873 in *Der Deutsche Pionier.* In the next four decades he produced a stream of books on American and principally American-German folklore, including *Folkloristische Streifzüge* (1899), *Nachklänge germanischen Glaubens und Brauchs in Amerika: Ein Beitrag zur Volkskunde* (1903), and *Amerikanischer Aberglaube der Gegenwart* (1913). A list of some thirty of his publications appears in the Pochmann-Schultz *Bibliography of German Culture in America to 1940* (1953).

In the twentieth century the distinguished work of Heinz Kloss in linguistic and ethnic history and Emil Meynen's studies of Pennsylvania German cultural geography and bibliography need no detailed analysis here. They are both basic, constantly used by scholars in many disciplines, and always useful as guides to further research.[24]

In the last decade, several new agencies have arisen in Pennsylvania to promote folk-cultural research. Several of these are regional historical and folk-cultural groups that directly or indirectly show the influence of the folklife approach of the Pennsylvania Folklife Society. The principal groups are (1) Goschenhoppen Historians, with its field of research in the historic "Goschenhoppen" area in Montgomery and adjoining counties north of Philadelphia, the oldest Pennsylvania German rural area in continuous settlement; (2) Historic Schaefferstown, a group planning an open-air museum for the Lebanon County area; (3) Community Historians, a Lancaster County group; and (4) the Council of the Alleghenies, centered in Upper Appalachia and in-

---

[23] See Mercer (1897). Mercer's work is discussed in Dunbar (1961).

[24] See especially Heinz Kloss (1929), still the best small anthology of Pennsylvania German prose; Kloss (1931); Kloss's maps of the Pennsylvania German settlements in Winkler (1935); Kloss (1937); Kloss (1952), especially the chapter on "Halbsprachen" (Pennsylfaanisch), pp. 119–126; and Kloss's chapter in Fishman (1966). The indispensable bibliography in the entire field of Pennsylvania German studies is Emil Meynen (1937); see also Meynen's important cultural-geographical study, "Das pennsylvanien-deutsche Bauernland" (1939).

volving parts of Pennsylvania, Maryland, Virginia, and West Virginia. Several new regional historical and folklife journals have been initiated by these groups, as for example, *The Goschenhoppen Region*, a quarterly that has now completed its first volume, 1968–1969.[25]

In 1966 the Commonwealth of Pennsylvania, through the instigation of Professor MacEdward Leach of the University of Pennsylvania, founded the Ethnic Culture Survey under the Pennsylvania Historical and Museum Commission. Henry Glassie, the first director of the survey, served from 1966 to 1969. Glassie, who was also state folklorist, has published distinguished work in American material folk-culture. He was succeeded in 1969 as head of the survey by David S. Hufford. For the history and plans of the state program, see MacEdward Leach and Henry Glassie, *A Guide for Collectors of Oral Traditions and Folk Cultural Material in Pennsylvania* (1968), which includes Pennsylvania German material and bibliography.

Finally, it should be mentioned that the Folklore and Folklife Program of the University of Pennsylvania has begun work on Pennsylvania subjects in connection with its research goals in American regional and ethnic folklore/folklife. In the planning stage is a full-fledged folklife institute on the model of the German and Scandinavian institutes of ethnography and regional history.

Folksong Research

For a detailed example of folklore research in one particular genre, I have chosen to discuss research in Pennsylvania German folksong traditions.

Pennsylvania German folk music is hardly represented in the commercial record catalogues; there is one nationally circulated album, George Britton's *Pennsylvania Dutch Folksongs* (Folkways Records FP615, 1955). Pennsylvania as a whole is scantily represented in the Archive of American Folksong in the Library of Congress, and of the published works on Pennsylvania German folk music there are only a few that are available for study: the Brendle-Troxell collection of 28 songs (out of 200 recorded) in George Korson's *Pennsylvania Songs*

[25] For these more recent movements, see Arthur J. Lawton (1967): Clarence Kulp, Jr. (1967); and Alta Schrock (1967).

and Legends (1949), the Boyer-Buffington-Yoder collection *Songs along the Mahantongo* (1951), Ruth L. Hausman's *Sing and Dance with the Pennsylvania Dutch* (1953), and Don Yoder's *Pennsylvania Spirituals* (1961).[26]

The major work on folksongs has been done by teams of field workers: for example, Brendle and Troxell, whose collection of some 200 songs has recently been transferred from disk to tape for analysis; Boyer-Buffington-Yoder, who worked in depth on the Mahantongo area of Schuylkill, Northumberland, and Dauphin Counties, Pennsylvania; Shoemaker-Frey-Yoder, who worked separately but published together under the auspices of the Pennsylvania Folklife Society; and Clarence Kulp, Jr., Robert C. Bucher, and Alan G. Keyser of the Goschenhoppen Historians, who have been recording folksong material (much of which is rare and of considerable value for comparison with the published collections) from the "plain" sectarians of the Goschenhoppen area north of Philadelphia. In addition, John A. Hostetler and C. Richard Beam have recorded religious folksongs. Hostetler worked among the Old Order Amish and Beam among the Old Order River Brethren.

The secular folksongs sung by Pennsylvania Germans deal with a wide variety of themes that reflect the history as well as the folk-culture of the group. Of historical interest are the songs dealing with the emigration and the political campaign songs. Among the latter there is the amusing parody of the *Doctor Eisenbart* song that circulated in the Delamater-Pattison gubernatorial campaign of 1891:

> *Der Dellemeeder kummt net nei,*
> *Zwilli willi wie kumm bumm!*
> *Der Bobby Pattison iss der Mann,*
> *Ass der Dellemeeder biede kann,*
> *Zwilli willi wie kumm bumm!*
> (Boyer, Buffington, Yoder 1951:187–188)

One large category is the type of humorous song sung by courting couples at the "snitzing-" and other work-parties of the nineteenth

[26] In addition there exist several early collections of Pennsylvania German folksongs without musical notation; see S. P. Heilman (1899); and John Baer Stoudt (1916).

century. These are essentially German imports and include such well-known songs as "Schpinn, schpinn, meine liewe Dochder," "Meedli, widdu heiere?," "Wie kumm ich an des Vaadershaus?," "Siss net alli Daag luschdich Leewe!," "Ich hab gedraamt die anner Nacht" (sung to the tune of "Oh Susanna"), "Zu der Lissie bin ich gange," and "Geschder waar der Michel do." (Boyer, Buffington, Yoder 1951: 59–83, 88–93) In addition there are children's songs, drinking songs, and various satirical materials dealing with American situations.

In the special area of religious folk music there are two genres that merit further study, the Amish slow tunes and the "bush-meeting" or German Methodistic spirituals. Much research has been done in both of these categories; in fact more effort has now been spent on the religious genres than on the secular ones.

The Amish *langsame Weisen* are the slow tunes of the curious *Ausbund,* ballads of martyrdom from the sixteenth-century Anabaptist movement that are still sung by the Old Order Amish. These are interesting to scholars from the standpoint of their archaic German and their archaic tunes. The *Ausbund* texts and hymnody have been analyzed by Rudolf Wolkan in *Die Lieder der Wiedertäufer* (1903). In the United States Joseph W. Yoder published in 1942 his transcription of thirty-five *langsame Weisen* as he recorded them in the Old Order Amish community (of which he was originally a member) in the Kishacoquillas Valley of Mifflin County, Pennsylvania. The volume is entitled *Amische Lieder* and was analyzed by George Pullen Jackson, the chief discoverer of the white spiritual tradition in the United States, in "The Strange Music of the Old Order Amish" (1945); and by J. William Frey in his chapter, "Amish Hymns as Folk Music" (1949) in George Korson's *Pennsylvania Songs and Legends* (1949). The historical background and literary analysis of the texts of the *Ausbund* has been presented in a lengthy paper by William I. Schreiber, "The Hymns of the Amish Ausbund in Philological and Literary Perspective" (1962a). Finally, with all this expressed interest by outsiders to the *Ausbund* hymns, the Mennonites themselves have published a symposium on the subject (P. Yoder, Bender, Grober, and Springer 1964).[27]

[27] For the *Ausbund* and its use in Mennonite and Amish sects, see *The Mennonite*

The Amish and the plain sectarian groups are only one small seg-
ment of the Pennsylvania German population. The largest groups
were and are the "church people," the *Kaerricheleit* (*Kirchenleute*),
who sang in German until the 1930's in some rural union churches.
Their hymnody, which does not lend itself to a folk interpretation,
was literary and their musical tradition was sophisticated and eventually marked by the use of pipe organ and choir. There was also a
third religious division of the Pennsylvania German population that
was practically a folk movement. This consisted of the sectarian groups
that arose from the interaction of the Anglo-American revivalist movements (in Pennsylvania principally Methodism) and the Pennsylvania
German culture. What resulted was a dozen or more sects that grew up
on Pennsylvania soil, such as the United Brethren, the Evangelical
Association (*Evangelische Gemeinschaft*), the Church of God, the
United Christians, the United Evangelicals, the United or Evangelical
Mennonites, the United Zion's Children, and the Heavenly Recruit
Association. These were, at least in part, Pennsylvania German linguistically, of the lower class economically, and Methodistic—even to
the shouting—in their piety. To use a biblical allusion, the hands were
Esau's but the voice was Jacob's. Beginning in southeastern Pennsylvania and western Maryland, these intensely missionary little sects
spread in the nineteenth century to the west, to the south, and to the
north (Ontario) with the Pennsylvania German diaspora. In the process they converted a great many of the nineteenth-century German emigrants who went to those areas.

Folkloristically, the most distinctive aspect of the bush-meeting culture was its hymnody. The songs they sang were white spirituals related in text and tune to the white spirituals of the southern uplands
and the Negro spirituals; instead of being in English, however, they
were couched in various levels of German from almost full-dialect to
almost literary Standard German.[28] The materials were "folk" in that

---

Encyclopedia, 4 vols. (1955–1959), especially the articles on "Ausbund," "Amish
Singings," "Chorister," "Church Music," "Hymnology," and "Tunes." For additional
bibliography on Amish hymnody, see Don Yoder (1969).

[28] A linguistic analysis of the texts of the Pennsylvania spirituals, which rates them
closer to High German than to the Pennsylvania German dialect, appeared in Albert
F. Buffington (1965).

they were traditionally diffused or spread from one part of the religious community to another; they were normally sung without books, and so precious were they to the community that they were still recordable in the 1960's in twelve counties of eastern and central Pennsylvania (see D. Yoder 1961).

For several reasons it is important that this body of folk or traditional hymnody be recorded and analyzed. First, the songs are the representatives, *par excellence,* of the hybrid English/German character of Pennsylvania German culture. Second, of all the rich folksong materials once cultivated by the Pennsylvania Germans they are, along with the traditional hymnody of the Old Order Amishmen and the Old Order Mennonites, the only still functional folksong element of the culture. The secular songs are still passively remembered by a few older singers; the folk hymns or spirituals still have a function in the community. Third, these spirituals underwent a cultural diffusion in two directions, (1) from the evangelical sects to the plain sects, and (2) from both of the latter to the Russian-German "brotherhoods" of Nebraska and the Dakotas. It is interesting to note that some of these brotherhoods still sing their own versions of certain Pennsylvania German spirituals that arose in eastern Pennsylvania 150 years ago through culture contact of the Pennsylvania Germans with Anglo-American revivalism (D. Yoder 1961:355, 421–422).[29]

For future research in the Pennsylvania spiritual it will become increasingly important to search out the variants still sung or at least passively remembered by older singers in the plain traditions. In certain cases the musical picture is far from simple. Clarence Kulp, Jr., who is at present studying the Brethren and Mennonite cultures, reports that there are occasionally four tunes for one text known to the old-fashioned singers: *Kaerriche-Weise* (Lutheran or Reformed tunes), *Mennischte-Weise* (Mennonite tunes), *Dunker-Weise* (Dunkard tunes), and *Maeddedischt-Weise* (Methodist tunes) (D. Yoder 1961:38).

Another important area for research on the Pennsylvania spiritual

---

[29] For Russian-German spirituals, see especially Elias Hergert (191–). For the background of the pietistic brotherhoods in Europe, see George J. Eisenach (1950), especially Chapter 10, "Evangelisation und Erweckungen."

is the singing patterns of the emigrant-German congregations of fundamentalist sects in the Midwest and Canada. A recent study of religion in the province of Alberta reports that as late as 1946 "a number of German Baptist and Evangelical United Brethren preachers were still holding services in German, especially in rural areas. It was this kind of bilingual preaching that made possible seventeen German-speaking congregations and an almost equal number of Slavic churches within the Alberta Pentecostal Assemblies of Canada" (Mann 1955: 33, 35, 99). The singing patterns as well as the preaching styles of these emigrant sects deserve full recording and analysis in their own right, apart from the fact that they represent to some extent cultural and religious influences from Pennsylvania German culture.

"New Folklore" Institutions

In the 1930's and 1940's there arose a number of new Pennsylvania German institutions that attracted much local interest in the dialect-speaking areas. These were of several types: (1) folk festivals, (2) *Versammlinge* and *Grundsow Lodges*, (3) dialect plays, (4) dialect radio programs, (5) liars' contests and dialect spelling bees, and (6) dialect church services. These were in a sense the layman's updated equivalent of the earlier ethnic societies. While they involved traditional or "old" folklore in part, they have been instrumental in creating a new kind of dialect folklore for the Pennsylvania Germans. Let us briefly examine each type.

1. The folk festivals have become the most spectacular institution of the period. They can be traced to several origins. George Korson's All-Pennsylvania Folk Festivals at Allentown in 1935 and at Bucknell University in 1936–1937 first brought Pennsylvania German dialect performers to statewide prominence. Also important were William S. ("Pumpernickle Bill") Troxell's Pennsylvania German Folk Festival (Allentown, 1936–1941) and his "Applebutter Boilings" started in 1942 at Dorney Park near Allentown.[30] The latter were open-air picnics with local Dutch atmosphere, gvien some of their flavor by the day-

---

[30] Troxell's significance for Pennsylvania German has been summarized in Alfred L. Shoemaker (1949); see also Rosenberger (1966:308–313).

long ritual of boiling down cider and *Schnitz* into the Pennsylvania German specialty "applebutter" (*Lattwaerrick*) in huge copper kettles over an open fire. A dialect program with emphasis on broad Dutch humor was usually the feature of the afternoon. Since the 1940's, the boiling of applebutter as a symbol of the Dutch culture has been added to local celebrations, town anniversaries, even flea markets in Pennsylvania towns; the small open-air picnic has grown into the huge, nationally attended Pennsylvania Dutch Folk Festivals at Kutztown and the Pennsylvania Dutch Days at Hershey.[31]

2. *The Versammlinge* (1933 ff.) are usually held on winter evenings (Kemp 1944). They are linguistically all-dialect affairs and usually offer an abundant Dutch dinner. The programs involve Dutch toasts, jokes, lay sermons, and humorous addresses (See R. Gilbert 1951, 1956*a*). The *Versammlinge* appeal to the urban Dutchman, the professional or business man who has "grown up Dutch" and enjoys hearing the dialect at least once a year. There are even fines imposed for speaking English, which adds to the fun.

Very similar is the *Grundsow Lodch* (or *Lodge*), which also first made its appearance in 1933 (see Troxell 1953). It is organized tongue-in-cheek as a mock fraternal order with officers bearing "made-up" dialect titles and a heavy meal for the brother *Grundsei*. Annual meetings are held on or near "Groundhog Day" in February. The new-folklore elements in both this and the *Versammlinge* include the humorous menus (*Fuderzettel*, to use the coined word).[32] While oc-

---

[31] For the Pennsylvania Dutch Folk Festivals, see Maynard Owen Williams (1952); and E. Estyn Evans (1959). The Kutztown festival format and its total concentration on regional culture has influenced other American festivals, notably the Low Dutch Festival at Newton, Kansas; the Allegheny Festival at Penn Alps, Grantsville, Maryland; the Goschenhoppen Festival in Montgomery County, Pa.; and the Schaefferstown Festival in Lebanon County, Pa.

[32] For example, the *Fuder Tzettle* in *Die Nin'd Yairlich Fersommlung und Fesht fon da Grundsow Lodge Nummer Ains on da Lechaw* (Allentown, 1942) includes such coinage as *Obsht Hawna Schwontz* 'Fruit Cocktail,' *Greena Shofe G'noddle* 'green sheep nuttles' (i.e., 'peas'), *Narfa Shtangel* 'celery,' *Bidderra Blauma* 'olives,' *'M Adam Sei Unnergang* 'apples,' *Uff Shtose Mints* 'after dinner mints,' and of course, *Tzae Blicker* 'toothpicks.' Some of these go back to earlier programs and were copied by other dialect assemblies. For a brief comparative analysis of this phenomenon, with copies of two *Fuder Tzettle*, see Kemp (1944:199–203).

casionally the "old" folklore of the Pennsylvania Germans appears in a few of the dialect speeches and in the jokes, for the most part the jokes are current American joke material dressed up in Dutch dialect. These institutions, of which there are perhaps twenty, could therefore be characterized as a reflection of American popular culture naturalized into a Dutch setting.

3. Dialect plays began in the 1880's with *Die Inshurans Bissness* and have continued down to the present. They have been a very successful and popular newer feature of Pennsylvania German culture. The humor involves poking fun at common human types in small communities in their Pennsylvania Dutch versions: the town gossip (*Schteddelrutsch*) who "rutsches" around the town spreading her news, the "funeral runner" who attends every local funeral for the funeral meal, and other recognizable types. These plays, which are presented chiefly by church and grange groups, are analogous both to the general American "home talent" play that enjoyed considerable popularity in the 1920's and to the Alpine folk-theater that pokes fun even at the Catholic clergy. The Reichard-Buffington study of this phenomenon (Buffington 1962) is the best introduction.

4. Dialect radio programs made up of both new and old folklore elements have made their appearance since the Second World War. At one time there were programs from Easton, Allentown, Reading, Lancaster, Sunbury, Lebanon, and elsewhere. One of the most popular was that of G. Gilbert Snyder, "Die Wunnernaas," which was broadcast *iwwer die Luft* every Sunday at 1 P.M., giving his Dutch auditors just time to get home from church and sit down by their radios for fifteen minutes of laughter.[33] The Wunnernaas employed a popular culture format with a modified disk-jockey approach. Listeners' birthdays were cited, records of German *Schuhplattler* bands played, and other "German-German" phenomena emphasized. Among the other popular programs were those of Professor Buffington ("Der Nixnutz")[34] at Sunbury, Alfred L. Shoemaker (" 'S Rote Gaisbort Schu-

---

[33] For G. Gilbert Snyder (1897–1956), see *The Pennsylvania Dutchman* 1, no. 2 (May 12, 1949): 1; also Rosenberger (1966:206–209).

[34] For a history of the *Nixnutz* program, a transcript of a sample program in

macher" at Reading, and Florence Baver (" 'S Bobbelmowl") at Easton. These were popular because they involved listening to oral dialect rather than the laborious process of trying to read printed dialect. In content the radio programs were in a sense the twentieth century successor of the nineteenth century humorous newspaper "Letter to the Editor" about which Heinz Kloss has written in detail (see Kloss 1931).

5. The liars' contests (*Liegner Matche*; see Winter 1949) and dialect spelling bees are similar to the *Versammlinge* in that they are usually held in the evening and involve interest in spoken dialect. These are sponsored by local town organizations and are partially supported by small cash donations. The liars' contests are analogous to tall-tale-telling sessions in the rest of the United States, and it always adds to the humor to find a preacher or two among the winners.

6. The dialect church services, or "commemorative services in the language of the fathers,"[35] are a further example of mixed new and old folklore. The churches in which they were (and are) held are the Lutheran and Reformed (United Church). They were, however, completely untraditional; it was only at informal or popular church gatherings such as that peculiarly American institution, the Sunday School picnic, that Lutheran or Reformed clergymen ever dared to speak their piece in dialect as men of the cloth.[36] Also, while the German Methodist sects did sing spirituals or "Dutch choruses" that were couched in a language halfway between dialect and *Hochdeitsch,* no Lutheran or Reformed church allowed this except one or two Low Church revivalist Lutheran churches of the "Gettysburg" persuasion. Hence today when one attends a commemorative service in the language of the fathers, instead of the German *Kernlieder,* which the older members of

---

dialect, and an autobiographical article by Albert F. Buffington, see *The Pennsylvania Dutchman* 1, no. 5 (June 2, 1949): 1; also Rosenberger (1966: 260–261).

[35] For dialect church services, see Russell W. Gilbert (1956*b*).

[36] Cf. the statement from the *Jugendfreund* in 1850, probably from the pen of S. K. Brobst: "Zu unserm Leidwesen haben wir schon zu verschiedenen Malen vernommen, dass Lehrer, die doch gut deutsch reden können, pennsylvanisch-baurisch-deutsch reden, wenn sie Knider unterrichten. Ja, wir hörten schon von Predigern, die z.B. bei Sonntagsschul-Festen sich einer ganz gemeinen Bauern-Sprache auf der Kanzel bedienten." For the context, see D. Yoder (1961: 114n.)

the congregation still could sing if they were asked to, one hears the congregation lifting to God the offering of the Anglo-American gospel song "I Need Thee Every Hour" ("Ich brauch dich alle Schtunn, Alle Schtunn ich brauch dich"); or the congregation of the big brick church on the hill joins in singing a Dutch version of "The Little Brown Church in the Vale." Again, popular culture has here supplanted folk culture.

Among the Evangelical United Brethren (now part of the United Methodist Church) the use of dialect sermons and singing at their *Deitsche Versammlinge* (which are church rather than secular gatherings) is more in accord with the group's history and character. They have recently introduced the additional incitement of a "dialect Sunday School lesson for the adult bible class."[37]

These comments on the newer dialect institutions of the twentieth century are not in any way to be considered derogatory. Like the analysis of the ethnic societies, the study of the newer dialect institutions is instructive when one is tracing the development of the ethnic consciousness of the Pennsylvania Germans. Their analysis however presupposes a strict separation of traditional folkloristic elements from those of the twentieth century.

Current research problems include (1) the relation of folklore to the breakdown of the folk-culture that began in the nineteenth century, (2) the stratigraphy of Pennsylvania German folklore, and (3) the problem of bilingual repertory.

Breakdown of the Folk-Culture

The folk-culture of the Pennsylvania Germans, which centered around the two worlds of church and sectarian religion, was formed in

[37] The movement appears to be spreading to the Lutheran and United churches as well. Dialect Sunday School classes were begun in 1968 at Huff's Union Church, Clayton, Penn. The interest was so great that on May 18, 1969, a Pennsylvania German Sunday School was held at the *Huffa Kaerrich* auditorium *om holver drei* to an audience of some four hundred persons. The lesson, which was given in fluent dialect by Superintendent Clarence G. Reitnauer, was based on Matthew 18:1–6, 11–14. The hymns sung included "Meh Leeb tzu Deer" (the gospel song, "More Love to Thee, O God"), "Wie Gross Duh Bisht" (Billy Graham's theme song, "How Great Thou Art"), and "Ich Brauch Dich alla Shtun."

the period from the Revolution to the Civil War through contact with the English language and culture. It began to fragment by the first half of the nineteenth century and has continued to break down to the present. Only scattered cultural remnants, such as cookery, continued use of the dialect, and deviant English usage, have survived in most areas. The obsolete barn and farmhouse architecture is fast being replaced by suburban patterns. The older folklore is still recordable but is in most cases no longer functional in a folk-community matrix.

This steady breakdown of folk-culture is a symptom of the disintegration of the folk-community as a whole. It has proceeded farther among the church people than among the sect people, although the latter are also being gradually weakened by the onslaught. The process consisted of Americanization, individualization, and secularization. The specific factors that combined to destroy the folk-culture were (1) Americanization in language, beginning with English schools in the 1830's and continuing in stepped-up measure in the twentieth century with radio, television, and the movement of population (especially of the men who have had wide contacts outside the culture through the national wars), and (2) pietistic individualism in religion as represented by Anglo-American revivalism, which broke up the old sense of churchly community.[38] This was a very subtle change. The older church community exhibited a "de-individualization of the individual," a process that went so far as to require separate church seating and separate doors for men and women. The new religious association began to insist that one is not born into a church and ministered to from birth to death through the sacramental system but that each individual must undergo a dateable conversion experience. These changes broke up family, church, and folk-community. Along with the insistence on conversion came a new pietistic morality that saw nothing good in the common "play elements" in life often associated with religious holiday celebration. With its temperance orientation this new morality condemned the country tavern, the country dance (the "frolick"), and the militia muster or *Baddalya,* 'battalion.'

[38] The same thing happened to folk-culture in Puritan New England due to the Great Awakening; see also Trefor M. Owen (1959: 23–26) for an analysis of the impact of Methodism on Welsh folk culture.

The Lutheran and Reformed majority churches among the Pennsylvania Germans met the challenge by eventually rejecting the revival system, although they later adopted its concomitants, the Sunday Schools, youth groups, mission societies, ladies' guilds, and men's brotherhoods. These provided socially permitted substitutes for the archaic folk peer groups.[39] At the present time the (Old) Mennonites[40] are in the process of adopting the whole revival system, including tent meetings, so that (as I have put it elsewhere) after 150 years the frontier has finally come back to Lancaster County. The Old Order Amish and the Old Order Mennonites are the last holdouts against this individualizing process in American Protestantism. They have never been completely Anglicized; they have never accepted revivals or conversion as a necessity; they have not even accepted Sunday Schools; and they have preserved a distinctly pre-revivalist, pre-temperance, folk-cultural morality that in some areas has carried along even the ancient folk-cultural system of "bundling" into the twentieth century. On a recent visit in an Amish community of central Pennsylvania, John Hostetler and I talked to the first Old Order Amishman on record who for pietistic reasons has become a non-tobacco smoker, which in the Old Order is, strangely enough, a first step toward secularization.

There are three main factors to note here: (1) the loss of High German as a cultural matrix among the majority of German speakers and the gradual replacement of the dialect by English; (2) the radical shift in religion away from the old community-based church that pre-

[39] Two antirevivalist approaches, the Reformed "Mercersburg Theology" and the Lutheran confessional movement, enabled the churches to withstand much of the revivalist impact even though large wings of both denominations became revivalistic for a time and set up separate colleges, seminaries, and church newspapers. This was also the cause of the earlier rivalry between Pennsylvania's two Lutheran seminaries, Gettysburg and Philadelphia. Gettysburg represented the "low-church" Methodistic and English influence, while Philadelphia was "high-church," confessional, anti-revivalist, and, for a time, pro-German Language.

[40] In eastern Pennsylvania the term "Old Mennonites" is used to designate the larger body of Mennonites, to distinguish them from both the "New Mennonites" or Herrites, a schism of 1812, and the "Old Order Mennonites," the latter still using horse-drawn transportation like the Amish. For these distinctions see *The Mennonite Encyclopedia* (1955–1959).

served basic elements of what German scholars call *religiöse Volks-kunde* or *kirchliche Volkskunde*; and (3) general American, in fact universal influences of the modern era that in all parts of the world have tended to break down the "little community" and submerge it in the "great cultural" tradition of industrialization, urbanization, move-ment of population, and greatly improved communications.[41]

At the present rate of disintegration of the folk-culture, the old dialect folklore as rooted in folk-community will be recordable a generation from now only among the sectarian communities of the strictest Old Order type. These are the only ones that have not yet "eroded" and moved toward our individualistic modern culture. The (Old) Mennonites already show little interest in present-day Pennsyl-vania German culture. Their world-view is that of eighteenth-century Pietism rather than of Pennsylvania German folk-culture; they may tell you, in Dutch accents, that they cannot speak the Dutch dialect and have no interest in being considered part of Pennsylvania German culture.[42]

The Stratigraphy of Pennsylvania German Folklore

It is an important historical task of the present day to separate and evaluate the sources of Pennsylvania German folklore. If one attends a *Versammlinge* meeting or a *Grundsow Lodch*, the homogeneous nature of Pennsylvania German culture soon makes itself apparent, from the pseudo-Dutch menus through the rousing singing of the "Schnitzelbank Song" (from charts published in Milwaukee) to "Schweet Adoline," "Deheem uff de alt Bauerei" (the Dutch version of "Home on the Range"), and even "Vergess net Pearl Harbor," which invaded the *Versammlinge* repertoire during the Second World War.

In the Pennsylvania German folksong world there are obviously elements of Continental Germanic origin and others that have come in at various times via acculturation. Among the Germanic elements, some, judging from their widespread prevalence and tenacity, must

---

[41] For general perspectives here, see Hermann Bausinger (1961).
[42] For present Mennonite attitudes to revivalism, see John A. Hostetler (1954).

have been part of the eighteenth-century emigrant culture, although in studying the field since 1951 I can no longer maintain (as Buffington, Boyer, and I did in *Songs Along the Mahantongo*, 1951:13–14) that even the majority of the Germanic songs are of eighteenth-century emigrant origin. Many songs of courting, drinking, and in each of the other categories that we established can be better accounted for if we assume that they were introduced by the nineteenth-century German emigrants, by the 48ers, the tramps,[43] and the urban Germans of the beer garden culture. This is an area that deserves careful study. Up to now, relatively little is known about the cultural relations of the Pennsylvania Germans with the emigrant Germans of the nineteenth century who settled in their communities. Not only was a larger proportion of the latter urban, but there was often a differential in education between the two groups that led the *Deitschlenner,* as the natives called the emigrants, to excel in such roles as clergymen and editors of German newspapers. Some of the earliest printed writings in dialect (newspaper letters) as well as a number of the later popular dialect newspaper columns were written by emigrant Germans such as Wollenweber, Conrad Gehring, and "Hansjörg." Nationally, it was the emigrant German population of the nineteenth century that added to the American Christmas celebration such customs as the Christmas tree (even if documented earliest among the Pennsylvania Germans).[44] We need trustworthy historical and culture-historical studies of these relationships.

Despite the influence of the emigrant Germans, it was Anglo-America that was responsible for most of the changes which took place in Pennsylvania German culture. Hybridization took place in every area of the culture—from barn and house architecture to cookery. While we still speak of the Pennsylvania German barn as a

[43] For the folk-cultural influence of the German tramps on Pennsylvania's rural scene, see the many articles by Victor C. Dieffenbach and others, in *The Pennsylvania Dutchman* and *Pennsylvania Folklife*. Tramps, like tinkers and itinerant labor in general, represented links with the outside world and brought news, gossip, songs, and lore into the homes of the rural people.

[44] See Alfred L. Shoemaker (1959), especially "The Christmas Tree in Pennsylvania," pp. 52–60; Albert Bernhardt Faust (1909: 383–385) came to much the same conclusion.

"Swiss" barn, the Swiss pattern of a combined house and barn under one roof was broken in America; there are even two-story stone barns that look suspiciously like Pennsylvania "Swiss" barns in Westmorland and adjoining counties of England. Even though the Pennsylvania Germans continued to relish *Sauerkraut, Schnitz un Gnepp, Buwe-schenkel*, and *Pannhaas*, they developed the English round fruit pie (which they called *Boi*, borrowing the very word)[45] to a fine art. In pioneer days and afterwards they often lived on cornmeal mush as much as their porridge-eating Scotch-Irish neighbors.

In the area of folklore there has been a constant Anglo-American influence, from the German broadside translations of "Wicked Polly" and "The Hunters of Kentucky" through "Oh Susanna" down to "Die Ford Maschin" and "Schweet Adoline." Even the most popular dialect literature genre, the newspaper letter, was essentially a borrowing. It reflected mid-nineteenth-century American humor as well as some folk patterns. Detailed linguistic studies have made the process of borrowing and hybridization reasonably clear. What we now need are detailed analyses of the basic forms of hybridization represented in what we have called Pennsylvania German folk-culture. This is especially urgent since the special interest groups and filiopietistic elements have neglected the issue of "cultural mixing" and for various motives have overemphasized the "Germanic" heritage.

The Study of Bilingual Repertory

This area too is in need of urgent attention. Unfortunately, when Boyer, Buffington, and I recorded folksong materials in the 1940's in the Mahantongo and Lykens (Hegins) valleys, little recording space was given to English songs. One of the informants, Willy Brown, Pennsylvania's "Papa Gernet,"[46] had an amazing dialect repertory; in

[45] In the acculturation process between British and Continental cookery patterns in Pennsylvania, the Continental *Kuchen* eventually lost out to the British "pie," without permanent damage to either the Pennsylvania German stomach or psyche.

[46] As I have (almost too enthusiastically) referred to him; see D. Yoder (1952). Willy Brown used to sing these songs, most of them beautifully obscene, for drinks in the Klingerstown Hotel barroom—following a classic folksinger pattern of an earlier era. The one or two songs we dutifully recorded have unfortunately never been published. Perhaps Gershom Legman's new journal of erotic folklore can use them.

addition, he could sing an almost equally astonishing number of English songs.

Aside from this and a few other limited studies, there has been very little interest in the scientific analysis of bilingual repertoires (or bilingualism in general) among the Pennsylvania Germans. Adequate information is available only for the Amish, who actually preserve the nineteenth-century Pennsylvania German pattern of trilingualism (see Frey 1945). It is to be hoped that work on problems of English/ European-language bilingualism, such as that being done at The University of Texas (see G. Gilbert 1970a, Pulte 1970), can also be initiated among the Pennsylvania Germans. The results should be of great interest to cultural historians and linguists alike.

Conclusion

First, there is an urgent need to make immediate, copious, and geographically well-chosen recordings of Pennsylvania German folklore in its dialect matrix. Second, all types of dialect studies should be combined without restriction with the full range of folk-cultural studies. Third, more emphasis is needed on the historical relationships within the Pennsylvania folk-culture between Pennsylvania German, Pennsylvania High German, and English. Fourth, folk-cultural analysis should be undertaken on German-language texts from Pennsylvania and the areas influenced folk-culturally from Pennsylvania. By "texts" is meant not only German poetry, but tombstones, house inscriptions, the texts (as well as the symbols) of the *Fraktur*, wills, account books, personal correspondence, spiritual testaments, baptismal letters, Bible records, prayers, and funeral texts. Fifth, the studies already made, combined with those suggested above, will prove useful for comparison with the acculturation of German folklore and language in the various older rural German settlements in the New World, such as those in Brazil, Argentina, Chile, and Nova Scotia.

At least I wrote him recently that until the Pennsylvania German returns are in, he had better hold the presses in regard to pornographic folklore. We can be given some credit for having recorded the songs at all; it is said that an earlier team of recorders, led by a man of the cloth, used to silence its singers when obscenity intruded. In this connection see Kenneth S. Goldstein (1964), especially pp. 56–59, 116–117.

DISCUSSION

————: What is the historical background of the folk-healing you mentioned? Was it brought from Europe or was it developed in this country? Is it still an important part of their culture?

YODER: Yes, it is important, despite the people who have tried to suggest that it does not really exist in the twentieth century. There are still dozens of practicing powwowers in eastern Pennsylvania, as well as in parts of central and western Pennsylvania where some degree of Pennsylvania German culture exists even though the dialect is hardly spoken any longer. These patterns are traditional. They form a part of the old European folklore that was brought over in the eighteenth century by the pre-Revolutionary migration to Pennsylvania, Maryland, and other areas of colonial German settlement. The powwowing charms are still recited in German. The monograph on Adolf Spamer's *Romanusbüchlein* (Nickel 1958), which describes the major traditional German charms from the Middle Ages, provides the European background of the Pennsylvania German charm books. An example of the latter is called the *Pow-Wow Book*, the first edition of which, *Der Lang-Verborgene Freund,* was published as early as 1820 in Reading, Pennsylvania. This was translated under the title of *The Long-Lost Friend* in several English versions. Even in English, though, the charms rhyme in such a way that it is possible to identify the translator as a Pennsylvania German. One of the most famous charms is the three worm charm: "The Virgin Mary traversed the land holding three worms in her hand; one was red, the other was black, the other was white." These fixed formulas had their beginnings in pre-Christian times. By the time they were first written down in the Middle Ages, we find them always set into a Christian frame. At the end of each charm, one must say what the Pennsylvania Germans call [di: dřaɪ hɛkʃtə na:ma] 'the three highest names,' the Trinitarian formula. After saying, "In the name of the Father and the Son and the Holy Ghost," one then adds, "help to this," pronounces the baptized name of the person, and formally closes with an "amen," thereby giving the charm the appearance of a prayer.

Despite the curious name *powwowing*, the practice has obviously not been adopted from the American Indians, as some people have maintained. The *Oxford English Dictionary* (1933:VII/1216) under the entries *powwow, powwower*, and *powwowing*, cites the first occurrences of these words in New England in the 1630's and 1640's. The Puritans, who had powwowers of their own, were the first to use the term. Whittier, in one of his earlier essays dealing with New England superstitions, presents compelling evidence that even among the Quakers in New England there were healers of this sort.[1] Although the term was widely used in the United States in the nineteenth century, in the twentieth century it seems to occur most frequently among Pennsylvania Germans.

One of the typical charms (to cure the bite of a snake), brought from Germany or Switzerland in the eighteenth century, reads "God has created all things and they were good. Thou only, o serpent, art damned. Cursed be thou and thy sting. Zing, zing, zing." This charm is unusual because of its direct address to the snake. As in primitive medicine, one should address the thing or do something to the thing that has caused the harm, e.g., when one is cut by an axe, something must be said to the axe or the axe should be greased, i.e., treated. At the end of the charm, the snake is cursed directly. I recently found several manuscript charms in Pennsylvania that, instead of the "zing, zing, zing," give the German "ziehen dein Gift, ziehen dein Gift, ziehen dein Gift."[2] These manuscripts then show three crosses, meaning not the sign of the cross in the Catholic sense, but rather, "In the name of the Father, the Son, and the Holy Ghost."

Even today, powwowers in Pennsylvania tend to use German instead of English when reciting the charms. Since powwowing is not

[1] See Whittier's essay, "Magicians and Witch Folk" (1904), especially pp. 401–402, 404–405.
[2] Possibly "zieh an dein Gift." See editor's note in connection with the illustration on pp. 24–25, Phares H. Hertzog (1967–1968). The German charm illustrated, done in Fraktur by or for Regina Selzser in 1837, reads in its entirety: "und gott hat alles erschaffen, was im himmel und auf erden ist, und alles war gud, nichts als allein die schlange hat gott verflucht, verflucht solst du bleiben, schlangen, geschwülst ich stelle dich, gift und schmerz ich döde dich, zian dein gift, zian dein güft, zian dein güft, amen X X X."

completely respectable, the orally transmitted charms are often difficult to record. The Protestant churches have not looked with favor upon this for four hundred years. It was at the time of the Reformation that folk-healing had to go underground; to Luther and the Reformers it was associated with some of the abuses in the saints' cults and healing shrines of Roman Catholicism. Wherever powwowing continued to exist in Protestant cultures, it went underground and became a secret practice, as it still is in Pennsylvania.

In Pennsylvania there are at present three grades of powwowers: the professionals, the domestic powwowers, and the witch doctors. The professionals support themselves by their trade. Although they have large clienteles, they do not advertise, since advertising brings them into conflict with the local medical associations. They are also not allowed to take fees, but everyone knows what their particular fee is. A domestic powwower would be, for example, the grandmother in the family, who knows how to "blow fire," to "stop blood," and so forth. Whereas the domestic powwower is completely respectable (after all, she is your grandmother), the professionals live on the fringes of society—marginal functionaries in the folklore-culture. The witch doctors go further in that they attempt to make counter-charms against witchcraft. All three types are derived directly from the Central European German or Swiss areas.

KLOSS: Has any research ever been done on the influence of the American Indians on the folk medicine of the Germans? The German traveler, Johann Georg Kohl, published a book in 1856 in which he described a family living in Bowmansville, Pennsylvania, that used an herb against snake bites first employed by an ancestor who had been cured by the Indians (Kohl 1856:537). As early as 1730, Johann Adam Gruber, one of the leading German sectarians, proposed to write a book on the folk medicine or the healing power of the American Indian (Sachse 1899:206). Therefore, there must have been considerable contact between the two groups.

YODER: Yes, there was contact but not in the occult or magico-religious type of folk-healing. That there was Indian influence on the herbal type of folk-healing is suggested by historical descriptions of herbs, the use of which was supposedly learned from the Indians. In addition, there are extensive anthropological monographs on medical practices among the Delawares and other Indians in Pennsylvania. These practives have not yet been compared with what is known of Pennsylania German herbal medicine.

ABRAHAMS: Is there any literature on the relationship between the German Americans in Pennsylvania and other ethnic groups? Has any kind of antagonism between the various ethnic groups been embodied in the lore?

YODER: Yes, much material exists on interethnic relations between the Pennsylvania Germans on the one hand and both the immigrants from the British Isles (their neighbors in the colonial period) and the Slavic immigrants of the coal-mining regions who came in the nineteenth century on the other. There is an unusually larger number of rhymes, jokes, and other lore regarding the conflict between the Pennsylvania Germans and the Irish. In the nineteenth century it was common to call any non-Pennsylvania German an *Eirischer* [ˈʔaiɾiʃɒ] rather than an *Englishman*. Although the Amish refer to anyone who is non-Amish as an *Englishman,* the other Pennsylvania Germans, the majority, use the word *Eirischer*, because of the juxtaposition of Pennsylvania German and Scotch-Irish settlements which was very common in colonial Pennsylvania. The Pennsylvania Germans also had rhymes directed against the Philadelphians, the *Städtler*, with whom the "country Dutchmen" came into contact at market. There are also some early jokes in the almanacs about the people in New Jersey. The Pennsylvania Germans had a special relationship with the New Jersey area. Occasionally, in order to improve their knowledge of English, a family would send one of its sons to work on a farm "in the Jerseys" [ɪn dɒ ltʃaɹʐiː]. This term is an old plural usage referring to the West Jersey and East Jersey of the colonial period.

WILSON: Many of the songs, rhymes, charms, and other Pennsylvania German folklore you have described have parallels among the Texas Germans.

YODER: It is just this type of comparative material that we are most interested in collecting in all the surviving German linguistic enclaves in the United States.

6. GERMAN AS AN IMMIGRANT, INDIGENOUS, FOREIGN, AND SECOND LANGUAGE IN THE UNITED STATES

HEINZ KLOSS

University of Marburg

IN EVERYDAY USAGE the concepts "immigrant language" and "indigenous language" overlap. Although we regard a person born abroad as being unambiguously an immigrant, and the son of native American parents of non-English mother tongue as being a member of an indigenous, settled linguistic minority, we think of a group consisting chiefly of the American-born children of immigrants as, in a way, belonging to both worlds. It is still partly an immigrant group—the U. S. Census of Population assigning it to the "foreign stock"—and partly already indigenous and rooted to the soil.

Even more extensive is the overlapping between the concepts of "second language" and "foreign language." Here, it is really a question of two concentric circles: a second language is actually only a special case of the general category "foreign language." A second language is not only read but spoken with some fluency. It fulfills an important and lasting function in the life of the person concerned. It may be the language used on the job or the language of free-time in clubs and churches.

In order to present a picture with reasonably clear contours I will treat these four terms in the following discussion not as overlapping but as sharply separated entities. Hence we will define (1) *immigrant language* as the mother tongue of those born abroad; (2) *indigenous language* as the mother tongue of all people born within the boundaries of the United States; (3) *second language* as a language which is not the mother tongue but which the speaker more or less fully controls and constantly uses in certain contexts; (4) *foreign language* as every language which is neither the mother tongue nor a second language.

German as an immigrant language is something which is relatively well known. In particular, there are four indexes which help us to visualize German in this role: (1) general statistics giving totals for the United States at large; (2) statistics and maps of geographical distribution; (3) newspapers and periodicals; (4) publications in book form.

From Germany alone, immigration amounted to:

1700–1820	0.2 million people
1820–1870	1.5
1870–1917	3.1
1920–1962	1.3
TOTAL	6.1

Prior to 1870 the overwhelming majority of German-speaking immigrants came from Germany itself. However, after 1870 (especially in the period after the 1880's) hundreds of thousands of Germans came from eastern and southeastern Europe. Even though the Censuses of Population since 1850 give the *origin* of the foreign born, this information was for a long time limited to the country of birth. In 1910, for the first time, the mother tongue was asked for. In that year it was found that 18 percent, in 1930 almost 28 percent, of all immigrants of German mother tongue did not come from within the boundaries of the German Empire. Also, among the people reported as born in Germany there were of course a certain percentage (in 1910 exactly 10 percent) with a non-German, mostly Polish, mother tongue. The number of foreign born of German mother tongue was:

Year	Total No.	Born outside Germany (Das Deutsche Reich)
1910	2,759,000	499,000
1930	2,260,000	601,000
1960	1,279,000	—

From 1961 to 1967 approximately 200,000 additional immigrants of German mother tongue came to the United States. Thus even today we still have impressive figures to deal with. Although German as an immigrant language has been equaled at the present time by Italian and has been greatly surpassed by Spanish (if we include the Puerto Ricans), it was previously the leading non-English language for long periods of United States history. In the eighteenth century it was the only significant non-English language; around 1850 it was still the language of about 70 percent of all non-English-speaking immigrants; and in 1880 it was still the usual language of 60 percent of them. Also, if we put together all figures for immigration since 1700, immigrants of German mother tongue constitute even today by far the largest subgroup, clearly surpassing speakers of Spanish and Italian.

In addition to general figures concerning the foreign born, these statistics also provide us with information about geographic subareas. Subtotals for individual states and counties that divide the foreign born by country of birth have been compiled since 1880.[1] Unfortunately, the figures that divide the foreign-born *by language* have been published only for entire states and not for individual counties. By way of compensation, we sometimes know that people in certain states who were born outside of Germany were almost without exception of German mother tongue. Most important in this respect are the Russian-born immigrants in the prairie states from North Dakota to Kansas. The same holds true for the Swiss in a few states, such as Wisconsin (but not California!).

Another method of surveying the geographic distribution of the immigrants is provided by maps of those organizations and organization types that we know to be limited chiefly to the foreign-born generation. This is the case, for example, with the secular German clubs in many states. I have plotted on maps the locations of these clubs for the year 1915. Such maps provide valuable information concerning

---

[1] Such information is given for example in Charles O. Paullin (1932), which maps the distribution of people born in Germany by county for the years 1880, 1900, and 1930. Records by county for the census years 1850, 1860, and 1870 were destroyed without ever having been published.

the distribution of the immigrants. Still, one must be careful about making hasty generalizations. When I inquired in Fredericksburg, Texas, in 1937 as to the number of members of the Gillespie County federation of German glee clubs who had been born in Europe, the reply was, "Only one, and he comes from Norway."

A fact brought out clearly by both the censuses of population and the maps of German associations is the ubiquity of the German immigrants. They can be found almost everywhere. Next to the Anglo-Saxon element (and naturally a very great distance behind it in most states), they are the only one to be represented in all states by sizeable groups. Nothing illustrates this more clearly than the fact that the well-known bibliography by Arndt and Olson[2] (1961) lists German-language periodicals or newspapers for all but four of the forty-eight contiguous states: New Mexico, Mississippi, Maine, and Vermont. Nevertheless, even in these four areas we know of the presence of German immigrants.

In one sense, the spatial and temporal spread of the German immigration was even greater than that of the Anglo-Saxons. Everywhere that another European colonial power appeared first on the scene of what was later to become the United States—Netherlanders and Swedes in the East, French in the South, Spaniards in the Southwest, Russians in Alaska and California—we find Germans in the service of the respective older colonial powers. The oldest Lutheran congregation whose sermons were held in German was founded in New Amsterdam in 1657. In New Sweden, German was an official language. In Louisiana there came into being the Côte des Allemands, 'German Coast,' which was later Gallicized and then Anglicized. In Alaska several place names remind us of German explorers who came in the service of the Czar. In Texas, too, the first Germans appeared

---

[2] A follow-up volume, "Deutsch-Amerikanische Zeitungen und Zeitschriften 1732–1968, Bd. 2: Argentinien, Bolivien, Brasilien, Chile, Dominikanische Republik, Ekuador, Guatemala, Guiana, Kanada, Kolumbien, Kostarika, Mexiko, Paraguay, Peru, Uruguay, Venezuela, Vereinigte Staaten von Nordamerika," is about to be published in Munich. The addenda for the United States constitute five hundred pages in typescript. For Canada, see also H. K. Kalbfleisch (1968).

before the declaration of independence from Mexico, the German settlement of Industry in Austin County being established as early as 1831.

We may even broaden our perspective. It is startling to observe that German is the only language spoken by immigrant groups in almost all parts of the New World, from Canada to southern Chile. It has strong roots in Paraguay and in the Mexican province of Chihuahua; it is the everyday language of very large settlements in Brazil and Argentina, and of small settlements in British Honduras, Venezuela, and Peru. With this in mind, we are not far off the mark in venturing the conclusion that German, because it is the only language spoken in all parts of the New World, is a truly Pan American language (Kloss 1930). But of course it exists in some areas only as an immigrant language that members of the first generation born in the New World no longer fully command.

In the United States, evidence for the existence and, to a limited extent, for the distribution of German immigrants is also provided by periodicals and books, since both are mainly, although not exclusively, products of the foreign born, even though the readership of these publications must have included many native-born Americans. For a time, second- and third-generation readers may have been in the majority, not to mention the users of school textbooks who were predominately native Americans.

For the American German press, we may refer to Arndt and Olson's bibliography (1961), a standard work of the highest quality. The only sizeable gap in the bibliography concerns a group born within the United States, the Pennsylvania Germans of the nineteenth century. The pertinent studies of Alfred L. Shoemaker for this period have not been sufficiently made use of.[3]

Unfortunately there is no parallel handbook dealing with the book production of the German Americans.[4] The extent and richness of such

---

[3] In *The Pennsylvania Dutchman*, e.g., Feb. 1, 1962, March 1 and 15, 1953, and Feb. 15, 1954.

[4] For the period up to 1830 there is the bibliography by Oswald Seidensticker, *The First Century of German Printing in America* (1893). Although this book is now obsolete, a large amount of additional data is said to have been compiled by Wilbur

a work, I am sure, would astonish its readers. Among the titles listed, there would surely be many volumes of poetry and numerous books on theology and church history. It is interesting to note though that, aside from books of a religious-ideological nature, there are apparently very few containing nonfiction or expository prose, especially scientific prose. Only in very isolated cases are there books dealing with topics in the natural sciences, medicine, technology, folklore, and world history. These are relatively most frequent in the period 1830 to 1860, often a product of the refugees of the 1830's, *die Dreissiger.*

Very striking is the immense quantitative and still greater qualitative significance accorded to ideological and religious literature by the German Americans.[5] Since, from the eighteenth century on, America was the place of refuge for a great variety of political and religious groups that could not maintain themselves in Central Europe, the literature of many ideological groups continued to flourish in North America at a time when it had become more or less forcibly silenced in Germany. Many of the most lively German American publications are of the latter type. The Protestant magazine *Der Deutsche Kirchenfreund,* for example, in which much of the ecumenical thinking of our time was anticipated, must certainly be ranked as one of the finest German-language periodicals in the United States. Among such thinkers as the Catholic Maximilian Örtel and the Anarchist Johannes Most, or among the Old Lutherans and the Methodists, can be found sparkling life and unique worlds of ideas.

Urgently needed is the compilation of either *one* great anthology of all ideological movements or a separate anthology for each of the main lines of thought, such as Old Lutherans, other Protestants, Roman Catholics, and Free Thinkers and leftist radicals. We should note, however, that the making of such an anthology is partly dependent upon the creation of the comprehensive bibliography described above.

Both phenomena, the abundance of ideological writings and the

---

Oda. A revised and expanded edition would be a desirable undertaking. Invaluable work has been done by Henry A Pochmann, compiler, and Arthur R. Schultz, ed. (1953).

[5] For a study of the stratification of German American literature, see Heinz Kloss (1934).

lack of other nonfiction prose, are intimately connected with the two main causes for the collapse of the linguistic position of the German language in the United States: the neglect of a higher education conducted in the German language and the ideological cleavages that resulted in almost as many separate groups as there were ideologies.

As early as 1819, John H. Livingston reproached the Pennsylvania German church bodies with being the only denominations in America that had not yet set up their own institutions of higher education (Livingston 1819:20–21). And in 1932 an American of German descent, Otto A. Stiefel, pointed out how far the German Americans had lagged behind the Anglo Americans in the promotion of universities.[6] To be sure, this criticism was directed more toward the liberals than to the orthodox Lutherans and the Catholics. Nonetheless, a certain lack of respect for intellect and schooling and the unwillingness to make sacrifices for the cultivation of secondary and higher education characterizes long stretches of German American history.

Much less clear is the evidence concerning the use of German as the language of an indigenous population born in the United States. The paucity of information commences with the statistics themselves. Only once, in 1940, were figures published for the mother tongue of the entire white population. They indicate that German was the mother tongue (as defined by the United States Census, the language of early childhood) for 1.6 million foreign born, 2.4 million members of the second generation, and 0.9 million members of the third or later generations.

These figures are, however, only of limited value, since they are made up of a representative sampling of only 5 percent of the population. There are also four supplementary statistical sources: (1) since 1880, official figures for the second generation, arranged according to country of birth of the parents, have been available; (2) for 1910 and 1960 we also have information on the mother tongue of the parents; (3) for 1906 and 1916 there are official figures on the language of church

---

[6] In an address to the German American National Congress; quoted in Heinz Kloss (1937: 275–276).

services;[7] (4) finally, for many Protestant church bodies—for example, the Missouri Synod Lutherans and the former Evangelical and Reformed Church—there are private, nongovernmental figures giving the language in which church services were conducted for both the whole denomination and for individual congregations (Gehrke 1935; Hofman 1966, 1968).

All these statistics show us that the German language, on the average, has died out more slowly than popular opinion on both sides of the ocean would have it. Also the Germans, compared with other ethnic groups, did not fare badly in this respect—at least not until World War I.

Three questions arise with respect to German as an indigenous language: (1) Where is it spoken? (2) What are the linguistic characteristics of the spoken language (3) To what extent was (is) it used in writing?

With regard to the first question, we could answer that German survives as a rule longer in the country and in small towns than in the larger cities. However, this is a generalization with many exceptions, as for example in large cities such as Milwaukee, St. Louis, Cincinnati, and Baltimore, where German has survived for generations.

If we really want to know where remnants of the German language are still in existence *today*, we first need maps of the German ethnic enclaves. These in turn can be derived from county statistics and from the lists of German Catholic, Lutheran, and other church congregations. The most informative of these maps prepared from such lists are those indicating the language of church services for a given year.

I have prepared a large atlas showing the locations of the significant German speech islands (or settlement enclaves).[8] Also, ethnic inventories have been prepared for single states, J. Neale Carman's *Foreign Language Units in Kansas* (1962) being an outstanding example.

The availability of a printed atlas covering the forty-eight contiguous states would contribute much to the solution of a further re-

---

[7] See United States (1910, 1919). The latter statistics have been so thoroughly ignored that the Bureau of the Census assured me in 1967 that such a language survey had never been carried out.

[8] Kloss, forthcoming. The outline of the atlas was first presented in Kloss (1939).

search problem to which several investigators have already devoted themselves: the recording and study of the rapidly disappearing German dialects in the numerous linguistic enclaves. The coordinator of this symposium, Glenn Gilbert, has prepared an atlas of Texas German (1971),[9] Reed and Seifert have compiled two atlases for Pennsylvania (1954; forthcoming), and Seifert has planned a further atlas for Wisconsin.[10] A special mapping of the distribution of the Old Order Amish, the Old Order Mennonites, and the Hutterites (the three ecclesiastical bodies which have remained almost completely German but which are made up almost entirely of native-born Americans) should prove especially valuable to dialectologists.[11]

Although we are primarily concerned with the dialects spoken in rural speech islands, we should also study the varying types of urban dialects that lasted for decades in several of the large cities with German districts. It would at least be worth the effort to determine whether speakers of such dilects may still be living. I am thinking especially of the legendary St. Louis "South Side Dutch" and the speech of the part of Cincinnati once called "Over the Rhine." But no less valuable would be carefully planned dialect studies in the cities where specific urban immigrant groups settled, for example Bavarians and Siebenbürger Sachsens.

Ralph Charles Wood has carried out extensive studies concerning the colloquial language of the indigenous German settlements in the United States. He should be given the opportunity to present to the American public the finished manuscript for his book, which by now numbers 250 pages in typescript. Up to now there has appeared only a short summary within the framework of the Mannhardt-Festschrift of 1958, in which Wood asserted that the article was "to be considered

---

[9] This atlas and those of Reed and Seifert are described in Wolfgang Viereck (1967).

[10] The proposed atlas is described in Lester W. J. Seifert (1951)

[11] Certain very small splinter groups can of course be discovered only by field investigation. An example is the surprising discovery in the early 1960's of remnants of the former Pennsylvania German speech island in the Shenandoah Valley of Virginia. See Smith, Stewart, and Kyger (1962), especially pp. 3–7, 243–247.

more of a program than as a finished achievement" (Wood 1958: 186).[12]

The question concerning the proportion of American-born authors in German American literature seems to me to be of great importance. Without doubt, a major part of this literature was written by immigrants. On the other hand there is no question that the proportion of native-born German Americans has been underestimated. Two regional groups have been especially important in this regard: the Pennsylvania Germans and the Texas Germans. In the case of the Pennsylvanians it is chiefly a question of their impressive dialect literature, which is unfortunately more praised than read. Just this year (1968) the dialect has reached its latest literary peak with the appearance of a Pennsylvania German translation of all four gospels from the pen of Ralph Charles Wood.

In addition to the dialect literature there was also a High German literature written by the Pennsylvania Germans in the nineteenth century. Since there was only a small market for books, High German writings appeared mainly in periodicals. Among the writers of the

---

[12] In a letter to me dated Oct. 20, 1968, Professor Wood wrote: "At first I wanted to call my book simply 'German as folk-language in America,' but now I do not know whether that is sufficient. What I have attempted to show is the history of the German folk-language and its present state as a product of settlement history, economic development (whereby I have strongly emphasized the role of a largely materialistic, egotistical speculation in land), church history, and political forces—and hence bound up with this, as the product of a natural, internal linguistic development. The mixture of 'diachronic' and 'synchronic' phenomena and the admission of data ('sociological, political, economic') which is not purely linguistically determined will perhaps cause objections on the part of one-sided structuralists in America, and even more so in Germany. . . . The picture is as follows: formation of an indigenous folk-language consisting of three main types (Pennsylvania German, Low German [*Plattdeutsch*], and High German) in small towns and in the country, with tendencies in that direction in some large cities; the main function of the latter being to bring together the newly-arrived immigrants and more or less to facilitate the exchange of ideas. . . . I have shortened the book considerably. . . . The table of contents reads as follows: 0. Foreword; I. Basic facts concerning the immigration and settlement of the Germans; II. The settlements and the speculation in land; III. Stylistic characteristics of the folk-language; IV. The three main types; V. Rise and fall of the German folk-language; VI. Texts."

time, the names of Brobst, Helffrich, and Trexler are outstanding.[13]
Many works still await discovery and analysis. There are, for example, indications that the early ecclesiastical and historical writings
of the Evangelical Association (Evangelische Gemeinschaft) are the
product of predominantly American-born authors writing in the German language. In 1936 in the Historical Museum of Albright College
in Reading, Pennsylvania, I discovered what is probably the only collection of these books.[14] At the time it was apparent that the German
instructor at the college knew nothing of these literary treasures, which
could have enriched his German classes with indigenous intellectual
history and local color.

German literature in Texas, to which both the second and third generations contributed, is written almost exclusively in High German.
Among the leading authors were the women writers: Hilde Walther,
Clara Rummel, and Clara Reyes. A fourth woman writer, Selma Metzenthin Raunick, is noted for her history of German Texan literature
(1929; 1935–1936). The regional peculiarities of the German literature written in Texas clearly refute the notion that the German immigrants in the United States were largely free of local connections and
culturally (or linguistically) little influenced by their American setting. Can there be anything more local, more unmistakably Texan than
the *Unfehlbare Wetterverse* ('unerring weather rhymes') by Georg
Oheim, who had come to America as a child?[15]

In addition to the Pennsylvania and Texas Germans there were
numerous American intellectuals prior to World War I whose ancestry
dated back to the German immigrants of the nineteenth century and
who used both their German mother tongue and English with equal

---

[13] Samuel K. Brobst (1822–1876) was the founder and editor of several leading
German-language periodicals. The chief works of William A. Helffrich are: *Geschichte . . . Berks Counties* (1891) and *Lebensbild . . . Predigerstand* (1906). The
latter was edited by N. W. A. Helefrich and W. U. Helffrich. For Benjamin F.
Trexlar, who died in 1922, see his *Skizzen aus dem Lecha-Thale* (1886).

[14] The collection has since been transferred to the Historical Society of the Evangelical United Brethren Church in Dayton, Ohio.

[15] The *Wetterverse* of Georg Friedrich Oheim appeared in the *Jahrbuch der Neu-
Braunfelser* [Tex.] *Zeitung* between 1905 and 1939. Oheim, who was born in 1865
and died in 1947, came to the United States in 1880.

fluency in their writings. Among the many German books which owe their existence to these authors we could mention, more or less at random, the works of the Catholics, Kenkel, Lochemes, and Rothensteiner, and of the Lutherans, Graebner, Grimm, and Zagel.[16] The subject matter treated by these authors ranges from a treatise on American birds (Nehrling 1891) to a critique of America (Scheffauer 1923, 1925).

A project worth considering would be to isolate the part of German-American literature written by American-born authors. This however is also dependent upon the proposed general bibliography of German books printed in America mentioned above. It is conceivable that the publication of an anthology of American-born authors who wrote in German would arouse increased interest in many students for their German language classes.

In this connection we should note that the incorporation of specifically national and even local motifs into German language classes is a pedagogical principle that has been adopted for the teaching of German in various countries. Even New Zealand possesses a small anthology of selections from German literature written in or about New Zealand. The book was designed to make German instruction at New Zealand universities more interesting and appealing to the students.[17]

---

[16] F. P. Kenkel, leader of the Roman Catholic *Centralverein*, wrote, among other things, *Der Schädel des Petronius Arbiter* (1898). Michael J. Lochemes, who went by the pseudonyn of Meik Fuchs, was noted as a poet. Johannes Rothensteiner, poet, wrote *Die literarische Wirksamkeit der deutsch-amerikanischen Katholiken* (1926). August L. Graebner wrote *Geschichte der lutherischen Kirche in Amerika* (1892). Alfred Ira (pseudonym of Alfred Grimm) and Hermann Zagel both wrote fiction; Zagel also narrated the story of his youth, *Aus Frühlingstagen* (1929).

[17] See John Asher (1956). The same pedagogical approach could be used in the United States; see Heinz Kloss (1957). It is said that a noted American professor of German always began his advanced classes as a matter of principle with the German version of the Declaration of Independence, which was published in advance of the English text by a German newspaper in Philadelphia on July 9, 1776 (Arndt and Olson 1961: 10). French language teachers have also repeatedly employed the "local motif technique." See the French reader, *France d'Amérique*, compiled by Simone de la Souchère Délery and Gladys A. Renshaw (1932), preface by Paul Claudel. Foreign Language Innovative Curriculum Studies (FLICS), in its experimental programs for the teaching of French in Michigan, has prepared a curriculum unit called " French Explorers in Michigan." Also interesting is the fact that in 1968 Louisiana Law No.

It would be a useful and rewarding task to prepare a number of anthologies of High German or Pennsylvania German literature. In 1954 I published a detailed proposal outlining a highly desirable anthology of Pennsylvania German prose, a project which was unfortunately never carried out (Kloss 1954).

With regard to the role that German has played in the United States as a nonindigenous language, there are no figures at our disposal which differentiate between *foreign language* (in the sense of a purely cultural object of study) and *second language* (i.e., a language involved in functional bilingualism). What the statistics do show is that, up to 1917, the study of German occupied a significant part of the school curriculum and thereby exerted considerable influence on the cultural life of the United States as a whole.[18] German was not only the most widely studied foreign language at universities and colleges but was also widely taught in high schools. In 1915, 25 percent of all high school students, namely 284,000, were studying German, as compared to 103,000 studying French, and 32,000 studying Spanish. Among those studying German there were naturally many students of German mother tongue. This was especially true of elementary school children studying German. In 1900 they amounted to about 600,000, of which 230,000 attended public schools. Of the latter, approximately one-quarter (i.e., 60,000) may not have been of German mother tongue (Kloss 1963:104). Thus it is clear that the FLES movement did not begin in 1922, as has been claimed (Kloss 1967a:29, 47–48). Prior

---

408 on the teaching of French in the public schools directed all public high schools to offer "at least one course in the culture and history of the French populations of Louisiana and other French-speaking areas in the Americas." The National Education Association (NEA), at its 1969 annual convention, adopted a resolution (C 13) stating that the NEA "believes that basic educational materials should portray our cultural diversity and the contributions of minority groups." National Education Association of the United States (1969:571). In the USSR it is becoming rather common to season the teaching of German by drawing on the literature written by German-speaking Soviet citizens. In 1970 this was made obligatory for German language classes in the high schools of Kazakhstan.

18 The standard sources for this assertion are Louis Viereck (1902), Charles Hart Handschin (1913), and Elijah W. Bagster-Collins (1930).

to the modern (second) FLES movement there was a first movement, the beginnings of which go back to the year 1839 and in which the main emphasis was on the cultivation of the mother tongue in bilingual localities. From the very beginning, and increasingly as the decades went by, pupils of English mother tongue shared in this teaching. These pupils were either from families with Anglo American parents or from German American families in which the parents still spoke German but whose children spoke English.

Even though the statistics are lacking, the following generalization seems historically justified: in 1900, wherever people of non-German mother tongue were studying German in the United States, they frequently attained such a command of the language that German became their second language. In the last few decades, on the other hand, German has remained in most cases a "foreign language" in the narrowest sense of the word, a language which can be read after a fashion but hardly spoken and not written at all.

Up to 1917, German in the United States enjoyed unequalled prestige as *the* language of education and learning. This was true not only in the natural sciences and technology but also in a great part of the humanities, for example linguistics and philosophy. For a span of many years, it was necessary to translate various important textbooks in chemistry, for example, from German into English. The ability to read German was indispensable in many disciplines; many university professors expected their students to be able to write a German summary of their readings. Professor Everett Cherington Hughes, a noted sociologist of the older generation, recently told me that as a student it was necessary for him to read and discuss papers in German dealing with such difficult authors as Georg Simmel and Max Weber. It was the custom for large numbers of American students to spend a considerable amount of time at German universities. Their preparation for this foreign study and its aftereffects could not help but influence the intensity of the students' learning of German in this country.

German instruction lasted in many cases much longer than it does today. Often it began in high school or even in elementary school. With such a background, college instruction could of course be planned and carried out with more intensity and variety.

A decisive factor was also the presence of a large German-speaking minority which at that time was by no means ready to give up its language at such a rapid pace. This attitude reinforced German instruction in three ways: (1) There were cities and rural areas where German was as much in everyday use as English. German in its heyday almost attained the position of an unofficial second language for the United States.[19] In this situation children of English mother tongue early came into contact with German outside the classroom. (2) The bilingual children from families in which the parents spoke German preferred German to any of the other foreign languages offered at the universities and thus helped to raise the level of German instruction. In 1900 Professor Otto Heller of Washington University in St. Louis wrote that, of his five German language and philology classes, one was designed for German Americans only and another for only Anglo American students at an advanced level together with German American beginners (Kloss 1962:156). (3) The number of college instructors of German mother tongue was considerably larger than today, partly because immigration from Germany was more extensive both absolutely and relatively, partly because German specialists were sought after even more than they are today due to the prestige of German research and scholarship, and partly because at that time there were still many American-born university instructors of German mother tongue.

In stark contrast to all this, it is the exception in the United States today when an American-born student learns German so well that it becomes a second language for him. Impressive as the figures are on the position of German in colleges and universities as compared with French and Spanish, they present an illusion of greater strength than exists in reality.[20] The simple fact that German has largely disappeared

---

[19] The *Report of the United States Commissioner of Education for the Year 1870* (1870:55) quotes a statement by one John Kraus from the *Washington National Republican* that "the German language has actually become the second language of our republic and a knowledge of German is now considered essential to a finished education." Cf. Heinz Kloss (1942:II, 684). Several authors have misquoted this statement as an expression of the commissioner's own opinion. Still there is reason to asume that Kraus belonged to the commissioner's staff.

[20] In 1965 enrollment in colleges and universities was 214,000 for German, 310,000 for Spanish, and 372,000 for French. High school enrollment, however, was 286,000 for German, 1,373,000 for Spanish, and 1,195,000 for French.

from high schools and elementary schools causes German instruction in the colleges to be relegated to the needs of beginners to a far higher degree than prior to 1917. Today, the goals of the German instructor are of necessity limited primarily to preparing his students to read German books and articles in their major field. In various natural sciences (especially in chemistry) German has still been able to maintain a moderately strong position.

Concerning the future of German instruction in the grades, decisions will have to be made regarding such problems as: (1) should future planning be directed predominantly to students of German ethnic descent or to any student regardless of his family background? (2) should educators be satisfied with simply introducing German as an object of study or should at least an attempt be made to create a modest number of bilingual schools? (3) should applications for financial support of such efforts be addressed to the American government (national, state, and local), to the German government, or to both?

The answer to the first question appears to have been already decided by the dogmatists who prefer to think in terms of "either-or" rather than "both-and." In February 1968 I was present at a lecture given in Bad Godesberg by one of the leading men of the Goethe-Institut in Munich, in which he explained that the teaching of German abroad rests exclusively on the magnetic attraction of Continental German culture. He maintained that the teaching of German has little or no correlation with the presence of German immigrants and their descendants overseas. This statement is exaggerated and certainly does not characterize the situation in countries such as Chile, Brazil, and Southwest Africa. Before World War I there was in the United States a definite relationship between intensity of German settlement and the effort put into the teaching of German. Today, however, it must be conceded that German FLES instruction has had relatively little success (i.e., has hardly been offered and even where available has aroused little interest) in those cities and counties of the Middle West in which the percentage of people of German ethnic descent is highest, such as southeast Wisconsin (including Milwaukee), St. Louis, and Cincinnati. Even the few German language schools are not infrequently more heavily patronized by children of monolingual English-speaking parents than by those of German-speaking parents.[21] Nevertheless there still exist American cultural institutions with a clearly discernible German American background. To take one example, the FLES instruction of the church schools of the Lutheran Missouri Synod has placed German in the first position among all foreign-language offerings. In 1965, 7,600 students at these elementary schools were learning German, 2,600 Spanish, and 1,600 French.[22]

The two-way dichotomy upheld in nineteenth-century America ("here are the German-speaking Americans and there are the Anglo Americans of non-German origin") has long been outmoded. It is true that there are some districts, such as those in central Texas, where the German language has largely or completely disappeared but where a certain vague consciousness of being of German descent lingers on. Nevertheless, the problem has been largely obviated by cultural assimilation. Of necessity, German instruction must be directed to all students regardless of their ancestry, but also without losing sight of the specific potentialities of regions with a strong German background.

Question two is of more immediate interest. Should all efforts to make instruction in German more widely available be limited to the treatment of German as a *branch of study*? Or does it make sense to work toward the establishment of at least a few schools in which German is employed as a second *medium* of instruction?

One avenue of approach here might be the FLES program. The promotion of German instruction within the FLES movement should certainly be continued. To make it more effective one might introduce German FLES programs in the areas of the country where remnants of the German linguistic enclaves have persisted to the extent that children are still able to use the language actively or passively. A survey

[21] This is the case in the German-language school founded in 1883 in Lawrence, Massachusetts (personal communication from its patron and promoter, Heinrich Rohrbach). See also Heinrich Rohrbach (1958).

[22] For a recent survey of all German *Sprachschulen* in the United States, see Heinz Kloss (1967a:94, 1967b). By way of comparison with the 7,600 Missouri Synod Students, it should be noted that in *public* elementary schools in 1960 there was a total of only 18,300 FLES students learning German.

of Kansas made in 1961 shows that FLES instruction in that year had scarcely touched the areas of the state where the German language is still alive (Carman 1961, 1962; Kreye 1961). In the last two decades over two hundred church schools have come into being among the Amish and among the Old Order Mennonites.[23] Perhaps the FLES idea could be introduced into such denominational schools. The anemic, mutilated written German of the Amish,[24] garbled and unintelligible as it sometimes is, could thereby be infused with new life so as to render it once again a vital, enduring component of their culture.

Up to now the FLES program has regrettably been completely restricted to the teaching of the foreign language as an *object* of study. In stark contrast to this short-sighted approach, the Soviet Union has been experimenting since 1948 with schools in which a foreign language is taught so intensively that it becomes the second language of the students. In these schools, which numbered about seven hundred in 1957, only the mother tongue was used as medium and object of instruction in the first year. In the second year, English, German, or French was introduced as a subject. In later years the foreign language gradually came to be employed as the medium of instruction for part of the other subjects. Through the use of this method it was hoped that the children would become truly bilingual (Ornstein 1958). Similar systems are common in certain other countries such as Luxemburg and Lebanon.

[23] Their school journal is the *Blackboard Bulletin*, published by the Pathway Publishing Corp. in Aylmer, Ontario. The Nov. 1967 and Nov. 1968 issues contain a school directory listing about 230 schools in the United States and 20 in Canada. Forty were founded by Old Order Mennonites. Almost 80 percent of the schools have come into being since 1960, some 60 in the 1950's and about 10 prior to 1950. The oldest was founded in Delaware in 1925.

[24] The following excerpts are indicative of the morphological change (disintegration) at work in Amish High German: "Er ergreifte neuen Mut and neuen Hoffnung. Er erstaunte sich als er Gedachte: Alles besteht in die Hände meines Herrn," from *Family Life* I, no. 4 (1968:32). "Ein bunten Vogel ist ein Vogel von viel verschiedene Färben. Einige Übersetzungen heißen es ein Räubervogel (ein zerreißenes Vogel), Welches sich ernährt auf andere Kreaturen und Blut. . . . Hier ist die Gemeinde Gottes abgebildet als ein fleckiges Raubevogel. . . . Der große sprenkliche Vogel ist in Wahrheit ein Hybrid welches hoch aufgestiegen ist und bald bereit zum Fall," *Family Life* I, no. 1 (1968:22).

In the United States the FLES movement has probably not achieved similar results anywhere, since it is usually restricted to the traditional pattern of three to five hours per week. To be sure, there have been a few isolated attempts outside of FLES to provide a greater intensity and duration of instruction. In the state of Virginia several courses in history were taught in French or Spanish in nine high schools during 1965–1966 and 1966–1967. The students enrolled were those who had had an intensive background in one of these two languages.

Although most of the experiments of this type that have been conducted by high schools in a number of other states have employed either Spanish or French, there have been a few attempts to use German, as for example in a core program at the University High School of Morgantown, West Virginia, at Carbon County High School in Price, Utah, and at a school in Sussex, Wisconsin.[25] There seems to be a definite tendency to set up high school curricula involving foreign-language instructional media that have little to do with the ethnic and linguistic composition of the student body; in other words, the presence of many English monoglots and of "other ethnics" seems to have little or no bearing on the language(s) chosen. In California and Pennsylvania, recent laws (1968) have even been enacted which explicitly permit the use of foreign languages in high schools. Along with Spanish and French, German should certainly have a place in such programs.

A notable experiment has been conducted at the college level; in 1963 the University of the Pacific set up "Elbert Covell College" in which a novel inter-American education program was offered with

[25] See Chester Christian (1967), especially Genelle Caldwell, "Report II: Teaching Content in a Foreign Language" (in Christian 1967: 42–56). Caldwell lists among her sources "Project OE–6–10–178, An Exploratory Study in Teaching World History in German, Board of Education, Common School District, Joint No. 16, Sussex, Wisconsin." On p. 53, she lists the following:

City and State	High School	Language	Topic
St. Louis, Mo.	Cleveland HS	French	Advanced geography
San Diego, Calif.	Point Loma HS	Spanish	World geography
Wilmington, Del.	Brandywine HS	Spanish	Latin American studies
Newton, Mass.	Newton South HS	French	Contemporary society
New York, N.Y.	St. Sergius HS	Russian	Russian literature, art, music, history

The same source gives a list of the Virginia high schools mentioned above.

Spanish as the chief teaching medium. This venture differed considerably from the Virginia experiment. The student body was of mixed linguistic background, with many students from Latin America enrolled, and English was reduced to a minor role.

Since 1953, the Massachusetts Institute of Technology has been conducting several of its courses in the humanities through the medium of French in a branch of study which was developed into a four-semester sequence. In contrast to the practice at Elbert Covell College, no native French-speaking students have ever been permitted to enroll in this program. [26]

In the Canadian province of Alberta a related question is being considered: are dual-medium schools desirable, indeed necessary, for the Anglo Canadians in order that at least a part of the population outside of Quebec can acquire French as a second language? In the United States, too, similar problems have arisen. In the last ten years the problem of bilingual schooling has become acute. Both ethnopolitical and pedagogical considerations are involved. We can attribute to ethnopolitics the fact that bilingual Spanish/English schools are rapidly being set up for the children of immigrants from Cuba, Puerto Rico, and Mexico as well as for children of American-born Spanish speakers. In the Commonwealth of Puerto Rico there are even public schools in which Spanish is the principal language of instruction and English only an object of study. Ethnopolitics may also be involved in the bilingual experiments initiated among the Acadians of northern Maine who still speak French. [27] Bilingual teaching has started at the Frenchville and St. Agatha public schools. The movement is also noticeable in other parts of New England where parochial schools have reduced, but never completely abandoned, their concept of bilingual teaching.

There is no reason why at least two or three experimental bilingual English/German schools could not be set up in the United States.

[26] In 1964–1965 there were 96 students at MIT registered in the program. See William F. Bottiglia (1965). Further information was contained in a letter to me from Bottiglia, dated May 15, 1968.

[27] Directed by the Franco-American Bicultural Research and Innovations Center (FABRIC). The French-speaking element in northern Maine is described in Heinz Kloss (1963:193–195).

Good locations for such schools might be Texas, eastern Pennsylvania, the Dakotas, or Wisconsin. Whether the conditions in Texas are more favorable (or less favorable) than elsewhere has yet to be determined. Regarding the question of German or American financial and technical backing for such an endeavor, it is significant that the German federal government established a German school in Washington, D.C., in 1961 and that negotiations for the establishment of a second school in New York have begun. Also, Bonn's surprising interest in the newly founded American Council on German Studies, with headquarters in Philadelphia, indicates a slowly growing awareness of the need for such schools on the part of the German Federal Republic. On the other hand, the United States Office of Education is becoming even more aware of the trends and traditions, the problems and the possibilities of bilingualism in America, and of the prominent role that the German language formerly played in this context. Witness the passing of the recent Bilingual Education Act (BEA),[28] or the establishment of the Advisory Committee on Bilingual Education, which was set up in compliance with Section 707 of the BEA.[29] Experiments have been planned and executed chiefly with Spanish, to a minor extent also with French, Navajo and other Indian languages, and in Michigan, with Polish and Dutch.[30] We should certainly initiate similar programs with German if at all possible. This should pose no problem since several of the ongoing projects are supported not by the BEA (whose limitation to linguistically handicapped children may render it applicable to only Amish and Hutterite German American children) but by other federal laws.[31]

[28] The provisions on bilingual education (sections 701–708) form part of Public Law 90–247, 90th Congress, House of Representatives 7819, Jan. 2, 1968, called the "Elementary and Secondary Education Amendments of 1967."

[29] The committee convened for the first time on Nov. 25–26, 1968. It is headed by Prof. Theodore Andersson, former chairman of the Department of Romance Languages at the University of Texas at Austin and long-time advocate of FLES and bilingual education programs.

[30] The Michigan experiments were conducted by Foreign Language Innovative Curricula Studies (FLICS) in Ann Arbor, Michigan.

[31] E.g., Title III (projects to accelerate creativity in education) and Title I (poverty programs) of the Elementary and Secondary Education Act (ESEA) of 1956, and

In summary, the projects that have been suggested here should proceed as follows:

1. Bibliographies and anthologies
   a. Bibliography of all German books printed in the United States since 1830
   b. (Based on *a*) anthology of German ideological writings, either one anthology for all ideological movements or separate anthologies for Old Lutherans, Catholics, and other groups
   c. (Based also on *a*) anthology of the German writings of American-born authors
2. Cultural and demographical atlases, linguistic atlases, and dialect investigations
   a. An atlas of the German settlements that arose as a result of immigration in the nineteenth and twentieth centuries
   b. Map of the German-speaking settlements of the (Old Order) Amish, (Old Order) Mennonites, and Hutterites
   c. Systematic collection of dialect samples and folk-cultural material, such as proverbs and songs, from all linguistic enclaves
3. A carefully planned pedagogical experiment in which German is made to function as the second teaching medium in two or three pilot schools

---

even the National Defense Education Act (NDEA) and the Educational Professional Development Act (EPDA).

7. A UNIFIED PROPOSAL FOR THE STUDY OF THE
GERMAN LANGUAGE IN AMERICA: DISCUSSION

PROPOSAL PRESENTED BY GLENN G. GILBERT

CHAIRMAN OF THE DISCUSSION: CARROLL E. REED

GILBERT: I would like to suggest that the participants in this discussion informally resolve that Dr. Kloss' "Atlas of Nineteenth-Century German Settlements in the United States" be given all possible support so that it may be published as soon as possible. The atlas, consisting of 102 maps and a 41-page introduction in English, deals with German cultural institutions in the United States on a state-by-state basis. Included are parishes or congregations where German was used in certain years as a language of religious services, the location of German clubs and fraternal organizations, and other data. Much of the immigration and language data is given by county, thus rendering the work invaluable for the location and study of the remaining rural speakers of German in this country. The publication of the atlas would mightily assist further undertakings in the fields of geography, sociology, history, demography, linguistics, and folklore.

REED: Many of us would be eager to obtain this material in order to plan research dealing with the language and culture of the German Americans. Such states as California, where studies of German culture are very few, could profit enormously from the atlas. [The resolution was then passed unanimously.]

GILBERT: I would like to present to you my conception of how a nation-wide study of the German dialects still spoken in the United States could be organized. The following has been purposely made rather general so that this body would be free to suggest needed modifications or changes. The first thing that should be done in a study of this sort would be to find the location of areas in the United States containing sizable numbers of German speakers. In addition to Dr. Kloss' unpublished atlas, it would benecessary to consult the United States and state censuses, especially the famous mother-tongue statistics contained in the United States Census of 1940. The use of the German language is closely correlated with the geographical spread of German cultural institutions: mutual aid societies, glee clubs, marksmanship clubs, gymnastic societies, churches, and so on. Also important are the geographical patterns of the teaching of German, inasmuch as such teaching can be shown to be predominant in certain sections of the country and neglected in others. Printed and manuscript descriptions of the Germans in the United States are of less value than the recent ethnic atlases and maps that have appeared in scattered books and newspapers. The latter show that the German language has survived into the present in compact rural areas in Minnesota, Wisconsin, Kansas, Pennsylvania, and Texas, among other states.[1] The small linguistic atlas published in 1954 by Reed and Seifert is being supplemented by a much larger word atlas by the same authors which will be published by Elwert Verlag in Marburg (Reed and Seifert, forthcoming).

Smaller areas of German speakers can of course be located by correspondence so that preliminary decisions may be made as to where fieldworkers could most profitably be sent. Through personal visits to the selected areas, trained or lay investigators would describe the German language spoken there and provide information on whether it is desirable to undertake a full-scale linguistic investigation. At the same

---

[1] See Kloss (forthcoming), Hofman (1966) and Hofman's later formulation (1968), Carman (1962), Jordan (1966, 1970), and Paullin (1932). Various useful maps have been published by the U.S. Census. Occasionally, midwestern newspapers publish maps of the distribution of ethnic elements on a state-wide basis. German publications such as the *Deutsches Archiv für Landes- und Volksforschung* (1937–1944) and the *Handwörterbuch des Grenz- und Auslandsdeutschtums* (1933–1938) have been largely ignored in the United States, even though they contain valuable cartographic and analytic studies of the German ethnic element in America.

time it would be necessary to compile bibliographies with an amount of annotation dependent upon the time, money, and other factors that are available. The bibliographies should include the following subject areas:

1. All linguistic studies of the German language in the United States.[2]

2. German/English languages-in-contact studies outside of the United States, that is, in Canada, British Honduras, Jamaica, South Africa, Southwest Africa, Tanzania, Australia, New Guinea, and New Zealand, among other places.

3. In considering the general methodology to be adopted in any such nation-wide, unified study of German as it still exists, we would want to include a perusal of what has been done in the Old World in German dialectology. The immense collections at Marburg, Münster, and elsewhere should be utilized to their fullest extent. We would not want to duplicate what generations of dialectologists have done before. General linguistic geography also has much to offer. Although Sever Pop's *La Dialectologie* (1950) is still the standard handbook in the field, it is unfortunately now rather out of date. The work of the last twenty years will have to be compiled from journal articles, proceedings of linguistic congresses, and excerpts from more recent books. Such work could also, incidentally, form the basis for a revision and updating of Pop's book. If funds were available, perhaps a revision and translation into English could proceed simultaneously. General linguistic geography in the United States will prove relatively easy to survey, since it is generally related to the work of Professor Kurath, his successors, McDavid and Atwood, and their students. Dialect lexicography should be studied, especially with regard to the methods and extent of the numerous dialect dictionaries in Germany and in the

---

[2] This has essentially been done by Wolfgang Viereck in a recent article, "German Dialects Spoken in the United States and Canada and Problems of German-English Language Contact, Especially in North America: A Bibliography," *Orbis* (1967, 1968). Unfortunately, his bibliography was not annotated; it certainly should have been. The introduction is very interesting, but it consists of only two pages. Also, there are gaps in it, so that a reworking of his bibliography plus annotation would be called for.

United States.[3] Important also is the new field of sociolinguistics, or perhaps we could call it social dialectology, as represented by McDavid, Fishman, and especially by Labov (1963, 1966, 1969; Labov et al. 1968).

Current work being done in bilingualism is also pertinent here, not only the classic books in the field by Haugen and Weinreich but newer studies by authors such as V. Vildomec and Wm. Mackey, the director of the recently organized institute for the study of bilingualism at Laval University in Quebec. Since bilingualism falls both within the province of sociolinguistics and psycholinguistics, literature from both branches of the science would have to be gone through carefully. The possible applications of generative transformational grammar to dialectology should be investigated. The whole problem of the geographical elicitation of syntactical patterns has for the most part been ignored in the past. The methodology suggested by David DeCamp (1964), by Sol Saporta of the University of Washington (1965), and by Samuel J. Keyser (1963), in his review of Kurath and McDavid (1959), raises many challenging possibilities for linguistic geography.[4] As dialectologists, of course, we cannot remain aloof from what is going on in linguistics, which is the parent discipline, and I think that we should pay more than just lip service to recent theoretical developments. The new ideas should be adapted to actual field situations. If the descriptive apparatus they provide seems superior to that used in the past, then we should by all means adopt it and not spare ourselves the effort of mastering whatever theoretical basis is necessary for such an undertaking.

Also important, I think, are the sampling methods used in the social sciences, techniques of estimating the characteristics of a large population on the basis of relatively small samples, techniques of polltaking, problems of random sampling versus judgment sampling, and so on. Dialectologists and linguistic geographers have failed to take advantage of the sampling methods available to them. For example, when I read in Sever Pop's *La Dialectologie* his description of the selection of in-

[3] The most important undertaking by far for American English is the "Dictionary of American Regional English" (DARE) being compiled under the direction of Frederic G. Cassidy at the University of Wisconsin.
[4] See also Donald Allen Becker (1967) and Wayne A. O'Neil (1968).

formants for the *Linguistic Atlas of Rumania* (1950: 723f.),[5] the
shortcomings of informant selection become appallingly clear. Nevertheless, we should keep in mind that the social situation in Rumania
in the 1920's and 1930's when these atlases were being made was of
course much different from that of the United States in the 1960's and
1970's. We can learn much from Mr. Harris and Mr. Gallup in this
respect.[6] If, on the basis of a small sampling, a good prediction can be
made concerning our next president, why can we not apply the same
techniques to find out what language is like? Traditionally, of course,
judgment sampling has been used almost exclusively in geographical
linguistics. However, the feasibility of random sampling has now been
demonstrated by Labov (1966). This type of investigation should be
followed up by all means.

Field methods—techniques of interviewing and working with informants—should all be carefully assessed. A question which has come
up previously in this symposium is, in what language shall we interview
the informants? Should we use High German, should the investigator
try to learn the dialect, should he use English, should he use a scrap-
book with pictures and drawings, should he use indirect elicitation techniques, or the approach developed by Labov (1963, 1966) or Stanley
Sapon (1953, 1957), and so on? Such problems should be carefully
thought out and a unified and consistent approach agreed upon, because obviously the questionnaire (if one is used) and the interviewing
techniques have much to do with the shaping of the results. That which
is built into the plan of investigation partly determines the results that
will be obtained. I think that dialectologists do not really face up to
that. In order to obtain more truthful results, the investigator must approach the field of inquiry with a minimum of preconceived notions.

As to the actual planning of the investigation, the theoretical background should be carefully thought out. What will be the general and
specific goals of the project? What will be the methods for achieving
these goals? What type of information about language is desired? It

[5] See also the discussion in Gilbert (1969), especially note 2.
[6] See Gallup (1948). For a general discussion of sampling methods in the social
sciences, see, for example, Selltiz, Jahoda, Deutsch, and W. Cook (1959), especially
chapters 6–8, "Data Collection."

may be that we are not primarily interested in the language itself but in the attitudes of the informants toward their language, something sociolinguists have shown us to be sometimes more important than a rote description of the language per se. I would recommend here a balance of the two types of data with a general approach modeled on Labov's study of English in New York City.

Aside from the methods for elicitation of information, the selection of the informants is of course very crucial. Here we have to make the basic decision: shall it be subject to judgment sampling, as has been done previously, or shall we use some type of random sampling, and if so, how can such a project be organized? Then, pilot studies would have to be made. Is the project workable? Will it come within the budget planned for the entire undertaking and its application? How do the informants react to the questionnaire and/or other elicitation methods employed? Are portions of the questionnaire impractical or unusable? Or are startling or unexpected results obtained? Does the interview proceed as expected? By yielding information on these and other problems, the pilot studies will serve as a bridge between the linguists steeped in their theory and the actual field situation.

The training of fieldworkers is very important. The fieldworker forms an integral part of the total interviewing situation, fully as critical as the elicitation methods and the selection of informants. This problem must have been in Professor Kurath's mind when he arranged for two noted European linguistic geographers, Jaberg and Jud, to come to the United States to hold a special summer seminar for the nine prospective fieldworkers for the *Linguistic Atlas of New England*. If sufficient money were available, the same thing could be done in our present situation. In other words, training and uniformity of approach and method on the part of the fieldworkers is highly desirable. To be sure, dialectologists are still debating about what constitutes a good fieldworker. Jules Gilliéron, pioneer linguistic geographer and author of the *Atlas Linguistique de la France*, thought that a layman (nonlinguist) would make a better fieldworker. The man should be a phonetician, to be sure, but should not know anything, or not very much, about the language he would be studying. Gilliéron was afraid that too much pre-knowledge on the part of the fieldworker would cause him to distort the data being gathered. Gilliéron's ideal fieldworker, then, is a *tabula rasa*, to be imprinted by the data with high fidelity, so to speak. Often, though, the opposite is the case. Gino Bottiglioni, the Italian linguistic geographer, performed all of his own work, as did S. A. Louw for the *Afrikaanse Taalatlas* [Linguistic Atlas of Afrikaans],[7] and numerous other linguists. They are fieldworkers, collators, editors, and sometimes even publishers of the works they produce.

Should the tape recorder be used? The first obvious answer to this is yes, by all means. The tape recorder is an indispensable instrument in dialectology today. Its presence, however, subtly or overtly alters the interviewing situation so that adjustments in the interview technique must be made to counterbalance potential biases. Many people refuse to be tape recorded. For random sampling this immediately creates a large non-respondent problem and drastically alters the characteristics of the hoped-for sample. To be sure, it is also possible to make candid recordings; present-day technology has made possible the miniaturization of the apparatus to the extent that recordings of excellent quality may be made from concealed machines and microphones. The legality of candid recordings for linguistic purposes is still in need of clarification, however.[8]

Should the aid of German universities, of German scholars and fieldworkers be enlisted? I would, of course say, by all means. But, again, this is expensive. Still more expensive are tape recorders, vehicles for transporting fieldworkers and other equipment needed in the field and at the data-collection point(s). The proposed project for American German could learn much from F. G. Cassidy's partially completed dialect dictionary of American English (see above). Perhaps the two projects could be closely coordinated. The administrative organization would involve numerous professors, fieldworkers, and assistants. A data-collection point or points would be necessary. Essential questions are: Where would the collected data be edited? Where would the records be archived? How much of the data should be published and in what form? Linguistic atlases, dialect dictionaries, and, in general, data-oriented rather than theory-oriented books usual-

[7] Louw (1959–1966). See also Louw (1941, 1948).
[8] See Gilbert (1969, note 1).

ly require large subventions for their publication. It is always advisable to obtain at least a promise of such a subvention in advance so that a situation will not arise in which the work is complete in manuscript but cannot be published, therefore remaining difficult of access to interested scholars. The design of the entire project must be drawn up in the form of a proposal and submitted to public and private philanthropic institutions in both the United States and Germany for financial support. Without such support the preliminary work will have been done for nothing and the entire undertaking will remain a mirage, in this case a tragic one for the German Americans, since we have before us essentially the last chance to record the characteristics of this rapidly disappearing language in the United States.

REED: Dr. Gilbert's remarks are open for discussion.

MOELLEKEN: I suggest we start at the end of Dr. Gilbert's outline. For instance, is there any institution that would sponsor such a program? Is there any institution that would make available the space needed for the collection of tapes and other equipment? Is it possible that the University of Texas might be interested in starting such a project? If not, we should perhaps begin by establishing some committees to investigate possible solutions.

REED: Looking over the history of projects of this kind, I feel quite uneasy in view of the problems involved in the establishment of such a center. The "Linguistic Atlas of the United States and Canada," for example, moved from Yale to Brown University, then to the University of Michigan, and is now housed in the University of Chicago. It has followed its directors around, more or less; many people have even lost track of it and know neither where it is located nor how to use its data collections. In other words, the atlas has not been institutionalized in a proper way. The cost of an atlas is considerable, and the availability of such funds for the advancement of American German studies is doubtful.

WILSON: In line with this same problem is the question of setting up a publishing repository, so to speak. The repository could be connected with an institutionalized archive. Perhaps one or several universities could act collectively to house the actual tape recordings and other pertinent written materials connected with the project. The participating universities should also be urged to finance and to sponsor the publication of an annual or quarterly journal. Among other things, the journal would undertake to publish selected sets of field data so that more comprehensive and far-reaching linguistic analyses could be undertaken by interested scholars no matter where they are located.

REED: A proposal of this kind was made by David Reed some years ago for the various records of the "Linguistic Atlas of the United States and Canada." Reed circulated one page (the page on which the *chesterfield*, 'soft,' occurs) of his so-called "preprints." Through a process similar to the Bruning Process or Xerox, such information was disseminated. Unfortunately the project lacked financial backing and was soon discontinued. This has been the fate of many such proposals. The Pennsylvania German material that Seifert and I collected is housed with the "Linguistic Atlas of the United States and Canada"; also, Seifert and I each have one copy. I am willing to turn over my copy to any responsible institution that would offer the facilities for a permanent archive. Do you think that the University of Texas at Austin would be willing to set up such an archive?

GILBERT: It might be possible.

REED: At least by the fact that this symposium is being held, the University of Texas has demonstrated more interest than any other university I know of. Much of the impetus, though, is attributable to the present members of the German Department. We do not know how it will be twenty years from now.

EICHHOFF: The idea of having the tape-recorded data transcribed and published right away arises of course from the feeling that one may collect large amounts of material but never see any of it published. If a scholar's efforts consist only of data collection in the form of tape recordings, this will not help him to become known and to enjoy the fruits of such recognition. On the other hand, the project described here would involve a huge number of transcriptions. Aside from the expense involved in procuring the necessary type fonts and special phonetic signs, the printing of such material would be a wasteful undertaking. Perhaps the procedure followed by the *Deutsches Sprach- archiv* in Germany would prove more useful. The *Archiv* has collected a great many tapes and has prepared transcriptions for a few of them that represent types of speech and geographical locations of great interest.

WERBOW: In the day of Xerox machines we need not think about publication in a normal way any longer nor fear a great deal of expense. We have on deposit here, for example, not only copies of all of the tape recordings made by Zwirner but also photostatic copies, Xerox copies, and photographic copies of various kinds of transcriptions of German made up to the year 1967. There are rough phonetic transcriptions, texts in *literarische Umschrift*[9] and in Standard German orthography. It would not be difficult to have these available at, say, five places in the United States so as to make them easily accessible to interested scholars. I think what we need to work toward is a consortium of universities which would be interested in putting this on a firm basis. One of the universities would be designated as the major depository; other universities would house duplicate collections. We certainly do not want to have one down here in Texas and no other in the country. It would be too expensive for people to travel. If there were one at Madison, Wisconsin, one or two on the East Coast, and one on the West Coast, this would probably prove satisfactory.

REED: The system developed by University Microfilms for their series of dissertation abstracts enables the interested scholar to obtain any doctoral dissertation from participating universities on microfilm or in Xerox form. A similar approach might be adopted here so that handwritten or typed transcriptions of tape recordings or copies of the recordings themselves could be made available in the same way. This has been the method used by Zwirner at the *Deutsches Spracharchiv*.

EICHHOFF: Of course only a few of the tapes in Münster have been transcribed.

REED: That is true.

EICHHOFF: I do not want to transcribe them all, and I am sure that the majority of people engaged in such work would think the same way. It is true that a large number of high-quality recordings must be made now, but only a few of these should be transcribed and the rest left for a time when the American German dialects are no longer in

---

[9] A literary, nonphonemic orthographic representation designed to render the dialect maximally intelligible to the reader who is familiar with the standard language.

existence. At that time a second decision can be made concerning the further preparation of the unedited tapes.

REED: A former colleague of mine in the anthropology department at the University of Washington prepared a good many drawers filled with handwritten records dealing with Indian languages of the Pacific Northwest. Although some of them are twenty-five years old, they have never been worked on. But at least the records are there; the Indian languages are gone. A similar process is taking place before our eyes with regard to the non-English European languages that have functioned for many years as second languages in this country. Your suggestion therefore seems very sound inasmuch as these American versions of European languages with long histories and weighty traditions will be preserved for posterity.

MICHAEL: Dialectology is not my field, but I have done considerable work involving the field recording of folk songs. I am curious about the notion of the transcription in general. Would it not be preferable to work only with the tapes? It strikes me as terribly laborious to put this into some sort of publishable form, that is, into written form. I grant you that very few people would want to sit down and transcribe dozens or hundreds of tapes; on the other hand, it seems so easy to make an audio-copy for fellow scholars.

REED: A considerable organization would be necessary to provide such copies on a large-scale basis. A whole tape library would have to be catalogued with audio-copies made available at fixed prices.

MICHAEL: Anything you did would require such a center and library.

REED: The University of Indiana for example possesses a center for the oral study of folklore.

EICHHOFF: The *Deutsches Spracharchiv* in Münster does not actually sponsor the recording of American German linguistic material, but it is nevertheless very eager to obtain copies of the originals we make here. Dr. Moelleken and I both send tapes to Münster. The storage of the originals and copies in different locations enhances their chances of survival and availability to the scholarly world. Other universities that wish to build up tape libraries may usually obtain copies very easily. The *Spracharchiv* even has a catalog from which the desired copies may be selected.

REED: Would it be too impractical to set up the center in Germany, say, at Marburg or Münster?

SCHULZ-BEHREND: I remember reading pleas for funds by Wrede and Wenker in Marburg around 1910: "If we only had one-tenth the cost of a battleship, we could do marvelous things in dialect studies." As it was, they were languishing in a basement and were not even enjoying full support of the university. You cannot expect much unless you ask much. Universities usually do not have much money. The institutions that *do* have money are German and American foundations. Needed is an evangelist of this cause, because the speakers themselves don't give a damn. Needed is an expert who is interested enough to seek the necessary funds and who can organize the work that must be done. There is nothing wrong with considering consortiums and depositories, but the center of action and research must be located in this country, not in Germany.

REED: I can say only "well roared, lion." In this connection the National Carl Schurz Association should also be mentioned. The only reaction now, if I may play the devil's advocate every time, is to say that the interest in promoting things concerned with the German language seems to suffer a fate more or less parallel to the use of German in the United States. If one asks a philanthropic foundation for financial support, there must be something concrete *to* support, something besides good words.

KLOSS: Quite recently the National Carl Schurz Association and the American Association of Teachers of German set up a joint board called the "American Council on the Study of German in America." The secretary-general, Mr. Deeken, and his associates in Philadelphia are mainly interested in promoting the teaching of German as a foreign language. However, if they can be convinced that the investigation of the German spoken by native Americans of native-born parentage would help promote the study or the teaching of the language, perhaps they would be willing to include such investigations among their goals. At the present time negotiations are being carried on between the American Council and authorities of the Federal Republic of Germany concerning further funds for the support of German teaching in the United States. Attempts should be made to have the plans that are being discussed here included in the negotiations. The proceedings of this symposium should be made available at once to the American Council.

REED: I assume it is the consensus of this group that there should be set up a center to be located in the United States and with sufficient financial backing.

WILSON: Is one center preferable to a number of regional centers? Does not the very size of the United States require the establishment of regional divisions?

MOELLEKEN: I think that it could be decentralized later on, after we have established such a center.

EICHHOFF: And what does it mean to have a center? Surely it will include adequate work space, several part-time faculty members with the Ph.D., graduate research assistants, and clerical assistants. If the project is connected with one professor, the physical collections should not be forced to change their location as the professor shifts from one university to the other. The center should have a full inventory of technical equipment and should have at its disposal the services of a recording engineer. The *Spracharchiv* in Münster even had two such engineers, who alternated with each other in the field and whose continuous monitoring of the tape interviews ensured an audio quality second only to an actual broadcast studio. Such considerations as these must also be carefully worked into the proposal.

REED: It was suggested, and I think there was a favorable response, that the University of Texas at Austin would be an ideal place, as far as any one location is ideal. Another possibility would be the University of Wisconsin at Madison.

SEIFERT: I do not know whether financial support can be found at the University of Wisconsin. Perhaps the Historical Society would be more amenable to such a proposal.

REED: What we need is space and a friendly, large German department that would supervise the undertaking over a period of many years.

SEIFERT: I have made arrangements with the Wisconsin Historical Society to take my records of Pennsylvania German, Wisconsin German, and collection of Americana Germanica at a time when I no longer shall want them. The Historical Society rather than the university would be a more likely sponsor for further work.

REED: No matter how much prestige a university or a German department has today, who knows what the situation will be a few decades from now? Compare the huge collections of the German Linguistic Atlas, which have been housed at Marburg since the 1870's, with the short sojourn of the collections of the "Linguistic Atlas of the United States and Canada" at the University of Michigan, for example. It would be highly desirable to have a director and a permanent staff that would make possible a considerable degree of continuity, provided that sufficient money were available over a period of years. There would also have to be a nonacademic staff that would presumably be supervised by an academic staff or at least coupled to a responsible departmental commitment. For some types of work only highly trained experts can qualify, and not just a series of amateurs who may be insufficiently trained.

SCHULZ-BEHREND: Professors are already overworked in the performance of their regular academic duties. You cannot expect a man to do two full-time jobs consistently. There may be a few hard-working, devoted men here and there, usually in academies or institutes of science with expert personnel who have the time to give out information and advice. On the other hand the typical answer of a professor will be, "See me next week—I'm too busy right now." My point is that the envisioned institute has to be organized and run like a museum. It will, in fact, be a language museum, not a teaching institution. Therefore I would advocate an entirely individual institute for German American language preservation and study, next door to a friendly German department.

REED: Some universities such as UCLA have folklore institutes that are more or less loosely attached to the regular departments of folklore.

WERBOW: An Institute of Texan Cultures was established at the 1968 HemisFair in San Antonio. It is the intention of the director, Henderson Shuffler, and his staff that the Institute remain as a permanent museum and research organization for the study of the diverse cultural components represented in Texas. Undoubtedly the Institute could be counted upon for certain kinds of support, a contribution toward a nation-wide effort.

REED: We have been discussing collections of linguistic materials. What about the study of folk culture and folklore? Do you think that folklore should go hand-in-hand with linguistics or should it be approached as a separate endeavor?

YODER: I have always felt that there is a middle ground here between the linguistic approach and the folklore approach. In some cases we are dealing with the same informants; some of the materials on the questionnaire might be combined so that questions designed to elicit exclusively linguistic information could be carefully interspersed with questions of a more general cultural and folkloristic nature.

REED: This would add a whole new dimension to the linguistic questionnaires that are now being used. The advent of tape recording makes the collection of great masses of linguistic and folkloristic material a relatively easy matter. In the days of handwritten phonetic transcriptions of the informants' responses, there simply was not sufficient time to note additional cultural data.

WERBOW: This actually brings us to point one again. After having talked in general about some possibilities for funding the proposed center, we should now turn back to the general and specific goals of the project.

MOELLEKEN: I should first like to introduce a third dimension, and that is, the possibility of help from the Canadian government. There is a large German colony in Canada that would certainly be interested in our endeavors. And since cultural minorities in Canada tend to receive considerable attention from the federal authorities, perhaps more so than in the United States, we might be able to find responsive ears for our plans.

REED: Let us remember the old adage: If you want something done, do it yourself. Thus I am hesitant about giving my neighbors the job. Although I am dubious that they could provide much money for the project, we could perhaps count on them for expert and competent help.

YODER: The National Museum of Canada has a very large ethnic culture involvement in various areas; it certainly might be interested in supplementing a project such as this by sponsoring the recording of German in Canada.

GILBERT: To go back to the suggestion of Dr. Wilson, there has been relatively little published in this field.[10] The journal that would seem most suited for the publication of such material, namely *PADS*, should be encouraged to print such articles in greater quality and quantity. The American Dialect Society has a standing committee on non-English languages in the United States headed by Einar Haugen; even so, articles such as Dr. Moelleken's recent contribution on Mennonite Low German in the Mexican province of Chihuahua are a rarity. We could perhaps urge Haugen to encourage more research and publication in this field, especially work dealing with German in America, a language that practically outweighs all other non-English language groups put together. I do not think that it would serve much purpose to attempt to start a new journal—there are too many already. Instead, the *PADS* or other journals, which we hope will serve as an outlet for our research, would be urged to expand its publication in the field of non-English languages.

REED: I have never heard of *PADS* refusing a reasonable article on American German. Even the *PMLA* maintains that its rather small number of German articles is due to the fact that there is a paucity of German scholars contributing such articles. There is really no problem as far as the printing of the results of research is concerned; the main questions are where are the contributors and who is willing to buy the journal. The more material of high quality that appears in print, the more the entire effort that we have been talking about will be stimulated.

SCHULZ-BEHREND: The official attitude on bilingualism in this country is beginning to change. In Texas we shall soon have Spanish

---

[10] This literature is being collected at Laval University at the International Center for Research on Bilingualism, under the direction of Professor William F. Mackey, and is also cited in extensive bibliographies by Haugen (1956; forthcoming), Weinreich (1968), Lambert (Peal and Lambert 1962, and other publications by Lambert), and others.

as a language of instruction on an equal basis with English. I see no reason why the descendants of German settlers could not receive the same kind of treatment. The federal government has become considerably more tolerant of foreign languages as a medium of instruction. The question is whether it is already too late for German. Despite the negative effect of two world wars, perhaps something could still be salvaged.

REED: I think that our chief interest here is research on transplanted German, not necessarily in increasing the use of the language.

SCHULZ-BEHREND: We should of course carefully distinguish the two goals. I just wanted the members of this group to know that we are experiencing a shift in attitude here.

REED: Since a considerable amount of money has been made available for improving the active use of certain foreign languages in this country, those research workers who are primarily involved in dialectology, bilingualism, and sociolinguistics would do well to interest their less theoretically minded colleagues in the practical applications of such research.

WERBOW: Ten million dollars has been allocated to Texas for bilingual teaching in Spanish and English. I think that the persons in charge of the bilingualism effort in Texas are aware of the existence of other languages that are spoken less widely than Spanish, and will focus on them in the next stage.

KLOSS: It is certainly not for a foreign visitor to voice an opinion as to where the headquarters of the prospective institute should be. However, I would like to point out two factors which speak in favor of Austin, first of all, the excellent connections which exist between the German department of the University of Texas and the *Institut für Deutsche Sprache* in Marburg and the *Deutsches Spracharchiv* in Münster. While I would be very much against having the seat of the whole project transplanted onto German soil, it is nevertheless imperative that there should be from the beginning close cooperation with kindred research centers in Germany. In the second place, Austin, as the capital of Texas, provides (at least potentially) a more broadminded atmosphere of linguistic toleration, primarily because of the strong Spanish heritage that is slowly coming into its own in the southwestern United States. This psychological factor should not be neglected; the presence of two widely spoken, important world languages in the state speaks strongly in favor of Texas over states such as Kansas or even Minnesota and Wisconsin.

REED: Perhaps Dr. Gilbert could suggest something that would be worthy of our immediate attention among the things he mentioned. One thing that seems imperative is a compilation of all questionnaires and check lists that have been used in the United States for the study of American German. With such information in hand we would be in a better position to make suggestions and decisions about future collections. As Dr. Gilbert said, in dialectology the outcome of field research is determined by the initial premises and research plan adopted. One must be very careful to avoid rigidity and to encourage flexibility and open-endedness.

GILBERT: I would say that there are two things that are urgently in need of discussion. Obviously it is impossible in dialectology, in linguistic geography, or in lexicography to obtain even a sketchy total picture of a language. In practice, even a large undertaking tends to be limited to a small part of the total grammar—to some aspect of syntax, morphology, lexicon, segmental phonology, suprasegmental features, basis of articulation, and so forth. Concerns more peripheral to linguistics such as semantics, bilingualism, attitudes of speakers toward their language, and, in general, the functioning of language in society and its role in the individual psyche are of course also legitimate. The project proposed here should, therefore, be essentially limited to some part of this great spectrum of linguistic phenomena. For example, lexicon could be emphasized throughout the study, or perhaps morphology (with a main interest being placed on changes undergone within the German morphology after the arrival of the speakers in this country). Or phonology may be thought of as paramount. The study of the phonemic systems of selected German dialects not only allows for convenient comparison of limited amounts of data but is also intrinsically interesting for the theory of innate conservatism of colonial languages as opposed to their propensity to change.

The second thing that should be discussed is the most important practical application of this project. In those areas of the United States where students entering elementary school, high school, and college still have enough knowledge of German so that they have some kind of advantage over students who do not have this background, how can we adjust our teaching (if there are enough of these students to make up a class) so as to build upon the background they already possess, instead of needlessly subjecting them to all the beginning German routines they already know? Dr. Eichhoff mentioned this morning that these students come to class with the idea that they have a great advantage over their fellow students and thus do not need to work very hard. He further observed that it is more often than not just these students who do badly in German classes. I do not think that is true at all. It is because the instructor expects them to do better. People who speak German and English are no more intelligent than people who speak only English. The good student, whether he has a German background or not, will soon realize that learning German is not an easy task and that much work will be required. A student who combines the advantages of a German background, good intelligence, and the desire to learn would be outstanding in any class, irrespective of its composition of students or teaching methods employed. Our pedagogical apparatus hardly provides for such students today.

REED: We could easily have as many theories as we have examples.

GILBERT: Let us go to the first question. What will be the goal of the proposed investigation within the whole realm of German language study?

WILSON: I do not believe that we should prescribe goals to each other; no one should direct that the first two or three years shall be devoted only to phonology, the next two years only to syntax, and so forth. Since each of us is interested in different aspects of the linguistic description of the American German dialects, the project would have to assume a more rounded or complementary character.

REED: When time runs out, the custom is that the chairman of an organization appoints a committee. I would recommend that the persons who are now most actively engaged in this work here in Texas constitute the chief members of this committee and that further members be selected to help and advise them. May I ask for a resolution on the part of this group which clearly expresses its confidence in such a plan and which designates Dr. Gilbert as the chairman of the committee. [The resolution passed unanimously.] Some of the proposals that have been made here may never be achieved. Even so, I think we have agreed on certain directions for research. Although the far-reaching program that Dr. Gilbert has outlined has little hope of being substantially realized any time in the near future, we can at least undertake to centralize the efforts of scholars and fieldworkers who are studying American German.

8. GERMAN FOLKLORE IN AMERICA: DISCUSSION

CHAIRMAN OF THE DISCUSSION: DON YODER

YODER: There are several areas where folk-cultural and linguistic questionnaires might possibly be combined to gather materials of interest to both disciplines. One of these areas is the recording of local place names, a procedure that is especially fruitful in regions of dense rural settlement such as that found in eastern Pennsylvania. Many interesting local names (*Flurnamen*) appear neither on county maps nor even on some of the more detailed topographical maps. There are names of hills, roads, fields, and streams, especially the smaller streams. In the process of recording such names in the area of Kutztown, Pennsylvania, I discovered for example a *Schmaltzgass'*, a *Wassergass'*, a *Hexegass'*, and so forth. The older people who are well-versed in these names can draw a map of the area and label the geographic features in their dialect. Knowledge of such names declines among the younger generation; nevertheless the names could still be elicited quite successfully by means of questionnaires or perhaps by regional maps in outline form to be filled in by the informant.

Closely related to the occurrence of the names are their varying pronunciations determined by geographical location. There are for example two Heidelbergs in Pennsylvania: [ˈheːdəlˌbařɪg] is in Lehigh County and [ˈhaɪdəlˌbařɪg] is further west. In Lancaster County the town of Manheim, which was named after the German [ˈmanˌhaɪm], is not pronounced [ˈmænˌhaɪm] by the local people; they say

[ˈmænɔm], even in English. This corresponds to the dialect pronunciation of *Mannheim* in the Palatinate, where one speaks of [ˈmanomɒ] for the people of Mannheim. Questions dealing with both local and supraregional names should be included in order to shed light on the geographical periphery in the world-view of the Pennsylvania Germans. For example, they pronounce *New York* as [naɪˈjařɪk].

There are also dialect names for people who live in certain localities in the Pennsylvania German country. In Montgomery County there is a *lower end* and an *upper end,* the people living in the *upper end* being referred to as the [ˌəð̥ɒlˀɛndɒ]. People in Berks County refer to the inhabitants of Schuylkill County across the Blue Mountain as the [ˌəβɒˈbařjɒ], 'the people across the mountain,' a fact that shows both a social and a linguistic divergence. The hill country across the Blue Mountain is inhabited by people of the lower economic stratum where sectarian religion and other characteristics of this economic group are present; the Berks County area to the south is quite different.

The pronunciation and orthographic changes of surnames might also be profitably included. After two centuries of isolated linguistic change most Pennsylvania German names can now be recognized at a glance. For instance, there exists the fascinating name *Harshbarger* in central Pennsylvania; it was originally spelled *Hirschberger*, but later came to be written *Harshbarger* in English because of the dialect pronunciation [ˈhaʃ bəřɣɒ]. Contrary to what most writers have stated, *Harshbarger* is not Americanized German; it simply represents a respelling according to dialect pronunciation.[1] Another example of linguistic change in surnames is *Bonebrake,* a Pennsylvania German name occurring in western Maryland. Such names were not spelled in accordance with the dialect pronunciation but were loan-translated into English for ease of pronunciation and possibly for social reasons. The process of loan-translation proceeded haphazardly; the original *Beinbrecht* was rendered as *Bonebrake* rather than *Bonebright*, whereas *Albrecht* has become *Albright*. Family names were thus altered in unexpected ways.

<hr/>

[1] "Dutchified Surnames," Allentown *Morning Call*, Sept. 21, 1946; for H. L. Mencken's comments on it, see *The American Language, Supplement II* (Mencken 1956:410–411).

A folk-cultural context for linguistic materials may be provided by asking directly for proverbial phrases, expressions, and superstitions, as wholes. We have for example in American folklore many euphemisms for going to the privy. One of the most common American English expressions is to say that you are "going to see your aunt." The Pennsylvania Germans possess an equally elegant expression that involves their attitude toward the Irish. They say something like this: [ɪç mʊs ˈnaosge: ʊn ɪn aɪɹɪʃ ɪˈlɛdəřə], 'I have to go out back and beat up an Irishman.'

Also of great interest is the recording of German church services in order to study the so-called "sermon German" or "Bible German," assiduously cultivated in the German sectarian and church worlds. For comparative purposes we should establish archives of tape recordings of German preaching services with the singing and the recitation of liturgical parts, the creeds in the more formal churches, and of course the whole service in the freer type of religious institutions. Among other things, this type of material sheds light on the process by which the High German language was altered to fit American conditions. Unfortunately, it is now almost impossible to record German services among the Lutherans and Reformed in Pennsylvania. I thought of this twenty years ago but was never able to begin the project. At that time there were preachers living who in their early ministry had preached every other Sunday (at least in Pennsylvania in the Union churches) in the "Pennsylvania High German" language. If these preachers were native to Pennsylvania it would have been valuable to record their reading of the Lutheran and Reformed services and prayers as they had been traditionally recited before the First World War or in the 1920's when such services were still a part of Pennsylvania German culture.

SEIFERT: Are you doing this in Pennsylvania now?

YODER: No, I never was able to make such recordings. I do not know if recordings were made of Thomas Brendle, whose German was exceptionally good. In any case, he would not be typical of the ordinary country boy who went away to seminary and whose High German, which he would use only for church, would be influenced considerably by his dialect background. A few of the ministers are still living who began preaching around 1910 and who for perhaps ten years gave a German sermon once every two weeks or once a month. The situation is more promising in western Canada, where German services are still fairly common among churchmen and sectarians, and in parts of the Middle West and in Texas.

Also in urgent need of systematic study are the singing styles of the German churches—not so much those of church groups who have a more sophisticated and general singing style, but of sectarian groups such as the Hutterites, the Old Order Amish, the River Brethren, the Old Order Dunkards, and the German Baptist Brethren. Each sect seems to possess patterns of singing and a body of hymnody in unique texts. Although the singing styles are of value both to the linguist and to the folklorist, very few of them have been studied.

The preaching styles as used in the pulpit vary from the *Kanzeldeutsch*, the "holy tone," the "language of Canaan," and other adjusted ways of speaking that many ministers had in the past, down to the chanted sermon found among the Old Order Amish, the Old Order Mennonites, and the Hutterites. It is considerably more difficult to record such material because of the closed nature of these sectarian services. For American English, there is a general project centered at the University of Virginia to study preaching styles. Although the project has investigated Negro and white southern preaching styles, for example, it has not attempted research in the field of non-English language preaching.

A final point of common interest to folk-cultural research and linguistics is the elicitation of life histories of informants speaking in their native dialects. Have you tried this approach with any of your informants?

SEIFERT: We try to get as much as they can remember. In Pennsylvania, informants were occasionally able to relate life histories with genealogies going back as far as five or six generations.

YODER: This would be carried on in the form of a conversation, I presume. You mentioned that there was often a thirty-minute warm-up before the actual questions were broached.

SEIFERT: We use the conversational form beginning with, "Could you give me the name of your father and mother, your mother's maiden name, parents' places of birth," etc. Later we would ask for the grandparents' names, including maiden names of female ancestors.

REED: Nothing was mechanically recorded.

SEIFERT: Usually we would transcribe their pronunciation of their names. Also, much of the genealogical information was available from written sources if we had wanted to pursue the matter further.

GILBERT: We might note that Professor Kurath in the *Linguistic Atlas of New England* (Kurath 1939–1943) included a concise life history of each informant. As for the work done in Texas and Kansas, we made use of the typescript questionnaire that was employed in Wisconsin (Seifert 1946a) and added to it the items that Haugen had used in his study of the Norwegian language in America (1953:645–653).[2] A rather long list of biographical questions was thus accumulated. The informants were encouraged to answer in their dialect on the tape. Even the speakers of dialects that we hardly understood were encouraged to speak in a type of monologue. Usually though, as far as the German language in Texas goes, we could follow more or less what they were saying.

MEYER: When I was teaching at Rice University in Houston I regularly asked all of my students to write about their family history. I would occasionally get long stories about how a grandfather was born in the same castle as Bismarck and how they were all noblemen. The *Adelsverein* seems to have provided all of its colonists with an aura of nobility so that when the old men began talking about it, everyone had become a nobleman. By this means I was able to collect a considerable amount of material for my Texas German novel. To the request for a life history were appended a few questions about superstitions such as walking under a ladder, breaking a glass, or spilling salt. Each student was able to give long lists of superstitions. Such an approach yields a great deal of material without ever having to leave the university grounds.

YODER: Both direct interviewing and postal questionnaires have proved useful in the collection of folklore materials. The folk-cultural institute in Amsterdam, for example, sends out detailed questionnaires

---

[2] Haugen's questionnaire has also been used to study the remnants of Norwegian in Texas; see Kjell Johansen (1970).

on foods, clothing, and many other aspects of folk-culture to a network of between twelve and fifteen hundred regular correspondents who complete the questionnaires and return them to the institute. I am working on a similar project at the University of Pennsylvania. There must be some way of designing the folkloristic questionnaires to simultaneously elicit systematic linguistic material.

With regard to Dr. Meyer's observation about the noble background of the Texas German families, there is a common genealogical myth in Pennsylvania also. If one asks an informant about his family, he will give the common reply that in the eighteenth century "three brothers came to Pennsylvania." Sometimes he will add that "one went north, one went south, and one stayed in Pennsylvania." This would be very difficult to document; it is simply a genealogical myth.

One of the main problems with the life-history approach is that the investigator gets a great deal of rambling material. The informant has to be guided, as you evidently have done. Have you also investigated the attitudes of the dialect speakers toward their own dialect?

SEIFERT: We asked our informants whether they use the dialect actively or whether it is a petrified language for them. In my studies of German in Wisconsin similar questions were posed.

EICHHOFF: Concerning the family histories of the German dialect speakers, there seems to be a great difference between Texas, Pennsylvania, and Wisconsin. Many of my informants in Wisconsin knew almost nothing about their family histories; some could not even state where their father had been born. Only in places where there had been a one hundredth or one hundred twenty-fifth anniversary and local genealogies had been restudied for the occasion would people show an interest in the history of their family.

YODER: That would seem to be a typical American attitude. Many Americans do not know their grandmothers' maiden names, much less those of the great-grandparents. However, in Pennsylvania there exists perhaps a more sharply developed genealogical sense, at least since the 1890's. There is a family reunion held every summer in the form of an all-day picnic. In Pennsylvania the family reunion becomes a kind of semireligious service. It is opened with prayer and a short religious preamble. After the patriotic addresses about the family there are the "closing exercises." The family reunion extends itself into the popular culture. Prizes are given to the people who come the longest distance, to the newest baby, to the oldest couple, and so on. The reunions began in Pennsylvania in the nineteenth century, and there is a highly developed family sense. Most Pennsylvanians of German background speak of the *Freindschaft* [ˈfraɪnˌʃaft], of "being in the *Freindschaft*," "I'm in his *Freindschaft*," and so forth. The *Freindschaft* involves the interesting genealogical concept of the larger or extended family. Some of the earliest American genealogies that have been written down were those of the Moravians and other sectarians of the eighteenth century. One of these was printed as early as 1764 and is supposedly the earliest printed German ethnic genealogy in Pennsylvania. This is extremely early for the United States.

With regard to the attitudes of the dialect speakers toward their dialect, I have corresponded about this with leading educators of Pennsylvania German background. I asked various people, including the president of Temple University, Millard Gladfelder, and Henry Gehman of Princeton Theological Seminary (both of whom grew up in dialect-speaking surroundings), to write frankly what their reaction had been to the use of the dialect in their early life and in public life. Their remarks were published in a recent issue of *Pennsylvania Folklife* (Gehman 1968; Gladfelter, Kreider, Spotts 1968). The types of materials we received were in some ways disappointing. As I had expected, the humorous side of the dialect was stressed. Most of my informants mentioned that they had been in Germany and were able to use their Pennsylvania German with great success. They tended to avoid discussing the conflict of Pennsylvania German with English and the possible social handicap a Pennsylvania German accent in English seems to create. *The Pennsylvania German Manual*,[3] which appeared in Kutztown in 1875, was not published in order to provide instruction in Pennsylvania German but rather to show Pennsylvania German students, especially those who were going out to be teachers, how to eliminate their Pennsylvania German accent. One of Horne's sentences for practice is, "The volunteers fired a volley down the valley," since he

---

[3] A. R. Horne (1875). The volume went through several editions.

knew the Pennsylvania German students would at first pronounce English [v]- as [β]-, the latter being the only voiced labial fricative occurring word-initially in their dialect.

I would like to quote an account that was discovered in a Lebanon newspaper of 1858,[4] which throws into sharp relief the tension and bitterness over the dialect from within the culture in Pennsylvania in the nineteenth century. It is the most extreme of the many proposals that the "Americanizing" forces of the nineteenth century developed to wipe out Pennsylvania German:

> Advances toward the desirable aim of a total disappearance of the German cannot, from the very nature of the case, be made in a very accelerated manner. The gravity of the German character does not readily respond to the stirring tone of an animated progressive quick-step; but rather chooses to listen to the soberation of the well tempered march of conservatism. The brogue, so strenuously adhered to by the Pennsylvania German, is a much cherished inheritance from generation to generation, and the progeny will but reluctantly part with the time-honored legacy of their forefathers. Radical remedies vigorously applied will, therefore, be of little avail. The cure must be effected by degrees and by mildly administering the English antidote. Our population is eminently stationary [still true of Lebanon County and the surrounding area]. The idea of willingly abandoning their place of birth, of transgressing the circumference of the narrow circle, to which they are attached by traditional as well as personal ties, is foreign to their mind. The intense love of locomotion, the cosmopolitan ubiquity which forms a prominent characteristic of the Anglo-American, does not rumple their equanimitous disposition with its restless impulses. Very few emigrate from Lebanon County.

This author's program was threefold: first, to encourage the "Pennsylvania German fledgling," by which he meant the young working man, to work several years outside of the Pennsylvania German area where he would be forced to learn English; second, to improve the teaching of English in rural schools by hiring teachers with non-Pennsylvania German accents from the Anglo-American population; third,

---

[4] The articles appeared in the Lebanon [Penn.] *Courier*, Jan. 29, 1858, and Feb. 26, 1858. They were republished, with an introduction by Alfred L. Shoemaker, in *The Pennsylvania Dutchman* 3, no. 15 (Jan. 1, 1952):2–3.

to lengthen the school term, for "what good are a few months of English when Dutch reigns solidly between terms?" His comments on the Pennsylvania German dialect are a classic example of the extreme Americanizing stance that was so common in the nineteenth century.

He continues in a still more negative vein: "As the inevitable product of this continued backward motion, we now have the degenerated, mutilated, confounded, hybrid creation which is made to answer the linguistic wants of the German districts of Pennsylvania. . . . Indeed, we boldly assert that the Pennsylvania Dutch is an anachronism, a rotten relic of national ties, severed many years ago and consequently superseded by those of the adopted country; a decrepit reminiscence of a semi-civilized epoch, unworthy of our age, which ought to be wiped off from existence."

Such pressure from within the culture continuing into the 1890's and the early 1900's, especially on the part of teachers and others interested in public education, resulted in a very negative attitude among some of the dialect speakers around 1900. We sometimes sense this today in recording materials from Pennsylvania Germans who have bridged the gap between the nineteenth and the twentieth centuries. Some of them were actually rather surprised in the 1930's when Pennsylvania German again became fashionable and numerous scholarly investigations of the dialect and culture were published.[5] It is possible to reconstruct the history of attitudes toward the language from newspapers, almanacs, and other printed and manuscript sources. Has similar work been done on Texas Germans? Have the nineteenth-century newspapers been systematically gone through for linguistic materials?

GILBERT: Almost nothing has been done.

YODER: It would be a tedious but extremely rewarding task. Another important source of historical documentation that should be mentioned is family letters. The Pennsylvania German dialect was never really used as a means of written communication. No one (at least not until the twentieth century renaissance of the dialect) wrote a completely Pennsylvania German letter to express his thoughts;

---

[5] See the footnotes to my paper in this book; also the listings in Otto Springer (1941).

letter writing never quite reached that stage. However, the High German which the people used in the nineteenth century and which some of the sectarians still use in the twentieth century is heavily influenced by dialect usage. Documents showing such influence could be studied to great advantage.

GILBERT: As Dr. Kloss has pointed out, the situation in Texas is basically different from that in Pennsylvania. German writers in Texas wrote only in High German, frequently in a stilted artificial language that could be termed "super High German." Even the German type font, Fraktur, was employed until the 1950's.

YODER: I am not speaking of the Pennsylvania German dialect literature published in newspapers beginning about 1810, but rather of High German correspondence composed by Pennsylvania German speakers if they did not wish to resort to English. In addition to the letters, Pennsylvania High German wills provide much valuable linguistic material. In the eighteenth century a Pennsylvania German was not allowed to record a will in any language but English; however, after 1800 wills written in German were permitted. County courthouses in eastern Pennsylvania contain numerous examples of German wills written by the person himself or by a neighbor. These wills give us vocabulary items for the entire material culture of the Pennsylvania Germans. Aside from the dialect names for items to be passed on to the heirs, the High German syntax is often influenced by dialect usage.

GILBERT: There exists an extensive literature that was published partly in this country and partly in Germany. In general it was designed to encourage emigration from Germany to Texas in the 1840's. Although most of this literature is completely in High German, there is one document preserved in the Barker Library of Texas History that was a kind of propaganda sheet issued by the Adelsverein and signed by a number of German farmers who had emigrated to Gillespie County, Texas (Stählen 1846). In the attempt to draw further settlers from Germany, the document is couched in a very folksy type of language, which remained unedited in order to preserve its propaganda value. Many of the linguistic features so characteristic of Texas German today may be found in this document of 1846.

YODER: There was also the Amish journal *Der Herold der Wahr-*

heit, a German and English bilingual publication. In the letters sent in by Amish German speakers there is much influence of English and the Pennsylvania German dialect.

MEYER: A possible source for Texas German are the Texas novels of Friedrich Strubberg (Armand).[6]

YODER: Some of the books written by the nineteenth-century German travelers contained long passages commenting on the type of German spoken in these settlements. Kohl (1856:539), for example, assigns the word *Buschdeutsch* to Pennsylvania German. Some of these accounts seem to be reliable, others are questionable or superficial. Nevertheless, they also should be collated for both the linguist and folklorist.

GILBERT: Do you find that German folklore materials can still be collected in those parts of Pennsylvania and other states where the German language is no longer spoken but where we know that it once existed?

YODER: German folklore lingers on in places where German is no longer spoken. The techniques of gathering German folklore under such circumstances are well documented in Helen Creighton's book, *The Folklore of Lunenburg County, Nova Scotia* (1950), which is one of the best examples of a generalized folklore approach to an old colonial German settlement in America apart from the Pennsylvania German area. The emigrants to Nova Scotia came from the area of the middle and upper Rhine, as did the bulk of the colonists who went to Pennsylvania. The Nova Scotian Germans emigrated to Halifax and to Lunenburg County in the 1740's and 1750's, bringing with them a folk culture remarkably similar to that of the Pennsylvania Germans.

---

[6] A complete list of editions and other pertinent information is to be found in Preston A. Barba (1913). The first story, *Amerikanische Jagd- und Reiseabenteuer* (Strubberg 1858), went through four editions between 1858 and 1901. Others were published only in newspapers, and still other material remained in manuscript. The total list runs to about twenty-five titles, most of them dealing with the Southwest, especially Texas. For instance, *Alte und neue Heimath* (1859) covers Fredericksburg in 1844 and 1845, two years before Strubberg's own residence there. While his technique is not that of the realistic novel, his experiences strike one as truer to reality than the fancies of Sealsfield, who has luscious wild peaches grow on his *Prairie am Jacinto* (Sealsfield 1841).

Although the nuances that one would obtain in Pennsylvania when recording folklore materials in the dialect are no longer present in Nova Scotia, the general outward shape of the eighteenth-century German folk culture is still very much in evidence. Even though knowledge of German in Lunenburg County disappeared several generations ago, the dialect names for German customs are still well known. The *Fastnacht* customs, the carnival customs, and the term *Freindschaft* are still in active use. It is thus apparent that German folklore, in the general sense, can be recorded in English from English-speaking people who do not know a sentence of dialect.

WILSON: With reference to Dr. Yoder's remark about the Pennsylvania German barber who asks his customer, "how do you want them," i.e., how do you want your hair cut, similar carry-overs of the German singular/plural system are also present in the English of people of Texas German descent. The Texas Germans also use the word *hair* as a plural and refer to it as *they*. Similarly, they say *cotton are* and have even formed a new singular in German *eine Kotte* [ˀaɪnə kʰotə], meaning a single boll. The same kind of change, but in the opposite direction, is shown by their use of *weeds* as a singular, evidently because of the German singular *Unkraut*.

YODER: Pennsylvanians also regard the word *coal* as a plural, as in *the coal are expensive this year*. Too little attention has been paid to the English spoken in areas of the United States populated by the descendants of Germans and other non-English language groups.

KLOSS: Richard Beam, the editor of the forthcoming Pennsylvania German Dictionary, has shown me a recent copy of the Amish periodical, *Blackboard Magazine*, which details the recent movement to found Amish parochial schools. Although it is published in Canada, most of the contributors seem to be living in the United States; it is certainly representative of Amish speaking and writing generally. Even though this and all other Amish magazines are largely in English, there are occasional items in High German. The language is even more mutilated than that which could be found in Amish magazines twenty or forty years ago. Sometimes it is unintelligible. It is not Anglicized, it is not petrified, it is not dialectized, it is simply disintegrating. There is something tragic about the process; they cling to a language that they can actually no longer make any use of. Nevertheless it may still be possible to link the Amish parochial schools with the FLES movement, but one must go about that very cautiously. Because of the delicate nature of the matter, such a link-up would have to be accomplished in a very personal way.

GILBERT: What help or benefit can we draw from the experience of German scholars who have collected European-German folklore? I am thinking here especially of the *Atlas der Deutschen Volkskunde* (Harmjanz and Röhr 1937–) and similar materials. Could these methods possibly be applied in part in our country, or do you think that we should start afresh and not overemphasize connections with the Old World?

YODER: We must remember that German folklore in the United States and Canada has flourished in an entirely different environment so that many of the methods used in the Old World are not applicable here. But the European recording programs, the idea of making direct ethnographic recordings and combining them with historical documentation could certainly be applied to the study of ethnic cultures in the United States. It is urgent that such work be undertaken immediately to preserve folk-cultural materials intimately bound up with non-English languages.

MEYER: We might note here that almost all of the African languages in this country have been lost as well as much of the African folk culture, which could have still been collected several generations ago.

YODER: Are linguistic geographers also interested in the vocabulary of rural architecture or folk architecture? This forms an important part of Pennsylvanian German studies. For instance, there are two words in English for the ramp that leads up into a Pennsylvania barn: *barn bridge* and *barn hill*. *Barn bridge* has a dialect analogue in [ˈʃɑɪᴅ| bʀɪkʼ]; I do not know whether there is an analogue for *barn hill*.

REED: This again points up the need for a careful study of how the proposed linguistic/folk-cultural questionnaires are to be combined.

WILSON: You are putting the cart before the horse. One must first carry out preliminary investigations without questionnaires. Once it is known that *barn bridges,* etc. exist, such items may be placed in a questionnaire.

YODER: For an investigation of national scope we should really use questionnaires from the very beginning. Fuller materials from these same informants may then be recorded for either linguistic or folk-cultural purposes at a later time.

SEIFERT: There is the danger that questionnaires will become so long that informants with sufficient time and inclination will be difficult to find.

YODER: There is no reason why an interview must be held in one sitting. More than one session is the ideal format for folk-cultural fieldwork.

SEIFERT: The very long questionnaire that Reed and I used in Pennsylvania was considerably shortened for the fieldwork done in Wisconsin in order to ease the problem of informant selection and to reduce bias.

YODER: The bias of availability would seem to strongly favor older people who are fortunately in many instances the very informants whom linguists and folklorists are most interested in. I found that in recording spirituals or "Dutch choruses" it was necessary to depend on the oldest people. The younger people sing only a chorus plus one verse; they know the individual choruses but not the intricate threading together of the text materials that make up the whole spiritual. This and other evidence indicates that for folk-cultural data, at least, the older people should comprise the majority of the informants. In the Pennsylvania German area Americanization is proceeding rapidly, creating a marked generation gap. In such cases, folk-cultural texts in their dialect setting must be collected from persons over a certain age.

WILSON: It is important to convince prospective informants that we are not normative language teachers interested in how many mistakes they make and just how bad their language is. The fact that Low German is not used in the sermons does not mean that it is not a perfectly viable means of communication.

YODER: In this country, hybridization of language and culture is the rule rather than the exception. Despite many years of social and technological change, the German dialects established in the eighteenth and nineteenth centuries have functioned as living, viable cultural units.

KLOSS: I would like to quote from an article I published in 1938, which is of interest in regard to German folklore of the nineteenth-century immigrants. The article was written after I had visited many German settlements in the United States on behalf of the Carl Schurz Memorial Foundation. A much longer report in English was also prepared but has unfortunately never been published. It was noted, for example, that Catholic localities had preserved richer folkloristic traditions than Protestant localities and congregations. In Indiana I was told about a place called Fulda and a nearby community called Mariah Hill but referred to by local residents as Mariahilf. The article then continues:

[They are] completely Catholic localities in which the children, who are starting school, know no English. Confessions are still conducted in the language of their fathers, but the church-school—in stark contrast to the nearby Lutheran-Franconian Haysville—omits German completely. These small Catholic areas are often notable for the unusual gayness and variety of their folk-cultural tradition. At Mariah Hill the people still shake rattles on Easter Saturday, the New Year is ushered in with gunshots, and a newly married couple cannot move into their new quarters without a shivaree (charivari). In the nearby town of Fulda, *Wurstfahren* was not discontinued until after World War I. On *Nikolaus* (December 5), in Germantown, Illinois, everyone dons a mask and visits his neighbors; the children recite a prayer and are rewarded with sweets. At weddings a terrible dissonance blares forth if no free beer is forthcoming. The shooting of guns at New Year's and the Easter rabbit are well known, and the Three Wise Men go around the town every year in traditional, inherited masks reciting a long Low German (*Plattdeutsche*) saying. This does not mean that there is a lack of colorful traditions in non-Catholic areas. In Fredericksburg, Texas there exists the custom of Sunday-houses, occasionally erected by churches on church property, for farmers (weekend houses for attending church in town), a tradition which represents the reverse of the city dwellers' country houses. Other customs of the town are masquerade balls for children and the pealing of the evening bells on Saturday evening at sunset. Brenham, Texas, the center of a Lutheran Low German region, celebrates a May festival every year.

I just wanted to givé an example of folkloristic traditions that were still in existence in the 1930's. If the customs themselves are no longer practiced, they might still be remembered so that their collection and study may still be undertaken at this late date.

YODER: In the case of the Pennsylvania Germans, medieval Catholic folk-cultural items have continued to function in a Protestant matrix. Surprisingly enough, the Amish who are thought to be ultra-Protestant have actually preserved much of the old Catholic church year from the Middle Ages. They still have for example *Altgrischtag* [ˀaltˈgrɪʃdag], December 6, and *Mikelstag* [ˈmɪkəlsˌdag], September 29, from which they date their Autumn Communion. The folk sense of time is very significant: the divisions of the day, the forenoon lunch, the five-meal system, and the names of certain days in the year. The Pennsylvania Germans have special dialect names for the two holidays in the Catholic church year relating to the cross—the finding of the cross by Saint Helena in the fourth century and the elevation of the cross. One is in May and the other is in September. Since May and September are represented in the Pennsylvania German almanacs by little crosses, these days are called the *Greitzlimoi* [grɪtsliːˈmoi] and the *Greitzliseptember* [graɪtsliːˌzɛpˈtɛmbɹ], names that were still recordable in the 1960's from some of the older dialect speakers. These last survivals of the medieval church year or the folk year, the old folk-cultural names for the seasons and other meteorological phenomena should definitely be investigated.

9. GERMAN PEDAGOGY AND THE SURVIVAL OF GERMAN IN AMERICA: DISCUSSION

CHAIRMAN OF THE DISCUSSION: HEINZ KLOSS

KLOSS: I would first like to take up the problem of the bilingual or dual-medium schools, i.e., the schools that use both English and a non-English language as media of instruction. The Foreign Languages in the Elementary Schools (FLES) movement may be called a forerunner of the present-day trend toward bilingual schools. Actually there are two movements, one major, the other minor. The former supports bilingual education for bilingual children or at least for schools with a linguistically mixed student body. The other movement favors bilingual schools for monolingual student bodies of English mother tongue. Among the general innovations that characterize the major movement is the Bilingual Education Act recently passed by Congress, a piece of legislation designed to help children who are not yet fully familiar with English.[1] A number of research centers have been set up under the auspices of the United States Office of Education to deal with the numerous problems arising from bilingual education. Such centers include the Early Childhood Bilingual Education Project at Yeshiva University directed by Dr. Vera John,[2]

[1] This hardly applies, however, to American children of German descent, with the possible exception of the Amish.
[2] Actually, the Yeshiva project deals chiefly with Puerto Rican children, but the general problems involved are of interest to bilingual education as a whole.

and the Foreign Language Innovative Curricular Study Center at Ann Arbor, Michigan.

The languages that have benefited from this new movement are chiefly Spanish and to a lesser extent Navajo, French, Portuguese, and Chinese. Speakers of Navajo at present exceed 100,000,[3] and various efforts are underway to have their language introduced into schools. While there is a project at the Center for Applied Linguistics to study the effects of different language media in Indian kindergartens, the United States Office of Education has actually sponsored the introduction of Indian languages in specific schools.

The effort to establish bilingual education for Spanish/English has of course been on a much greater scale than for Navajo/English.[4] There are also a number of French/English bilingual schools, although French was seldom regarded as an important immigrant language in the United States. In 1968 the state legislature of Louisiana passed four laws favoring the reintroduction of the French language; the most important of these provides for the teaching of French beginning in the first grade.[5] Contacts were established between Quebec and Louisiana to aid in the revival of French. The movement in favor of French extended chiefly to the Acadians of southwestern Louisiana. The Creoles of French descent, who originally came directly from France and who now live in New Orleans or surrounding areas, have largely given up the French language and therefore remain relatively unaffected by the new laws.

Among the Acadians in northern Maine along the New Brunswick border, bilingual education in French and English has also been introduced. Due to the isolation of the Acadian settlements around Van Buren in northeastern Maine, the inhabitants remain fully bilingual.

[3] See the figures given in Gaarder (1968:86–87).

[4] In the school year 1969–1970 the U.S. Office of Education will be funding 76 bilingual programs, of which 90 percent will be Spanish/English and 2 or 3 Navajo/English.

[5] In 1968, act no. 408 of the Louisiana legislature provided for the teaching of French in the public schools; no. 458 for the foundation of a nonprofit French-language television station; no. 409 for the creation of a *Conseil pour le développement de la Louisiane Française*; no. 1968 reconfirmed the right to print public documents and publish public notices in both English and French.

In 1942 French was reintroduced into public schools in Van Buren, and approximately six years later a FLES program was set up. Quite recently, fully bilingual schools have been established.

The Foreign Language Innovative Curricular Study Center (or FLICS), mentioned above, has received a grant under Title III of the ESEA Act to sponsor a large number of bilingual or bi-dialectal school programs. Some are designed for monolingual children of recent Hispano-American immigrants; others support the teaching of Polish among children of Polish descent whose Polish has become at best a second language.[6] Even more progressive is the program called "Dutch Language and Heritage," which was launched in Holland, Michigan, among the Anglicized descendants of Dutch Reformed immigrants. It transcends the limits established by the Bilingual Education Act. The children at Holland, Michigan, are not in need of pedagogical assistance with their English; instead, their parents are bent upon restoring the ancestral tongue. A similar procedure might be followed in order to provide instruction in German to children of German descent from rural and urban areas of the United States where the German language is still widely spoken by older people. While children of Latin American descent in the Southwest and even of French descent among the Acadians in Louisiana and northern Maine are still largely monolingual, the situation of the children of German descent seems to be similar to the situation of the French ethnic group in New England, which represents the third and fourth generation descendants of immigrants from Quebec.

Concerning the minor movement, there are two examples I would like to cite. In Virginia, courses in history in nine high schools were taught in French or Spanish starting in 1965–1966. "The students enrolled were those who had an intensive background with one of these two languages. The classes were organized as part of a pilot study of the Division of Research of the Virginia Department of Education. . . . [Pre- and post-testing] were conducted in order to ascertain

6 This program, which is called "Polish language and heritage," is functioning in collaboration with such Polish-American institutions as St. Mary's College in Orchard Lake, Michigan, St. Florian's High School in Hamtramck, and Madonna College in Livonia.

the amount of progress achieved by the students in both language and history. . . . The results have since been analyzed and made available in mimeographed form. The classes offered were world history, world in the twentieth century, history of France, and history of Latin America."[7] Several of these classes are continuing although the official and formal pilot study has been ended. The project is significant because it involves state and not federal initiative. In California similar teaching methods have recently even been explicitly authorized by law in the so-called Short Bill, which passed the assembly on July 17, 1968.[8]

Since 1953, the Massachusetts Institute of Technology has been conducting some of its courses in the humanities in the French language. These courses, which have become a permanent part of the curriculum, have been developed into a four-semester sequence. Since no native speakers of French have ever been permitted to enroll, one of the primary aims of the courses is to enable students of English mother tongue to become fluent in both languages. In quizzes and examinations students may use either French or English, but essays must be written in French.

Both the major and the minor movements are of considerable significance in the context of what we are to consider today. It is not for me to say that an effort on behalf of German ought to be made. Its technical feasibility has been demonstrated by the precedents mentioned above. Could we not expand the proposal that the German language be recorded and analyzed in all notable German settlement areas in the United States to include certain pedagogical experiments on a small scale along the lines outlined above? If a few dual-medium schools on the elementary or high school level are a success, the movement will spread almost automatically. Because of the work of Professor Theodore Andersson, who is not only in charge of the Spanish bilingual education project in Texas but also favors the strengthening of other

[7] According to a letter received from the Virginia Department of Education; see also Caldwell (1967:50–53).

[8] The main provision of the Short Act states that "pupils who are proficient in English and who, by successful completion of advanced courses in a foreign language or by other means, have become fluent in that language may be instructed in classes conducted in that foreign language."

non-English languages,[9] Texas may prove to be the best site for such English/German dual-medium schools.

PHILLIPS: As a member of Professor Andersson's staff, I want to make it known that we are strongly in favor of enlarging the scope of the Spanish/English bilingual education project to include other languages.

WILSON: In Germany, the principle that the child has a right to receive instruction in his mother tongue seems to be upheld more strongly than in the United States. In South Schleswig, for example, there are Danish schools for the Danish minority; conversely, in North Schleswig there are German schools for German children. And yet, in the United States we are only now in 1968 thinking timidly of establishing one or two schools in all of the fifty states.

KLOSS: In nearly the whole of Europe the principle is recognized that children have a right to be educated in and through their mother tongue.

GILBERT: How can you explain the fact that the federal government spends much more money for Spanish, French, and Navajo than it does for German, despite the very large number of German speakers still living in this country?

KLOSS: There are two major reasons. First, very few children of German descent are not fully proficient in English upon entering school. Second, there is a lack of self-assertion on the part of the German Americans. As I have pointed out previously (Kloss 1966), the German element in this country is suffering from a "psychological shock and block," a direct outcome of the two world wars.

GILBERT: The statement that you made about the Dutch language in Michigan is very significant. The large amount of money that the federal government is authorized to spend in support of certain types of bilingualism is now being used for the first time for the benefit of students who already know English very well but who also wish to continue their ancestral Dutch. It has been my experience that one of the main problems in financing any study dealing with the German-Americans, whether it be a pedagogical experiment, dialectology, or

---

[9] Such as French, German, Czech, and Polish.

folklore collection, is that these people are generally not poverty strick-en. They do not live in ghettos. They do too well. Hence from the standpoint of the government they stand low on the list of priorities for study or research support. This is actually one of our worst obstacles.

KLOSS: I am afraid you are right.

REEVES: Since my field involves working with bilingual children, I would like to mention a different aspect of this problem. I have found that we are at present not in need of more information about "what bilingualism is" among children and adults, nor even "how does one set up a FLES program or a dual-medium school." What we need from the remaining German/English bilinguals in the United States is a description of the outstanding characteristics of their standard lan-guage, colloquial language, and dialects, so that linguists and edu-cators may write programs specifically designed for the German-American bilingual child. Based on the linguistic description of the German dialects in Texas made by Dr. Gilbert, we are presently en-gaged in the formulation of a specially designed curriculum for col-lege freshmen with a bilingual background. The curriculum will be designed to prepare such students in one semester to read German prose usually studied in junior and senior courses. Because of the depend-ence of well-designed language curricula upon accurate linguistic descriptions of the language that the students speak before they enter the university, it would be wise to consider pedagogical applications in any research design for recording and analyzing the German lan-guage in the United States.

SCHULZ-BEHREND: Let me play the devil's advocate for a minute. First assumption: language equals political loyalty. Whoever spoke German was loyal to the Kaiser; later he was a Nazi. Second assump-tion: language equals culture, with a capital C. Third assumption: English equals Americanism, up to and in excess of 100 percent.

I will not take the time here to refute these arguments one by one. For those of us, though, who wish to encourage and preserve bilingual-ism and multilingualism in the United States, what is it that we really expect language to do? I think the bias of this group is that we expect knowledge of a second language to alter people in the direction of being cultured individuals, that is, humanists or at least humanistically oriented people. If we equate language knowledge with culture, we shall again be disappointed. What are our goals? Or if more than one goal is desired, what system of priorities shall be set up? Any loss of a second language is doubtless a pity, but how much so? In this country the English language has in general much greater prestige than German. Therefore, the loss of German is not overly regretted. Furthermore, many immigrant parents must have reasoned that if the choice is between maximum proficiency in one language or partial proficiency in two, then the child should definitely be a monolingual English speaker, thus avoiding any of the psychological problems of bilingualism, not to mention its political implications. There are a number of serious problems involved here, and the foremost of these is what do we expect the second language to do for our children, for our citizens?

WILSON: Disregarding the complexity of the question itself, we should note that attitudes toward language certainly play an important role here. In my opinion the old attitude that speaking German is a handicap should be combated. Recent research in bilingualism has shown differently.[10]

SCHEER: Is it correct that, in order to become a citizen of this country, a person must be able to read and write English?

PHILLIPS: An applicant is now expected to be literate, in English or in some other language, in order to become an American citizen.

GILBERT: To come back to Dr. Schulz-Behrend's very fundamental and deep-going criticisms of the assumptions that we made in wishing these things to be so, we should note that the literature on bilingualism reflects two main schools of thought. The first is represented by those who believe that it is better for a person to be a native speaker of one language and not have his abilities diluted by overly extensive knowledge of other languages. The other school claims that whatever a person may lose by not mastering the one language exceedingly well is more than outweighed by the mastery of two languages. This is the basic debate which has been going on, as you well know, and which

---

[10] See especially Elizabeth Peal and Wallace Lambert (1962); also Joshua A. Fishman (1965) and A. Bruce Gaarder (1965).

has not been unambiguously resolved either way. Since the majority of us teach German, we are fully aware of the struggles adults go through to acquire a foreign language. The advantages of a personal bilingualism established in childhood for students and adults at a later age are enormous. Because of the heterogeneous cultural history and make-up of the population of the United States, it would be not only in accord with our tradition but also to our political advantage among the nations of the world to aid and encourage the relatively few speakers of foreign languages that remain within our borders. We should positively maintain from the outset that the advantages of bilingualism outweigh possible disadvantages. Regarding the role that bilingual citizens will play in the future, the period of any conceivable challenge to the dominance of English in this country is long past. No non-English language in the United States could possibly be of any danger to English, except for perhaps Spanish in certain regions. From the national point of view, these surviving immigrant languages are esoteric curiosities. The checkered linguistic history of Alsace or Rumania has no counterpart here. Linguistic diversity is becoming the rare exception, and aside from Spanish, which has a vitality unmatched by the other languages, knowledge of less widely spoken languages can always be of value to the state. I cannot imagine any diversity or a linguistic, cultural, or national fragmentation stemming from the training of bilingual citizens in German and in other languages. Such training can only be of advantage to our country and to the persons speaking these languages.

PULTE: I think perhaps the policy of the Mexican government with regard to bilingualism and literacy might be of interest. It is probably correct to say that there was a time when a policy was advocated in Mexico that would have led to the extinction of the indigenous languages in the hope that this would facilitate the development of literacy in Spanish. More recently there seems to have been a change in policy, however, and I think that the conclusion is being reached that literacy in Spanish can best be achieved by first bringing about literacy in the various native languages.

KLOSS: We should not confuse the issue of bilingual education with that of language maintenance. Under certain circumstances, the detour via the mother tongue may be a short-cut to assimilation. Undoubtedly some people at the United States Office of Education favor bilingual education for this reason. In the case of the Indians in both the United States and Mexico, it seems obvious that the effort to Hispanicize or Anglicize them through the medium of Spanish or English has failed largely because of the complete neglect of the mother tongue. There is historical and experimental evidence which leads us to believe that assimilation can be brought about more fully and rapidly if instruction in the primary grades is in the mother tongue.[11]

————: There has always been strong pressure on immigrants to adapt to the customs and language of the United States. In recent times, however, minority groups have become more vocal in claiming their constitutional rights and have been instrumental in the rediscovery of ethnic cultures and languages. The German language might possibly benefit from this renewed interest in our ethnic origins. The United States is coming of age. As we personally and our country grow older, we like to discover our roots. Such interest, however, usually does not go so far as the wish to maintain bilingualism or to recreate it where it has already disappeared. If we consider ourselves students of the humanities and humanitarians, we would do well to examine the literature on the psychological conflicts that often arise in childhood bilinguals.

KLOSS: Miss Reeves, you mentioned the possibility of designing teaching materials for specific small dialect groups in certain geographic areas. Are we of the opinion that this task should fall within the program of our newly founded committee, or should it remain outside its scope?

WERBOW: We should note here that Gilbert's dissertation (1963) and his other studies (1965a, 1965b, 1970a) form a basis for exactly the kind of material we need for Texas German. If someone should want to convert this data into practical teaching materials, it could very well be done.

REEVES: A linguistic description of, say, Mennonite Low German would be more valuable if it were couched in terms of a contrastive

[11] See, for example, the Mexican experience as described by A. Castro-de-Fuente (1955).

grammar of the dialect as compared to Standard German. Since many, if not most, of the differences belong to the surface structure, the methods devised for Texas German speakers might possibly be used with a minimum of modifications for Mennonite Low German or for any other American German dialect.

EICHHOFF: I see no reason to expend so much time and effort on the German dialects with a corresponding neglect of Standard German. It is simply not economically feasible to prepare separate teaching materials for the hundreds of German dialects spoken in this country. And even if such an attempt were made, who would benefit from it, the children or the government? Do we want the children to be trained in two languages for their psychological, cultural, and economic benefit, or do we simply want to provide the government with a large pool of foreign-language speakers?

Regarding the statement made by Dr. Wilson that children in Germany are educated in their mother tongue, this is no more true in Germany than it is in the United States. A large part of the population in Germany never spoke High German; nevertheless, such speakers are educated exclusively in High German, never in Low German.

MOELLEKEN: Miss Reeves was not advocating that the dialect should be taught; rather, she wanted to point out that it is important for us to recognize and try to predict the difficulties dialect speakers encounter when learning the standard language.

KLOSS: The idea is to facilitate access to Standard German. With the one possible exception of Pennsylvania German, which may have some standing of its own, the target language would be Standard German in all cases.

EICHHOFF: According to what you are saying, the children would have to know three languages: the dialect, Standard German, and English. They would thus be forced to learn two foreign languages.

KLOSS: Who?

EICHHOFF: I mean the very children we are trying to help, those who speak a dialect at home and who must then learn Standard German and English.

KLOSS: You have misunderstood the pedagogical role of the dialect. It is a means to an end, not an end in itself.

WERBOW: Is there information concerning whether the Texas Germans (and the speakers of German in other areas of the country as well) have perhaps been disadvantaged by their bilingual background in the same way that speakers of Spanish or Acadian French or black speakers of nonstandard English have been handicapped by their situation? An interesting sociological comparison could be made in this regard. Perhaps Dr. Wilson can report on possible tendencies of the Texas Germans to follow such occupations as tradesman, craftsman, electrician and plumber, rather than certain other occupations.

WILSON: From my experience with the German speakers of Lee and Fayette Counties, Texas, it is very evident that they suffer no handicap whatsoever. They learn English early and well. Although a certain amount of German interference is present in their English, it results in no obvious social discrimination. The people of German descent are well off and pursue the whole range of occupations open to Americans of purely English background.

BOGGS: As far as German is concerned, would it not be better to say that you are in disagreement with current pedagogical methods here in the United States?

KING: One objection to the whole drift of this discussion is that bilingual school systems have rarely been successful when imposed from above. Those which function well come into existence because the local inhabitants have demanded them. In Schleswig-Holstein, for example, the presence of Danish schools is a sign of the strong nationalistic feeling of the Danes and their desire to preserve their language and culture. Such a feeling certainly does not exist among the Texas Germans nor, for that matter, among most other German speakers in the United States. Even the linguistically much stronger Spanish-speaking communities in the Southwest do not support their language to the degree that would be necessary to insure its survival.

WILSON: Actually, the converse is true. Our monolingual school system is forced onto the people. They were not asked if they wanted to maintain a bilingual school system.

KING: If they were given a choice they would undoubtedly select monolingual English schools.

REEVES: No choice is legally possible, since it is against Texas state law to give instruction in any language except English. Many other states, such as California, have the same restrictions. To teach a subject in a foreign language, one must have special permission from the state Department of Education. Foreign language classrooms are considered an academic subject and not an area of instruction.

GILBERT: Dr. Kloss, you have made a study of the linguistic situation in Ireland and in Israel, among other places, where there has been an attempt to impose bilingualism from above. What has been the success of these attempts?

KLOSS: It has been successful in Israel, but for a number of reasons has worked less satisfactorily in Ireland. There was a real need for a *lingua franca* in Israel, whereas in Ireland, English already fulfilled that function.

Regarding the advantages and disadvantages of bilingualism, I think the primary question should not be whether bilingualism is beneficial, but whether it is inevitable. In the case of the non-English-speaking population in this country it is inevitable; the problem is not whether it can be avoided but whether it can be maintained at a level at which it is not detrimental. One of the main reasons for teaching pupils of Mexican descent in the primary grades in both languages is that educators now largely accept experimental findings showing that bilingualism is less harmful if both languages are diligently cultivated.[12] It is much more detrimental if the school cultivates only the second language and not the home language of the pupils.

PULTE: Regarding Dr. King's comment, there is at least one rather large group of German-Americans who would favor the establishment of German schools for their children: the Old Order Amish. It might prove rather difficult to provide for such schools, however, since the Amish seem to be opposed to the concept of public schools and would likely be unwilling to accept public funds and meet the requirements that would be set up.

KLOSS: Their attitude has changed greatly during the last ten years. There are now a considerable number of parochial day schools staffed

[12] Cf., among others, Chester Christian (1967), and Andersson and Boyer (1970). For an illustration taken from a foreign country, see M. Ramos, J. V. Aguilar, and B. P. Silayan (1967).

with teachers of Amish background. While the only language of instruction is English, some German is still being taught in an informal way. Most of the teachers have received no systematic training in German and would perhaps welcome aid and advice from the outside, provided it does not interfere with their way of life, including of course their basic concept of what education should consist of.

BOGGS: In light of what you have been saying, may I answer that, since German speakers are not in any way disadvantaged because of their language background, the justification for teaching languages in a foreign-language or bilingual atmosphere is not so much a matter of changing stereotypes (i.e., of more "democracy" in Germany than in America) as simply a matter of pedagogical practices and attitudes in this country. In other words, one must inquire into the aims of the education offered children of grade school and high school age. Do we want to give them more and better job opportunities? Do we want to make them productive so that they will be able to enjoy the material benefits of this country, or do we aim to provide them with a solid education that is at the same time more liberal? This is the real problem in teaching German, is it not? We have bilingualism in its relation to language teaching on the one hand and changing pedagogical attitudes on the other hand. The goal, of course, of all of us who are interested in teaching German should be to change the attitudes of educators responsible for grade and high school curricula.

GILBERT: This has a direct bearing on German instruction at all levels, especially the college level. The National Carl Schurz Association, for example, as Dr. Kloss has said before, has apparently abandoned the idea that German can be taught in bilingual schools. It has recently received a large grant from the *Volkswagenstiftung* to improve the teaching of German as a foreign language. Some people consider the word "improve" to mean preventing the decline of German teaching from assuming alarming proportions. What we are discussing here has a direct bearing on the future of German language study in this country.

MOELLEKEN: There is a very strong tendency in the United States to abandon certain requirements on the college level, and it is usually the foreign languages that first come under attack. In the light of such developments, it might be helpful if this group could draw up a statement or a resolution embodying some of the reasons why German should be continued as a required subject on the college level. If adequately distributed, it could serve the individual German department to advance proper arguments in defense of its position.

EICHHOFF: I still have not really heard to whose benefit this eternal bilingualism would be.

KLOSS: Frankly, it has to do with the needs of society at large. In this regard, the interests of the individual seem to be subordinate to the needs of the state.

EICHHOFF: I see. So then it would be necessary to set up a Russian community . . .

KLOSS: If one would find gold in this country but not silver, would one import silver in order to bury it and then remine it? The fact that there is no silver should not prevent us from reaping the harvest in gold, if there is any. In other words, the absence of Russian-speaking communities should not prevent the United States from making use of the language resources that do exist.

EICHHOFF: I see. In other words you are saying that the general approach of the National Carl Schurz Association is not correct. But what is wrong with achieving a monolingual English-speaking population and then introducing German as a foreign language? Most of the remaining German speakers in the United States speak dialects, not the standard language. An attempt to teach students two new languages, English and Standard German, will not succeed.

KLOSS: We have examples from a number of other countries which show that it can be done.

————: I am amazed that no one has mentioned the bilingual situation in Dade County, Florida, in the last six or seven years. Spanish speakers from Cuba are being taught in both English and Spanish with such marked success that the study of Spanish has aroused wide interest among the monolingual English-speaking population in southern Florida. Could we not learn much from the positive achievements and the mistakes of this project?

KLOSS: The Dade County bilingual school system has been described at great length in a recent article by Bruce Gaarder (1967).

MEYER: Before the First World War, bilingual Spanish/English schools in San Antonio, Corpus Christi, and elsewhere in Texas were commonplace.

KLOSS: I do not remember criticizing the policies of the National Carl Schurz Association. However, I would strongly recommend adding the concept of bilingual schooling to the overall goal of promoting the teaching of German generally. Perhaps we should request our committee to draw this up in the form of a resolution.

EICHHOFF: Was the committee not directed to devote its full attention to the German *language* in America in its folk-cultural setting? The teaching of Standard German, the *Bühnenaussprache,* should be only a peripheral concern of the committee. Achieving trilingualism among American students is a costly, unattainable goal that we should have nothing to do with.

KLOSS: I see. It is for that reason that I asked Dr. Gilbert whether he felt that the problem of pedagogy should be considered by the committee.

GILBERT: Although I think that the concern of the committee should be limited to the topics which Dr. Eichhoff has just restated, I would be glad to take up this problem outside of the work of the committee. Miss Reeves is writing her dissertation on methods of teaching Standard German in high school to speakers of Texas German in Fredericksberg. Studies of this type can be expanded, and with sufficient financing and interest they can be converted into experimental pedagogical programs. I will investigate this further if you wish.

REFERENCES

Appel, John J. 1955. Immigrant historical societies in the United States. Dissertation, University of Pennsylvania.

———. 1962. Marion Dexter Learned and German American Historical Society. Pennsylvania Magazine of History and Biography 86(3).287–318.

Andersson, Theodore, and Mildred Boyer. 1970. Bilingual schooling in the United States. Austin, Texas: Southwest Development Educational Laboratory.

Arndt, Karl J. R., and May E. Olson. 1961. German-American newspapers and periodicals 1732–1955; history and bibliography. Heidelberg: Quelle & Meyer.

Asher, John Alexander. 1956. Des Erdballs letztes Inselriff. Munich: Max Hueber.

Bachman, Calvin George. 1942, 1961. The Old Order Amish of Lancaster County. Pennsylvania German Society 49, 60. Lancaster, Penn.

Baerg, Marjorie. 1960. Phonology and inflections of Gnadenau Low German; a dialect of Marion County, Kansas. Dissertation, University of Chicago.

Bagster-Collins, Elijah W. 1930. History of modern language teaching in the United States. Studies in modern language teaching, pp. 3–96. New York: Modern Foreign Language Study and the Canadian Committee on Modern Languages.

Barba, Preston A. 1913. The life and works of Friedrich Armand Strubberg. Americana Germanica 16. Philadelphia: University of Pennsylvania.

———. 1949. In memoriam; Edwin Miller Fogel. Pennsylvania German Folklore Society 14.175–181.

———. 1953. Pennsylvania German tombstones; a study in folk art. Pennsylvania German Folklore Society 18. 1–228.

———, and Eleanor Barba. 1939. Lewis Miller, Pennsylvania German folk artist. Pennsylvania German Folklore Society 4.1–40.

Baur, Gerhard. 1967. Die Mundarten im nördlichen Schwarzwald. Marburg: Elwert.

Bausinger, Hermann. 1961. Volkskultur in der technischen Welt. Stuttgart: W. Kohlhammer.

Becker, Donald Allen. 1967. Generative phonology and dialect study; an investigation of three modern German dialects. Dissertation, University of Texas at Austin.

Bender, Ruth. 1929. A Study of the Pennsylvania German dialect as spoken in Johnson County, Iowa. MA thesis, University of Iowa.

Birmelin, John. 1938. Gezwitscher; a book of Pennsylvania German verse. Pennsylvania German Folklore Society 3.1–156.

———. 1951. The later poems of John Birmelin. Edited by Preston A. Barba. Pennsylvania German Folklore Society 16.7–155.

Borneman, Henry S. 1937. Pennsylvania German illuminated manuscripts. Pennsylvania German Society 46.

———. 1953. Pennsylvania German bookplates; a study. Pennsylvania German Society 54.

Botkin, B. A., ed. 1944. A treasury of American folklore. New York: Crown Publishers.

Bottiglia, William F. 1965. Humanities in French at M.I.T. Modern Language Journal 49.354–358.

Boyer, Walter E., Albert F. Buffington, and Don Yoder. 1951. Songs along the Mahantongo. Lancaster: Pennsylvania Dutch Folklore Center.

Brackmann, Albert. SEE Deutsches Archiv für Landes- und Volksforschung. 1937–1944.

Brendle, Thomas R., and William S. Troxell. 1944. Pennsylvania German folk tales, legends, once-upon-a-time stories, maxims, and sayings spoken in the dialect popularly known as Pennsylvania Dutch. Pennsylvania German Society 50.

———, and Claude W. Unger. 1935. Folk medicine of the Pennsylvania Germans; the non-occult cures. Pennsylvania German Society 45.1–303.

Britton, George. 1955. Pennsylvania Dutch folksongs. Folkways Records FP615.

Brumbaugh, G. Edwin. 1930. Colonial architecture of the Pennsylvania Germans. Pennsylvania German Society 41.1–60.

Brunvand, Jan Harold. 1968. The study of American folklore; an introduction. New York: W. W. Norton.

Buffington, Albert F. 1937. Pennsylvania German; a grammatical and linguistic study of the dialect. Dissertation, Harvard University.

———. 1939. Pennsylvania German; its relation to other German dialects. American Speech 14.276–286.

———. 1948. Linguistic variants in the Pennsylvania German dialect. Pennsylvania German Folklore Society 13.217–252.

———. 1949. Linguistic variants in the Pennsylvania German dialect. The Pennsylvania Dutchman 1(5).1.

————, ed. 1962. The Reichard collection of early Pennsylvania German dialogues and plays. Pennsylvania German Society 61.

————. 1965. "Dutchified German" spirituals. Pennsylvania German Society 62.

————, and Preston A. Barba. 1954. A Pennsylvania German grammar. Allentown, Penn.: Schlechter.

Caldwell, Genelle. 1967. Report II; teaching content in a foreign language. Reports; bilingual education; research and teaching, Nov. 10–11, 1967, p. 42–56. Edited by Chester Christian. El Paso, Texas.

Carman, J. Neale. 1961. Germans in Kansas. American German Review 27(4).4–8.

————. 1962. Foreign-language units of Kansas; historical atlas and statistics. Lawrence: University of Kansas Press.

Castro-de-Fuente, A. 1955. The teaching of modern languages; a volume of studies. Problems in Education 10. 281–287. Paris.

Christian, Chester, ed. 1967. Reports; bilingual education; research and teaching, Nov. 10–11, 1967. El Paso, Texas.

Conference on Non-English Speech in the United States. 1942. American Council of Learned Societies. Bulletin no. 34 (March 1942).

Creighton, Helen. 1950. The folklore of Lunenburg County, Nova Scotia. Ottawa: E. Cloutier.

Davise, Wallace E. 1955. Patriotism on parade; the story of veterans' and hereditary organizations in America, 1783–1900. Cambridge, Mass.: Harvard University Press. [Harvard Historical Studies 66.]

DeCamp, David. 1964. Creole language areas considered as multilingual communities. Colloque sur le multilinguisme [Symposium on multilingualism], pp. 227–231. Lagos, Nigeria: Commission de Coopération Technique en Afrique.

Délery, Simone de la Souchère, and Gladys A. Renshaw, comps. 1932. France d'Amérique. Chicago: University of Chicago Press.

Deutsches Archiv für Landes- und Volksforschung. 1937–1944. Edited by Albert Brackmann, Hugo Hassinger, Friedrich Metz, and Emil Meynen. 8 vols. Leipzig: S. Hirzel.

Dictionary of American Biography. 1957. 11 vols. New York: Scribner.

Donnelly, Dale Jack. 1969. The Low German dialect of Sauk County, Wisconsin; phonology and morphology. Dissertation, University of Wisconsin.

Dornbusch, Charles H. 1956. Pennsylvania German barns. Pennsylvania German Folklore Society 21.

Doroszewski, Witold. 1938. Język polski w Stanach Zjedoczonych A. P. [The Polish language in the United States of America]. Warsaw: Nakł. Tow. Naukowego Warszawskiego.

Dunbar, Gary S. 1961. Henry Chapman Mercer, Pennsylvania folklife pioneer. Pennsylvania Folklife 12(2).48–52.

Dyck, Henry D. 1964. Language differentiation in two Low German groups in Canada. Dissertation, University of Pennsylvania.

Eikel, Fred, Jr. 1966–1967. New Braunfels German. American Speech 41.5–16, 254–260; 42.83–104.

Eisenach, George J. 1950. Das religiöse Leben unter den Russlanddeutschen in Russland und Amerika. Marburg: H. Rathmann. [A German translation of Eisenach, George J. 1948–1949. Pietism and the Russian Germans in the United States. Berne, Indiana: Berne Publishers.]

Evans, E. Estyn. 1959. A Pennsylvanian folk festival. Ulster Folklife 5.14–19. [Reprinted (1961) in Pennsylvania Folklife 12 (1).44–48.]

Everest, Kate A. 1892. How Wisconsin came by its large German element. Collections of the State Historical Society of Wisconsin 12.302. SEE ALSO Kate Everest Levi (1898).

Family Life. 1968. 1(1).22; 1(4).32. Aylmer, Ontario.

Faust, Albert Bernhardt. 1909. The German element in the United States. Vol. 2. Boston: Houghton Mifflin.

Fishman, Joshua A. 1965. Bilingualism, intelligence, and language learning. Modern Language Journal 49.227–237.

———, et al. 1966. Language loyalty in the United States. The Hague: Mouton.

Fogel, Edwin Miller. 1915a. Beliefs and superstitions of the Pennsylvania Germans. Americana Germanica, new series, 18. Philadelphia: Americana Germanica Press.

———. 1915b. Supplement to beliefs and superstitions of the Pennsylvania Germans. Philadelphia: Americana Germanica Press. [pp. 345–357, "for private distribution, not for public perusal."]

———. 1925. Proverbs of the Pennsylvania Germans. Pennsylvania German Society 36.1–222.

———. 1940. Of months and days. Pennsylvania German Folklore Society 5.

———. 1941. Twelvetide. Pennsylvania German Folklore Society 6.

Fourquet, Jean. 1952. The two e's of Middle High German. Word 8.122–135.

Frey, J. William. 1941. The German dialect of eastern York County. Dissertation, University of Illinois.

———. 1942. A simple grammar of Pennsylvania Dutch. Clinton, South Carolina: private edition.

———. 1945. Amish triple-talk. American Speech 20(2).85–98.

———. 1949. Amish hymns as folk music. Pennsylvania songs and legends, pp. 129–162. Edited by George Korson. Philadelphia: University of Pennsylvania Press.

Gaarder, A. Bruce. 1965. Teaching the bilingual child; research, development, and policy. Modern Language Journal 49.165–175.

———. 1967. Organization of the bilingual school. Journal of Social Issues 23(2).110–120.

———. 1968. Education of American Indian children. Monograph Series on Language and Linguistics 21.83–96. Georgetown University.

Gallup, George Horace. 1948. A guide to public opinion polls. 2nd ed. Princeton, New Jersey: Princeton University Press.

Gehman, Ernest G. 1949. Lautlehre der pennsylvania-deutschen Mundart von Bally, Pennsylvania. Dissertation, University of Heidelberg.

———. 1963. Pennsylvania German in the Shenandoah Valley. Allentown Morning Call, March 16, 23, 30.

Gehman, Henry Snyder. 1968. What the Pennsylvania Dutch dialect has meant in my life. Pennsylvania Folklife 17(4).8–11.

Gehrke, William H. 1935. The transition from the German to the English language in North Carolina. North Carolina Historical Review 12.1–19.

Gibbons, Phebe Earle. 1872. "Pennsylvania Dutch," and other essays. Philadelphia: J. B. Lippincott.

Gilbert, Glenn G. 1963. The German dialect spoken in Kendall and Gillespie Counties, Texas. Dissertation, Harvard University.

———. 1964. The German dialect of Kendall and Gillespie Counties, Texas. Zeitschrift für Mundartforschung 31.138–172.

———. 1965a. English loan words in the German of Fredericksburg, Texas. American Speech 40.102–112.

———. 1965b. Dative versus accusative in the German dialects of central Texas. Zeitschrift für Mundartforschung 32.288–296.

———. 1969. Review of The social stratification of English in New York City, by William Labov. Language 45.469–476.

———. 1970a. The phonology, morphology, and lexicon of a German text from Fredericksburg, Texas. Texas studies in bilingualism, pp. 63–104. Edited by Glenn G. Gilbert. Berlin: Walter de Gruyter.

———, ed. 1970b. Texas studies in bilingualism; Spanish, French, German, Czech, Polish, Sorbian, and Norwegian in the Southwest; with a concluding chapter on code switching and discourse structure in American Swedish. Berlin: Walter de Gruyter.

———. 1971. Linguistic atlas of Texas German. Marburg and Austin: Elwert Verlag and University of Texas Press.

Gilbert, Russell W. 1951. The oratory of the Pennsylvania Germans at the Versammlinge. Susquehanna University Studies 4.187–213.

———. 1956a. Pennsylvania German Versammling speeches. Pennsylvania Speech Annual 13.3–20.

———. 1956b. Religious services in Pennsylvania German. Susquehanna University Studies 5.277–289.

Gladfelter, Millard E., Homer L. Kreider, and Charles D. Spotts. 1968. Symposium on the Pennsylvania Dutch dialect. Pennsylvania Folklife 18(1).44–48.

Glassie, Henry. 1965–1966. The Pennsylvania barn in the South, Pennsylvania Folklife 15(2).8–19; 15(4).15–25.

———. 1968. Pattern in the material folk culture of the eastern United States. University of Pennsylvania Monographs in Folklore and Folklife 1. Philadelphia.

Görzen, Jakob W. 1952. Low German in Canada; a study of "Ploudîtš" as spoken by Mennonite immigrants from Russia. Dissertation, University of Toronto.

Goldstein, Kenneth S. 1964. A guide for field workers in folklore. Hatboro, Penn.: Folklore Associates.

Graebner, August L. 1892. Geschichte der lutherischen Kirche in Amerika. Part I. St. Louis, Missouri: Concordia Publishing House.

Graeff, Arthur D. 1946. The Pennsylvania Germans in Ontario, Canada. Pennsylvania German Folklore Society 11.1–80.

Gumperz, John J. 1954. The Swabian dialect of Washtenaw County, Michigan. Dissertation, University of Michigan.

Haldeman, Samuel S. 1872. Pennsylvania Dutch; a dialect of South German with an infusion of English. London and Philadelphia: Philological Society of London and Reformed Church Publication Board.

Halle, Morris. 1962. Phonology in a generative grammar. Word 18.54–72.

Handschin, Charles Hart. 1913. The teaching of modern languages in the United States. United States Bureau of Education Bulletin 1913, no. 3. Washington, D.C.

Handwörterbuch des Grenz- und Auslandsdeutschtums. 1933–1938. Edited by Carl Petersen and Otto Scheel. 3 vols. Breslau: Ferdinand Hirt. [Discontinued at the letter M.]

Harmjanz, Heinrich, and Erich Röhr, eds. 1937. Atlas der deutschen Volkskunde. Marburg: Elwert. [New series edited by Mathias Zender.]

Hart, Henry. 1881. Samuel Stehman Haldeman; a memoir. The Penn Monthly, August 1881, pp. 1–26.

Haugen, Einar. 1942. Problems of linguistic research among Scandinavian immigrants in America. American Council of Learned Societies Bulletin 34.615–637.

———. 1953. The Norwegian language in America; a study in bilingual behavior. 2 vols. Philadelphia: University of Pennsylvania Press.

———. 1956. Bilingualism in the Americas; a bibliography and research guide. Publication of the American Dialect Society 26. University, Alabama: American Dialect Society.

———. Forthcoming. Bilingualism, language contact, and immigrant languages in the United States; a research report 1956–1970. To appear in

Current Trends in Linguistics, vol. 10. Edited by Thomas A. Sebeok. The Hague: Mouton.

Hausman, Ruth L. 1953. Sing and dance with the Pennsylvania Dutch. New York: E. B. Marks.

Hays, H. M. 1908. On the German dialect spoken in the Valley of Virginia. Dialect Notes 3(4).263–278.

Heilman, S. P. 1899. The old cider mill. Lebanon County Historical Society Proceedings 1.209–242.

Helffrich, William A. 1891. Geschichte verschiedener Gemeinden in Lecha und Berks Counties, wie auch Nachricht über die sie bedienenden Prediger, vornehmlich über die Familie Helffrich, der Ursprung und Ausbreitung in Europa, nach authentischen Quellen, und deren Immigration und Verbreitung in Amerika, nebst einem Rückblick in das kirchliche Leben Ostpennsylvaniens. Allentown, Penn.: Trexler and Hartzell.

———. 1906. Lebensbild aus dem pennsylvanisch-deutschen Predigerstand; oder Wahrheit in Licht und Schatten. Edited by N. W. A. and W. U. Helffrich. Allentown, Penn.: private edition.

Hense-Jensen, Wilhelm, and Ernest Bruncken. 1900–1902. Wisconsin's Deutsch-Amerikaner. 2 vols. Milwaukee: Die Deutsche Gesellschaft.

Hergert, Elias, ed. 191-(?). Der köstliche Schatz. 10th ed. Portland, Oregon: A. E. Kern.

Hertzog, Phares H. 1967–1968. Snake lore in Pennsylvania German folk medicine. Pennsylvania Folklife 17(2).24–25.

Hockett, Charles F. 1958. A course in modern linguistics. New York: Macmillan.

Hoffmann, Walter James. 1888–1889. Folklore of the Pennsylvania Germans. Journal of American Folklore 1.125–135; 2.23–35, 191–202.

———. 1889a. Grammatic notes and vocabulary of the Pennsylvania German dialect. Proceedings of the American Philosophical Society 26.187–285.

———. 1889b. Folk-medicine of the Pennsylvania Germans. Proceedings of the American Philosophical Society 26.329–352.

———. 1899. Folklore and language of the Pennsylvania Germans. Washington, D.C.

Hofman, John E. 1966. Mother tongue retentiveness in ethnic parishes. Language loyalty in the United States, by Joshua A. Fishman et al., pp. 127–155. The Hague: Mouton.

———. 1968. The language transition in some Lutheran denominations. Readings in the sociology of language, pp. 620–638. Edited by Joshua A. Fishman. The Hague: Mouton. [A revised version of Hofman 1966.]

Holtzman, Jerome. 1961. An inquiry into the Hutterian German dialect. M.A. thesis, University of South Dakota.

Horne, A. R. 1875. Pennsylvania German manual, for pronouncing, speaking, and writing English; a guide book for schools and families. Kutztown, Penn.: T. K. Horne.

Hostetler, John A. 1954. The sociology of Mennonite evangelism. Scottdale, Penn.: Herald Press.

————. 1961. Amish family life; a sociologist's analysis. Pennsylvania Folklife 12(3).28–39.

————. 1963–1964. Folk scientific medicine in Amish society. Human Organization 22.269–275.

————. 1968. Amish society. Rev. ed. Baltimore: Johns Hopkins Press.

Huch, C. F. 1909. Oswald Seidensticker. Philadelphia Deutscher Pionier-Verein Mitteilungen 12.18–25.

Hull, William I. 1935. William Penn and the Dutch Quaker migration to Pennsylvania. Philadelphia: Swarthmore College Monographs on Quaker History, No. 2.

Humboldt, Wilhelm von. 1836. Über die Verschiedenheit des menschlichen Sprachbaues. Berlin: F. Dümmler.

Hymes, Dell. 1966. Two types of linguistic relativity (with examples from Amerindian ethnography). Sociolinguistics, pp. 114–167. Edited by William Bright. The Hague: Mouton.

Iobst, Clarence F. 1939. En Quart Millich un en halb Beint Raahm. Pennsylvania German Folklore Society 4.3–63.

Jackson, George Pullen. 1945. The strange music of the Old Order Amish. Musical Quarterly 31.275–288.

Johansen, Kjell. 1970. Some observations on Norwegian in Bosque County, Texas. Texas studies in bilingualism, pp. 170–178. Edited by Glenn G. Gilbert. Berlin: Walter de Gruyter.

Jordan, Terry G. 1966. German seed in Texas soil. Austin: University of Texas Press.

————. 1970. Map of population origins in rural Texas. Map supplement no. 13, Annals of the Association of American Geographers 60(2).

Kalbfleisch, H. K. 1968. The history of the German language press of Ontario, 1835–1918. Münster, Westfalen. [= Studien zur Publizistik, Bremer Reihe, Deutsche Presseforschung, vol. 2.]

Kauffman, Henry J. 1946. Coppersmithing in Pennsylvania. Pennsylvania German Folklore Society 11.83–153.

Kehlenbeck, Alfred P. 1948. An Iowa Low German dialect. Publication of the American Dialect Society 10. University, Alabama: American Dialect Society.

Kemp, A. F. 1944. The Pennsylvania German Versammlinge. Pennsylvania German Folklore Society 9.187–218.

Kenkel, Frederick Philip. 1898. Der Schädel des Petronius Arbiter. Chicago: Mayer and Miller.

Keyser, Samuel J. 1963. Review of The pronunciation of English in the

Atlantic states, by Hans Kurath and Raven I. McDavid, Jr. (1959). Language 39.303–313.

Kieffer, Elizabeth Clarke. 1945. Henry Harbaugh, Pennsylvania Dutchman, 1817–1867. Pennsylvania German Society 51.1–365.

Kloss, Heinz, ed. 1929. Lewendiche Schtimme aus Pennsylveni. Stuttgart and New York: Ausland und Heimat Verlags-Aktiengesellschaft, B. Westermann.

———. 1930. Deutschamerikaner-Panamerikaner. Neue Zeit 12(18).5–7.

———. 1931. Die pennsylvania deutsche Literatur. Mitteilungen der Akademie zur wissenschaftlichen Erforschung und zur Pflege des Deutschtums. Deutsche Akademie, no. 4, Nov. 1931, section 7, pp. 230–272.

———. 1934. Deutschamerikanisches Schriftum. Dichtung und Volkstum 35.399–403.

———. 1937. Um die Einigung des Deutschamerikanertums. Berlin: Volk und Reich Verlag.

———. 1938. Die Unberührten, die Verlorenen, die Ringenden. Deutschtum im Ausland 21.176–181.

———. 1939. Über die mittelbare kartographische Erfassung der jüngeren deutschen Volksinseln in den Vereinigten Staaten. Deutsches Archiv für Landes- und Volksforschung 3.453–474.

———. 1942. Das Volksgruppenrecht in den Vereinigten Staaten von Amerika. Vol. 2. Essen: Essener Verlagsanstalt.

———. 1952. Die Entwicklung neuer germanischer Kultursprachen von 1800 bis 1950. Munich: Pohl & Co.

———. 1954. A plea for an anthology of Pennsylvania German prose. 'S Pennsylfawnisch Deitsch Eck. Allentown Morning Call, Oct. 30 and Nov. 6.

———. 1957. Deutsche Sprachpolitik im Ausland. Sprachforum 2.8–9.

———. 1962. Die deutschamerikanische Schule. Jahrbuch für Amerikastudien 7.141–175.

———. 1963. Das Nationalitätenrecht der Vereinigten Staaten von Amerika. Vienna: Wilhelm Braumüller.

———. 1966. German-American language maintenance efforts. Language loyalty in the United States, by Joshua A. Fishman et al., pp. 206–252. The Hague: Mouton.

———. 1967a. FLES; zum Problem des Fremdsprachenunterrichts an Grundschulen Amerikas und Europas. Bad Godesberg: Verlag Wissenschaftliches Archiv.

———. 1967b. Deutscher Sprachunterricht im Grundschulalter in den Vereinigten Staaten. Auslandskurier 8.22–24.

———. Forthcoming. Atlas of nineteenth-century German settlements in the United States. Marburg: Elwert.

Knortz, Karl. 1899. Folkloristische Streifzüge. Oppeln: G. Maske.

———. 1903. Nachklänge germanischen Glaubens und Brauchs in Amerika; ein Beitrag zur Volkskunde. Halle an der Saale: H. Peter.

———. 1913. Amerikanischer Aberglaube der Gegenwart. Leipzig: T. Gerstenberg.

Kohl, Johann Georg. 1856. Reisen in Canada und durch die Staaten New York und Pennsylvanien. Stuttgart: J. G. Cotta.

Korson, George. 1949. Pennsylvania songs and legends. Philadelphia: University of Pennsylvania Press.

———. 1960. Black rock; mining folklore of the Pennsylvania Dutch. Pennsylvania German Society 59.

Kranzmeyer, Eberhard. 1956. Historische Lautgeographie des gesamtbairischen Dialektraumes. Vienna: Böhlus.

Kratz, Henry, and Humphrey Milnes. 1953. Kitchener German; a Pennsylvania German dialect. Modern Language Quarterly 14.184–198, 274–283.

Kreider, Mary C. 1957. Languages and folklore of the "Hoffmansleit" (United Christians). MA thesis, Pennsylvania State University.

———. 1961. Dutchified English; some Lebanon County examples. Pennsylvania Folklife 12(1).40–43.

Kreye, George W. 1961. German instruction in Kansas. American German Review 27 (April–May). 9–11.

Kriebel, Howard Wiegner. 1904. The Schwenkfelders in Pennsylvania. Pennsylvania German Society 13.

Kulp, Clarence, Jr. 1967. The Goschenhoppen historians. Pennsylvania Folklife 16(4).16–24.

Kurath, Hans, director and ed. 1939–1943. Linguistic atlas of New England. Providence, Rhode Island: Brown University.

———, and Raven I. McDavid, Jr. 1959. The pronunciation of English in the Atlantic States. Ann Arbor: University of Michigan Press.

Labov, William. 1963. The social motivation of a sound change. Word 19.273–309.

———. 1966. The social stratification of English in New York City. Washington, D.C.: Center for Applied Linguistics.

———. 1969. Contraction, deletion, and inherent variability of the English copula. Language 45.715–762.

———, Paul Cohen, Clarence Robins, and John Lewis. 1968. A study of the non-standard English of Negro and Puerto Rican speakers in New York City. Final Report. Coöperative Research Project No. 3288, Office of Education. New York: Columbia University.

Lambert, Marcus B. 1924. A dictionary of the non-English words of the Pennsylvania-German dialect. Pennsylvania German Society 30.

Landis, Henry Kinzer. 1939. Early kitchens of the Pennsylvania Germans. Pennsylvania German Society 47.

————, and George Diller Landis. 1944. Lancaster rifle accessories. Pennsylvania German Folklore Society 9.107–184.

Lawton, Arthur J. 1967. Living history. Pennsylvania Folklife 16(4).10–15.

Leach, MacEdward, and Henry Glassie. 1968. A guide for collectors of oral traditions and folk cultural material in Pennsylvania. Harrisburg: Pennsylvania Historical and Museum Commission.

Learned, Marion Dexter. 1888–1889. The Pennsylvania German dialect. American Journal of Philology 9.64–83, 178–197, 326–339, 425–456; 10.288–315.

————, director. 1911. The American ethnographical survey; Conestoga expedition, 1902. Americana Germanica 12. Philadelphia: Publications of the University of Pennsylvania.

————. 1915. The German barn in America. University of Pennsylvania lectures delivered by the members of the faculty in the free public lecture course, 1913–1914, pp. 338–349. Philadelphia.

Lehmann, Winfred P. 1962. Historical linguistics; an introduction. New York: Holt, Rinehart and Winston.

Lehn, Walter I. 1957. Rosental Low German; synchronic and diachronic phonology. Dissertation, Cornell University.

Levi, Kate Everest. 1898. Geographical origin of German immigration to Wisconsin. Collections of the State Historical Society of Wisconsin. 14.341–393. SEE ALSO Everest (1892).

Lewis, Brian A. 1968. The phonology of the Glarus dialect in Green County. Dissertation, University of Wisconsin.

Lick, David E., and Thomas R. Brendle. 1923. Plant names and plant lore among the Pennsylvania Germans. Pennsylvania German Society 33. 1–300.

Livingston, John Henry. 1819. An address to the Reformed German churches in the United States. New Brunswick, New Jersey: Myer.

Lohr, Otto. 1933. Die deutsche Sprache in Nordamerika im 17. Jahrhundert. Mitteilungen der deutschen Akademie 1. 95–96.

Louw, Stephanus Andreas. 1941. Taalgeographie; inleidende gedagtes oor dialekstudie. Pretoria: J. L. van Schaik.

————. 1948. Dialekvermenging en taalontwikkeling, proewe van Afrikaanse taalgeografie. Kaapstad: A. A. Balkema.

————. 1959–1966. Afrikaanse taalatlas. Pretoria: Universiteit van Pretoria.

Mang, Lawrence H. 1954. A German dialect spoken in the Edenwold-Balgonie area of Saskatchewan, Canada. MA thesis, University of Washington.

Mann, William Edward. 1955. Sect, cult, and church in Alberta. Toronto, Ontario: University of Toronto Press.

Mencken, Henry Louis. 1956. The American language, supplement 2. New York: A. A. Knopf.

The Mennonite Encyclopedia. 1955–1959. 4 vols. Hillsboro, Kansas: Mennonite Brethren Publishing House.

Mercer, Henry C. 1897. The survival of the mediaeval art of illuminative writing among Pennsylvania Germans. Proceedings of the American Philosophical Society 36.424–433.

Meynen, Emil, comp. and ed. 1937. Bibliography on German settlements in colonial North America, especially on the Pennsylvania Germans and their descendants, 1683–1933. Leipzig: Otto Harrassowitz.

———. 1939. Das pennsylvanien-deutsche Bauernland. Deutsches Archiv für Landes- und Volksforschung 3.253–292.

Mierau, Eric. 1965. A descriptive grammar of Ukrainian Low German. Dissertation, University of Indiana.

Miller, Cora. 1966. A phonological and morphological study of a German dialect spoken near Freeman, South Dakota. MA thesis, University of Nebraska.

Miller, Daniel. 1903. Pennsylvania German 1. Reading, Penn.: private edition.

———. 1911. Pennsylvania German 2. Reading, Penn.: private edition.

Moelleken, Wolfgang W. 1966. Low German in Mexico. Publication of the American Dialect Society 46.31–39.

———. 1967. Diaphonic correspondences in the Low German of Mennonites from the Fraser Valley, British Columbia. Zeitschrift für Mundartforschung 34.240–253.

Moll, Lloyd A. 1947. Am schwarze Baer. Pennsylvania German Folklore Society 12.9–146.

Moulton, William G. 1960. The short vowel systems of northern Switzerland. Word 16.155–182.

———. 1963. Phonologie und Dialekteinteilung. Sprachleben der Schweiz, 75–86. Bern: Francke.

National Education Association of the United States. 1969. Addresses and proceedings of the 107th annual meeting, June 30–July 5. Washington, D.C.

Nehrling, Henry. 1891. Die nordamerikanische Vogelwelt. Milwaukee: G. Brumder.

Newell, William Wells. 1883, 1903. Games and songs of American children. New York: Harper and Bros.

Nickel, Johanna, ed. 1958. Historisch-philologischer Kommentar zu einem deutschen Zauberbuch. Veröffentlichungen des Instituts für deutsche Volkskunde 17. Berlin: Deutsche Akademie der Wissenschaften zu Berlin.

Nitzsche, George E. 1941. The Christmas Putz of the Pennsylvania Germans. Pennsylvania German Folklore Society 6.1–29.

O'Neil, Wayne A. 1968. Transformational dialectology; phonology and syntax. Zeitschrift für Mundartforschung. Beihefte, neue Folge 4.629–638.

Ornstein, Jacob. 1958. Foreign language training in the Soviet Union; a qualitative view. Modern Language Journal 42.382–392.

Oswald, Victor A., Jr. 1949. The phones of a Lehigh County dialect of Pennsylvania German. Dissertation, Columbia University.

Owen, Trefor M. 1959. Welsh folk customs. Cardiff: National Museum of Wales.

Owens, J. G. 1891. Folk-lore from Buffalo Valley, central Pennsylvania. Journal of American Folklore 4.115–128.

Oxford English Dictionary. 1933 edition. Vol. 7. Oxford: The Clarendon Press.

Paullin, Charles O. 1932. Atlas of the historical geography of the United States. Washington, D.C. and New York: Carnegie Institution and American Geographical Society.

Peal, Elizabeth, and Wallace Lambert. 1962. The relation of bilingualism to intelligence. Psychological Monographs 546.

Petersen, Carl. SEE Handwörterbuch des Grenz- und Auslandsdeutschtums. 1933–1938.

Pochmann, Henry A., and Arthur R. Schultz. 1953. Bibliography of German culture in America to 1940. Madison: University of Wisconsin Press.

Pop, Sever. 1950. La dialectologie. 2 vols. Louvain: private edition.

Postal, Paul M. 1968. Aspects of phonological theory. New York: Harper and Row.

Pulte, William, Jr. 1970. An analysis of selected German dialects of north Texas and Oklahoma. Texas studies in bilingualism, pp. 105–141. Edited by Glenn G. Gilbert. Berlin: Walter de Gruyter.

Ramos, M., J. V. Aguilar, and B. P. Silayan. 1967. The determination and implementation of language policy. Philippine Center for Language Study Monograph Series 2.36–43.

Rauch, Edward H. 1879. Rauch's Pennsylvania Dutch hand-book. Mauch Chunk, Penn.: private edition.

Raunick, Selma Metzenthin. 1929. A survey of German literature in Texas. Southwestern Historical Quarterly 33.134–159.

———, comp. 1935–1936. Deutsche Schriften in Texas. 2 vols. San Antonio: Freie Presse für Texas.

Reed, Carroll E. 1942. The gender of English loan words in Pennsylvania German. American Speech 17.25–29.

———. 1943. The German dialect of southeastern Pennsylvania. Bulletin of the New England Modern Language Association 5.26–31.

———. 1947. The question of aspect in Pennsylvania German. Germanic Review 22.5–12.

————. 1948a. The adaptation of English to Pennsylvania German morphology. American Speech 23.239–244.

————. 1948b. A survey of Pennsylvania German morphology. Modern Language Quarterly 9(3).332–342.

————. 1949. The Pennsylvania German dialect spoken in the counties of Lehigh and Berks; phonology and morphology. Seattle: University of Washington Press.

————. 1953. English archaisms in Pennsylvania German. Publication of the American Dialect Society 19.3–7.

————. 1957. Die Sprachgeographie des Pennsylvaniadeutschen. Zeitschrift für Mundartforschung 25.29–39.

————. 1961. Double dialect geography. Orbis 10.308–319.

————. 1967. Loan-word stratification in Pennsylvania German. German Quarterly 40.83–86.

————, and Lester W. J. Seifert. 1941. The Pennsylvania German dialect spoken in the counties of Lehigh and Berks. Dissertations, Brown University.

————. 1954. A linguistic atlas of Pennsylvania German. Marburg: private edition.

————. Forthcoming. Wordatlas of Pennsylvania German. Marburg: Elwert.

Reed, Carroll E., and Herbert F. Wiese. 1957. Amana German. American Speech 32.243–256.

Reichard, Harry Hess. 1918. Pennsylvania Dutch dialect writings and their writers. Pennsylvania German Society 26. 1–400.

————. 1940. Pennsylvania German verse. Pennsylvania German Society 48. 1–299.

————. 1944. John Baer Stoudt, D. D.; an appreciation. Pennsylvania German Folklore Society 9.221–229.

Reinert, Guy F. 1948. Coverlets of the Pennsylvania Germans. Pennsylvania German Folklore Society 13.1–215.

Report of the United States Commissioner of Education for the year 1870. 1870. Washington, D.C.: U.S. Government Printing Office.

Robins, Robert Henry. 1967. A short history of linguistics. Bloomington: Indiana University Press.

Rohrbach, Heinrich. 1958. Lawrence's German school. American German Review 24 (April–May). 27.

Rosenberger, Homer T. 1966. The Pennsylvania Germans, 1891–1965. Pennsylvania German Society 63.

Rothensteiner, Johannes [John Ernest]. 1922. Die literarische Wirksamkeit der deutsch-amerikanischen Katholiken. St. Louis, Missouri: herausgegeben von der Schriftleitung der "Amerika."

Rupp, William J. 1946. Bird names and bird lore among the Pennsylvania Germans. Pennsylvania German Society 52.

Rush, Benjamin. 1789. An account of the manners of the German inhabitants of Pennsylvania. Columbian Magazine or Monthly Miscellany 3 (Jan. 1789), pp. 22–30.

Sachse, Julius Friedrich. 1899. The German sectarians of Pennsylvania, 1708–1800. Philadelphia: private edition.

Sapir, Edward. 1921. Language. New York: Harcourt, Brace & Co.

Sapon, Stanley Martin. 1953. A methodology for the study of socio-economic differentials in linguistic phenomena. Studies in Linguistics 11.57–68.

———. 1957. A pictorial linguistic interview manual [PLIM]. Columbus, Ohio: American Library of Recorded Dialect Studies, Ohio State University.

Saporta, Sol. 1965. Ordered rules, dialect differences, and historical processes. Language 41.218–224.

Schach, Paul. 1948. Hybrid compounds in Pennsylvania German. American Speech 23.121–134.

———. 1949. The formation of hybrid derivatives in Pennsylvania German. Symposium 3.114–129.

———. 1951. Semantic borrowing in Pennsylvania German. American Speech 26.257–267.

———. 1952. Types of loan translation in Pennsylvania German. Modern Language Quarterly 13.268–276.

———. 1954. Die Lehnprägungen der pennsylvania-deutschen Mundart. Zeitschrift für Mundartforschung 22.215–222.

Scheffauer, Herman George. 1923. Das Land Gottes. Hannover: P. Steegemann.

———. 1925. Das geistige Amerika von heute. Berlin: Ullstein.

Schirmunski, Viktor M. [Victor Zhirmunskij]. 1962. Deutsche Mundartkunde. Berlin: Akademie Verlag.

Schmeller, Johann Andreas. 1821. Die Mundarten Bayerns grammatisch dargestellt. Munich: K. Thienemann.

———. 1827–1837. Bayrisches Wörterbuch; Sammlung von Wörtern und Ausdrücken mit urkundlichen Belegen. 4 vols. Stuttgart: J. G. Cotta.

Schreiber, William I. 1962a. The hymns of the Amish Ausbund in philological and literary perspective. Mennonite Quarterly Review 36(1).36–60.

———. 1962b. Our Amish neighbors. Chicago: University of Chicago Press.

Schrock, Alta. 1967. The council of the Alleghenies. Pennsylvania Folklife 17(1).2–9.

Schwarze, William N., trans. 1941. Early Christmases in Bethlehem, Pennsylvania (1742–1756); transcriptions of items from the Bethlehem diary relating to early celebrations of Christmas in Bethlehem, Pennsylvania. Pennsylvania German Folklore Society 6.1–35.

Sealsfield, Charles [Karl Postl]. 1841. Das Cajütenbuch oder nationale Charakteristiken. Elberfeld: J. Bädeker. [Die Prairie am Jacinto is the first novella in this book.]

Seidensticker, Oswald. 1893. The first century of German printing in America, 1728–1830. Philadelphia: Schaefer & Koradi. [Reprinted in 1966. New York: Kraus Reprint Corp.]

Seifert, Lester W. J. 1946a. Wisconsin German questionnaire. Typescript, University of Wisconsin.

————. 1946b. Lexical differences between four Pennsylvania German regions. Pennsylvania German Folklore Society 11.155–169.

————. 1947. The diminutives of Pennsylvania German. Monatshefte für deutschen Unterricht 39.285–293.

————. 1951. Methods and aims of a survey of the German language spoken in Wisconsin. Transactions of the Wisconsin Academy of Sciences, Arts and Letters 40.201–210.

Selltiz, Claire, Marie Jahoda, Morton Deutsch, and Stuart W. Cook. 1959. Research methods in social relations. Rev. ed. New York: Holt, Rinehart & Winston.

Selzer, Barbara. 1941. A description of the Amana dialect of Homestead, Iowa. MA thesis, University of Illinois.

Shelley, Donald A. 1958–1959. The Fraktur-writings or illuminated manuscripts of the Pennsylvania Germans. Pennsylvania German Folklore Society 23. 1–375.

Shoemaker, Alfred L. 1940. Studies on the Pennsylvania German dialect of the Amish community in Arthur, Illinois. Dissertation, University of Illinois.

————. 1949. Pumpernickle Bill, dialect writer. Pennsylvania Dutchman 1(4).1.

————. 1959. Christmas in Pennsylvania; a folk-cultural approach. Kutztown: Pennsylvania Folklife Society.

Smith, Elmer Lewis, John G. Stewart, and M. Ellsworth Kyger. 1962. The Pennsylvania Germans of the Shenandoah Valley. Pennsylvania German Folklore Society 26. 1–278.

Springer, Otto. 1941. A working bibliography for the study of the Pennsylvania German language and its sources. 2nd rev. ed. Mimeographed, University of Pennsylvania, Department of Germanic Languages.

————. 1943. The study of the Pennsylvania German dialect. Journal of English and Germanic Philology 42.1–39.

Stählen, C. 1846. Neueste Nachrichten, Erklärungen und Briefe der Auswanderer von Texas. Heilbronn: A. Ruoff.

Starr, Frederick. 1891. Some Pennsylvania-German lore. Journal of American Folklore 4.321–326.
————. 1895. Pennsylvania Germans (Moravians). Journal of American Folklore 8.
Stoudt, John Baer. 1906. Pennsylvania-German riddles and nursery rhymes. Journal of American Folklore 19.113–131.
————. 1916. The folklore of the Pennsylvania Germans. Pennsylvania German Society 23, part 2.
Stoudt, John Joseph. 1937. Consider the lilies how they grow. Pennsylvania German Folklore Society 2.
————. 1951. Pennsylvania German folklore; an interpretation. Pennsylvania German Folklore Society 16.157–170.
————. 1955. Pennsylvania German poetry 1685–1830. Pennsylvania German Folklore Society 20.
————. 1966. Pennsylvania German folk art; an interpretation. Pennsylvania German Folklore Society 28.
Strubberg, Friedrich Armand. 1858. Amerikanische Jagd- und Reiseabenteuer aus meinem Leben in den westlichen Indianergebieten. Stuttgart: J. G. Cotta.
————. 1859. Alte und neue Heimath. Breslau: Trewendt.
Swetnam, George. 1965. Sex; the missing fascicle. Keystone Folklore Quarterly 10(4).155–171.
Thomas, William Isaac, and Florian Znaniecki. 1918–1920. The Polish peasant in Europe and America. 5 vols. Boston: R. G. Badger.
Trexler, Benjamin F. 1886. Skizzen aus dem Lecha-Thale. Allentown, Penn.: Trexler and Hartzell.
Troxell, William S. 1953. The first Grundsow Lodge. Pennsylvania Dutchman 4(12).4.
Trubetzkoy, N. S. 1931. Phonologie und Sprachgeographie. Travaux du Cercle Linguistique de Prague 4.228–234.
University of Pennsylvania Newsletter, Department of Germanic Languages. 1959. 2.42–59.
United States. 1791. First census of the United States; 1790. Philadelphia: Childs and Swaine.
————. 1853. Seventh census of the United States; 1850. Washington, D.C.
————. 1864. Population of the United States in 1860; compiled from the eighth census. Washington, D.C.
————. 1872. The statistics of the population of the United States, . . . compiled from . . . the ninth census (June 1, 1870). Washington, D.C.
————. 1883. Statistics of the population of the United States at the tenth census (June 1, 1880). Washington, D.C.

————. 1895. Report on the population of the United States at the eleventh census; 1890. Part 1. Washington, D.C.

————. 1901. Twelfth census of the United States; 1900; population. Vol. 1, part 1. Washington, D.C.

————. 1910. The United States Bureau of the Census; religious bodies, 1906. Washington, D.C.

————. 1913. Thirteenth census of the United States, taken in the year 1910. Vol. 1. Population 1910. Washington, D.C.

————. 1919. United States Bureau of the Census; religious bodies, 1916. Washington, D.C.

Viereck, Louis. 1902. German instruction in American schools. Report of the Commissioner of Education for the Year 1900–1901, 1.531–708.

Viereck, Wolfgang. 1967. German dialects spoken in the United States and Canada and problems of German-English language contact especially in North America; a bibliography. Orbis 16.549–568.

————. 1968. Supplement to the bibliography published in Orbis 16.549–568 (1967). Orbis 17.532–535.

Wayland, John Walter. 1907. The German element of the Shenandoah Valley of Virginia. Charlottesville, Virginia: private edition.

Weinreich, Uriel. 1954. Is a structural dialectology possible? Linguistics today, pp. 268–280. New York: Linguistic Circle of New York.

————. 1968. Languages in contact; findings and problems. 6th printing. The Hague: Mouton.

Weygandt, Cornelius. 1929. The red hills; a record of good days outdoors and in, with things Pennsylvania Dutch. Philadelphia: University of Pennsylvania Press.

————. 1939. The Dutch country; folks and treasures in the red hills of Pennsylvania. New York: D. Appleton Century Co.

————. 1953. Pennsylvania Dutch cultivation. Pennsylvania Dutchman 5(1).3.

Whittier, John Greenleaf. 1866, 1904. Magicians and witch folk. Margaret Smith's journal; tales and sketches. The writings of John Greenleaf Whittier, Riverside edition. Vol. 5, pp. 399–411. Boston: Houghton, Mifflin & Co.

Whorf, Benjamin Lee. 1941. The relation of habitual thought and behavior to language. Language, culture, and personality; essays in memory of Edward Sapir, pp. 75–93. Edited by Leslie Spier, A. Irving Hallowell, and Stanley S. Newman. Menasha, Wisconsin: Sapir Memorial Publication Fund.

Williams, Maynard Owen. 1952. Pennsylvania Dutch folk festival. National Geographic 102(4).503–516.

Wilson, H. Rex. 1958. The dialect of Lunenburg County, Nova Scotia. Dissertation, University of Michigan.

Winkler, Wilhelm, ed. 1935. Pfälzischer Geschichtsatlas. Neustadt an der Haardt: Verlag der Pfälzischen Gesellschaft zur Förderung der Wissenschaften.

Winteler, Jost. 1876. Die Kerenzer Mundart des Kantons Glarus. Leipzig: C. F. Winter.

Winter, Jack W. 1949. 'S Pennsylfawnish Deitsch Liegner Match. Pennsylvania Dutchman 1(19).4.

Wisconsin. 1886. Tabular statements of the census enumeration . . . of the state of Wisconsin . . . 1885. Madison: Democrat Printing Co.

Wittke, Carl. 1957. The German language press in America. Lexington: University of Kentucky Press.

Wolkan, Rudolf. 1903. Die Lieder der Wiedertäufer. Berlin: B. Behr.

Wood, Ralph Charles. 1958. Zur Problematik der deutschen Volkssprache in Nordamerika. Weltweite Wissenschaft vom Volke; Festgabe für J. W. Mannhardt, pp. 185–189. Vienna: R. M. Rohrer.

———. 1968. The four gospels translated into the Pennsylvania German dialect. Pennsylvania German Society, new series, 1.7–184.

Wust, Klaus. 1965. Review of The Pennsylvania Germans of the Shenandoah Valley, by Elmer Lewis Smith, John G. Stewart, and M. Ellsworth Kyger. Virginia Magazine of History and Biography 73.202–203.

Yoder, Don. 1952. Willy Brown of Mahantongo; our foremost folksinger. Pennsylvania Dutchman 4(2).3.

———. 1961. Pennsylvania spirituals. Lancaster, Penn.: Pennsylvania Folklife Society.

———. 1963. The folklife studies movement. Pennsylvania Folklife 10(4).43–56.

———. 1969. What to read on the Amish. Pennsylvania Folklife 18(4).17.

Yoder, Joseph W. 1942. Amische Lieder. Huntingdon, Penn.: Yoder Publishing Company.

Yoder, Paul M., Elizabeth Bender, Harvey Graber, and Nelson P. Springer. 1964. Four hundred years with the Ausbund. Scottdale, Penn.: Herald Press.

Zagel, Hermann H. 1923. Aus Frühlingstagen. Peoria, Illinois: private edition.

Zehner, Olive G. 1953. Cornelius Weygandt. Pennsylvania Dutchman 5(1).2.

Ziegler, Charles Calvin. 1936. Drauss un Deheem. Pennsylvania German Folklore Society 1. 9–73.

INDEX

Acadians: and bilingual schools, 125, 165–166. SEE ALSO French language
An Account of the Manners of the German Inhabitants of Pennsylvania: 72
Adams County, Pennsylvania: Germans in, 15
Adelsverein: and Texas Germans, 152; and written Texas German, 157
Advisory Committee on Bilingual Education: 126
Africa: German language in, 121, 130
African folklore. SEE folklore, African
Afrikaanse Taalatlas: and the training of fieldworkers, 134
Alaska: German immigrants in, 109
Alberta: and Pennsylvania German folksong research, 91; and bilingual schooling, 125
Alberta Pentecostal Assemblies of Canada: 91
Albright College: American German literture in Historical Museum of, 116
Alemannic: and Pennsylvania German, 18–20
Alleghenies. SEE West Virginia Alleghenies
Allentown, Pennsylvania: 74–75, 91, 93
All Pennsylvania Folk Festivals: 91
Alsace: 18, 171
Alsatian vocalism: and linguistic theory, 6
Amana German: dialect differentiation of, 7; study of, 10
America: and the study of linguistic behavior, 6–7, distribution of German immigrants in, 110
American Low Saxon German: 10

American Association of Teachers of German: 139
American Council on German Studies: 126
American Council on the Study of German in America: 139
American Dialect Society: 143
American Ethnographical Survey of 1902: 73
American Folklore Society: and the study of American ethnic groups, 83–84
American German: dialectology of, 3, 9; and linguistic behavior, 6–7; and European bilingual contacts, 8; study of, 9–10, 43, 135–136, 141; recommendations for a comprehensive description of, 43–45; front-rounded vowels in, 67; and the *Deutches Spracharchiv*, 138–139; nineteenth-century writers on, 158; teaching materials for, 173. SEE ALSO Franconian, American, Hanoverian Low German; Holstein dialect; Palatine German, American; Pennsylvania German; Sauk County Low German; Sugar Grove German; Swabian German; Swiss German, American; Texas German; Virginia German; Wisconsin German
American German press: in Wisconsin, 49; bibliographies of, 110
American Philosophical Society Proceedings: 84
Americans. SEE Anglo-Americans; Latin Americans
American Germans: in Wisconsin, 51; literature of, 110, 111, 115; and bilingual schools, 174. SEE ALSO Hutterite German Americans; Nova Sco-

tian Germans; Palatines; Pennsylvania
Germans; Texas Germans; Wisconsin
Germans
Amerikanischer Aberglaube der Gegenwart: 85
Amische Lieder: and Pennsylvania German folksong research, 88
Amish: and Pennsylvania German, 16, 36, 37; resettlement of, 60; folksong research among, 88; trilingualism among, 101; and education, 123, 126; German written by, 157–158, 159; preservation of Catholic traditions by, 163. SEE ALSO schools, Amish parochial
—, Old Order: songs of, 87, 88, 90, 151; and breakdown of Pennsylvania German folk culture, 97; and distribution of spoken German, 114; and linguistic atlases, 127; religious services of, 151; and bilingual schools, 175
"Amish Hymns as Folk Music": and Pennsylvania German folksong research, 88
Am Schwarze Baer: 82
Amsterdam: and methods of obtaining folklore data, 152–153
Anabaptists: 88
Anarchists: 111
Andersson, Theodore: and bilingual education, 167–168
Anglo-Americans: revivalism among, 89, 90, 96; and Pennsylvania German culture, 71, 73–74, 99–100; preaching styles of, 151
Anglo-Saxon immigrants: distribution of, 109
Ann Arbor, Michigan: Swabian colony near, 10; and bilingual education, 165
Appalachia, Upper: 85–86
Appel, John J.: and American ethnic group societies, 83
Applebutter Boilings: and Pennsylvania German folklore, 91–92
architecture: supplanting of Pennsylvania German styles of, 96; and Pennsylvania German folklore, 99–100, 160; and combined folklore and linguistics studies, 160
Archive of American Folksong: 86
Argentina: German language in, 110

Armand. SEE Strubberg, Friedrich
Arndt, Karl J. R.: and the distribution of German immigrants, 109; bibliography, 110
art. SEE folk art
Atlas der Deutschen Volkskunde: 160
atlases: linguistic, 56–57; ethnic, 129
Atlas Linguistique de la France: 133
"Atlas of Nineteenth-Century German Settlements in the United States:" potential value of, 128
Atwood, E. Bagby: and linguistic geography, 130
Ausbund: and Pennsylvania German folksong research, 88
Austin, Texas: 144–145
Austin County, Texas: early German settlement in, 110
Australia: and linguistic behavior, 6; and German/English contact, 130
Austria: and dialect studies, 6; and German in Wisconsin, 47, 52

Bachman, Calvin George: 80
Baddalya: 96
Baden: immigration to the United States from, 18, 51–52
Baerg, Marjorie: and structural descriptions of American German, 9–10
Baltimore, Maryland: 113
Baptist Church. SEE German Baptist Church
Barba, Preston A.: and dialectology, 9; and the study of Pennsylvania German language, 14, 74; as a student of Marion Dexter Learned, 73; and the study of Pennsylvania German culture, 74, 82
Baur, Gerhard: and sociolinguistics, 6
Bavarian immigrants: in Wisconsin, 51–52; in urban areas, 114
Bavarian speech area: and linguistic theory, 6
Baver, Florence: and dialect radio program, 94
Bayrisches Wörterbuch: 3
Beam, C. Richard: and Pennsylvania German language and culture, 76, 87, 159
Beliefs and Superstitions of the Pennsylvania Germans: 73

Bender, Elizabeth: and Pennsylvania German folksong research, 88
Bender, Ruth: and dialectology, 9
Berks County, Pennsylvania: linguistic geography of, 21–31; and complex distributions of lexical differences, 32, 33, 34; and the origin of Pennsylvania German, 35–37; dialect of, compared to Virginia German, 61, 62; and dialect names, 149
Berlin Township, Wisconsin: German language in, 50
Bible German: 150
Bibliography of German Culture in America to 1940: 85
Bilingual Education Act: 126, 164, 166
bilingual contacts: and resettlement to America, 8
bilingualism: and Pennsylvania German, 7–8, 91, 100–101; and levels of usage, 8; and front-rounded vowels, 67–68; and education, 119, 120, 125–126, 164–178 *passim*; and the study of German in America, 131; official attitudes toward, 143–144, 171; cultural problems of, 169–171, 174; inevitability of, 175; in other countries, 175
Bird Names and Bird Lore among the Pennsylvania Germans: 80
Birmelin, John: and Pennsylvania German, 82
Blackboard Magazine: 159
Black Rock: Mining Folklore of the Pennsylvania Germans: 81
Blue Mountain: as a boundary of German settlement, 15–16; and dialect names, 149
"'S Bobbelmowl": and dialect radio, 94
Borneman, Henry S.: and Pennsylvania German folk art, 80–81
Bottiglioni, Gino: and the training of fieldworkers, 134
Boyer, Walter E.: and folklore research, 87, 99, 100–101
Brandenburg, Germany: immigrants to Wisconsin from, 51, 52
Brazil: German language in, 110, 121
Brendle, Thomas R.: and Pennsylvania German folklore, 80, 86, 87; and Pennsylvania German religious services, 150

Brenham, Texas: German folklore in, 162
Brethren: and Pennsylvania German folksong research, 89, 90 SEE ALSO Evangelical United Brethren; Old Order River Brethren
British Honduras: German language in, 110, 130
Britton, George: 86
Brobst, Samuel K.: and American German literature, 116
Brown, Willy: bilingualism of, 100–101
Brown University: as a depository of the "Linguistic Atlas of the United States and Canada," 135
Brumbaugh, G. Edwin: 80
Bucher, Robert C.: 87
Bucknell University: All Pennsylvania Folk Festival at, 91
Bucks County, Pennsylvania: as a boundary of German concentration, 17; as part of eastern region of Pennsylvania German, 20–21; and complex distributions of lexical differences, 33, 34; and origins of Pennsylvania German, 35, 36; dialect of, compared to Virginia German, 61
Bucks County Historical Society: 84
Buffington, Albert E.: and dialectology, 9; and the study of Pennsylvania German, 14, 19, 76, 82, 100; and Pennsylvania German folklore research, 76, 87, 93, 99, 100–101; radio program of, 93
bundling: 97
Buschdeutsch: 70, 158

California: Swiss immigrants in, 108; German immigrants among the Russians in, 109; foreign-language education in, 124, 167, 175
Canada: migrations of American Germans to, 7, 81–82; and folksong research, 81–82, 91, 160; and American German, 110, 130, 142–143; value of recording German religious services in, 151
Canadian Germans. SEE American Germans; Nova Scotian Germans
Carbon County, Pennsylvania: linguistic geography of, 21, 28, 31; and complex

distributions of lexical differences, 33
Carl Schurz Memorial Foundation: 162.
SEE ALSO National Carl Schurz Association
Carman, J. Neale: and German speech islands in Kansas, 113
Cassidy, F. G.: and the study of American German, 134
censuses: value of, in locating German speech islands, 129
Center for Applied Linguistics: and bilingual education, 165
Centre County, Pennsylvania: as a boundary of German concentration, 17
Chester County, Pennsylvania: predominance of non-Germans in, 15
Chihuahua, Mexico: German language in, 110, 143
Chile: German language in, 110, 121
Chinese language: and bilingual education, 165
The Christmas Putz of the Pennsylvania Germans: 82
churches: dialect services in, 91, 94–95; and American German, 112–113, 123, 129. SEE ALSO Alberta Pentecostal Assemblies of Canada; Amish; Anabaptists; Brethren; Dunkards, Old Order; Evangelical and Reformed Church; Evangelical United Brethren; German Baptist Brethren; German Baptist Church; Grundsow Lodges; Heavenly Recruit Association; Lutheran Church; Lutherans, Freistadt; Mennonites; Methodist Church; plain sectarians; Protestant churches; Reformed Church; River Brethren; Roman Catholic Church; Slavic churches; Union churches; United Christians; United Evangelicals; United Zion's Children
Cincinnati, Ohio: American German in, 113, 114; German FLES in, 121–122
Colonial Architecture of the Pennsylvania Germans: 80
Calumet County, Wisconsin: preservation of German in, 52
Community Historians: 85
Conestoga Valley: and the American Ethnographical Survey of 1902, 73
Consider the Lilies How They Grow: 82
Coppersmithing in Pennsylvania: 82

Corpus Christi, Texas: bilingual schools in, 178
Côte des Allemands: 109
Council of the Alleghenies: 85–86
Coverlets of the Pennsylvania Germans: 82
crafts: of American Germans, 82, 84
Creighton, Helen: and the collection of German folklore, 158
Creoles: and bilingual schools, 165
Cuba: and bilingual schooling, 125, 177
Cumberland County, Pennsylvania: as an area of early German settlement, 15

Dade County, Florida: bilingual education in, 177
Dakotas, the: and Pennsylvania German folksong research, 90; and bilingual schools, 126. SEE ALSO North Dakota
Dane County, Wisconsin: disappearance of the Rhineland dialect in, 52
Danish language: 168, 174
Daughters of the American Revolution: and Pennsylvania German ethnic societies, 83
Dauphin County, Pennsylvania: linguistic geography of, 21–29; and complex distributions of lexical differences, 33, 34; folksong research in, 87
Dayton, Rockingham County, Virginia: study of German in, 59
Dayton German: compared to German in other areas, 60, 62–64; isolation of, 64; front-rounded vowels in, 64–68
DeCamp, David: and linguistic geography, 131
Deitsche Versammling: dialect services at, 95
Deitschlenner: and Pennsylvania German folklore, 99
Delamater-Pattisan campaign: 87
Delaware County, Pennsylvania: predominance of non-Germans in, 15
de Saussure, Ferdinand: 4
Deutsche Dialektgeographie: 4–5, 6
Der Deutsche Kirchenfreund: and American German religious literature, 111
Der Deutsche Pionier: and the study of Pennsylvania German folklore, 85
Deutsches Spracharchiv: and the dissemination of tape-recorded data, 136–137;

availability of American German linguistic material from, 138–139; technical staff of, 140; and Austin, Texas, as the site of a center for German American studies, 144
dialect lexicography. SEE lexicography, dialect
La Dialectologie: confusion of dialectology and dialect geography in, 5; and the study of German language in the United States, 130; and informant selection, 131
dialectology: and American German, 3; origins of, 3–6; and structural analysis, 5; confusion of, with dialect geography, 5; and social structures, 5–6; defined, 6; and speech records, 8–9; and extralinguistic information, 9; methods of, 10–11; and Pennsylvania German, 80, 82; and the study of German language in America, 130, 131; and bilingual education, 144; limits of, 145
A Dictionary of the Non-English Words of the Pennsylvania German Dialect: 19, 80
Doctor Eisenbart: 87
Dodge County, Wisconsin: 55
Dodge County Pioneer: 56
Dornbusch, Charles H.: and craft studies of Pennsylvania Germans, 82
Dorney Park, Pennsylvania: and the new Pennsylvania German folklore, 91
Drauss un Deheem: and dialect study of Pennsylvania German, 82
die Dreissiger: nonfiction writings by, 111
Dunkards, Old Order: songs of, 151
Dunker-Weise: and Pennsylvania German folksong research, 90
The Dutch Country: Folks and Treasures in the Red Hills of Pennsylvania: 73–74
Dutch languages: and bilingual education, 126, 166, 168
Dutch Reformed immigrants: and bilingual education, 166
Dyck, Henry D.: and dialectology, 9

ESEA Act: and bilingual education, 166

Early American Industries Association: 84
Early Childhood Bilingual Education Project (Yeshiva University): 164
Early Kitchens of the Pennsylvania Germans: 80
Easton, Pennsylvania: dialect radio at, 93, 94
Eastphalian dialect: preservation of, in Wisconsin, 52
Eck. SEE *'S Pennsylfawnisch Deitsch Eck*
education: in German language, 118–126, 145–146, 162; bilingual, 125–126; and the location of German speech islands, 129; designing materials for, 172–173. SEE ALSO bilingualism; schools
Eikel, Fred, Jr.: and structural descriptions of American German, 9–10
Elbert Covell College: and Spanish language education, 124–125
England: and Pennsylvania German folklore, 100
English, archaic: and Pennsylvania German, 7–8
English, Standard: and the disappearance of German influences on English in Wisconsin, 56
English language: and German in Nova Scotia, 7; and bilingualism, 8, 125–126, 143–144, 159, 164–178 *passim*; and linguistic influences on American German, 18–19, 35, 36, 37, 53, 56–57, 67, 149, 158; and Pennsylvania German, 24, 28; and complex distributions of lexical differences, 32–33, 33–34; and the decline of German in Wisconsin, 50; and trilingualism in Wisconsin, 51; and Standard German in Wisconsin, 54; ability of American German speakers to use, 54, 154–156; and German in Virginia, 59; American German folklore in, 96, 97, 101, 159; and education, 119, 123, 125–126, 162, 164–178 *passim*; translation of *La Dialectologie* into, 130; and informant interviews, 132; and theoretical framework of linguistic investigations, 133; and the study of American German, 134; study of preaching styles in, 151; and attempts

to eradicate Pennsylvania German, 155–156; and legal documents in Pennsylvania, 157; and minority group assimilation, 172

English-language press: compared to German-language press in Milwaukee, Wisconsin, 49

Ethnic Culture Survey (Pennsylvania): 86

ethnic societies: study of Pennsylvania German folklore by, 76–86; in America, 83

euphemisms: in Pennsylvania German, 150

Europe: German-speaking immigrants from, 107–110 *passim*; German dialectology in, 130; mother tongue education in, 168

Evangelical and Reformed Church: and German as an indigenous American language, 113

Evangelical Association: and Pennsylvania German folksong research, 89; American German literature by, 116

Evangelical Mennonites. SEE United Mennonites

Evangelical United Brethren: and Pennsylvania German folksong research, 91; dialect church services of, 95. SEE ALSO Brethren; United Methodist Church

Evangelische Gemeinschaft. SEE Evangelical Association

FLES. SEE Foreign Languages in the Elementary School

Faroese: used in generative analysis, 11

Fastnacht customs: in Nova Scotia, 159

Fayett County, Texas: 174

fieldworkers: training of, 133–134

The First Century of German Printing in America, 1728–1830: 72

Fishman, Joshua A.: and the study of sociolinguistics, 131

Flurnamen: value of recording, 148

Fogel, Edwin M.: and Pennsylvania German folklore, 73, 82

folk art, Pennsylvania German: studies of, 80–81, 82; and Henry C. Mercer, 84–85

folk culture. SEE folklore

folk festivals: 91–92

folklore: pioneer studies of, 73; writings on, by German Americans, 111; and linguistics, 142, 148, 160–161; and the recording of local place names, 148–149; methods of obtaining data on 152–153; German, 158; African, 160; study of, in America, 160

—, Pennsylvania German: research in, 71; study of, by ethnic societies, 76–86; folksong research in, 86–91; new institutions of, 91–95; recommendations for the study of, 95, 100, 101; sources of, 98–100

Folklore and Language of the Pennsylvania Germans: 84

"Folk-Lore from Buffalo Valley, Central Pennsylvania": 84

The Folklore of Lunenburg County, Nova Scotia: 158

"Folklore of the Pennsylvania Germans": 84

The Folklore of the Pennsylvania Germans: 80

Folklore Society (British): 83

Folkloristische Streifzüge: 85

"Folk Medicine of the Pennsylvania Germans": 84

Folk Medicine of the Pennsylvania Germans: The Non-Occult Cures: 80

folksongs, Pennsylvania German: research in, 86–91; religious, 87, 88–91; and the sources of Pennsylvania German folklore, 98–100; and bilingualism, 100–101; in English, 100–101. SEE ALSO songs, religious

Foreign Language Innovative Curricular Study Center (Ann Arbor, Michigan): 165, 166

Foreign Languages in the Elementary School: origins of, 118–119; and German-language education, 121–124; and Amish parochial schools, 160; and bilingual schools, 164; in Van Buren, Maine, 166

Foreign Language Units in Kansas: and the survival of German as a spoken language, 113

Forty-Eighters: and Standard German in Wisconsin, 51

Fourquet, Jean: and linguistic theory, 6

Fraktur: as folk art tradition, 84–85; and

the study of Pennsylvania German folk culture, 101
The Fraktur-Writings or Illuminated Manuscripts of the Pennsylvania Germans: 82
France: and bilingual education, 167
Franconian: and the development of Pennsylvania German, 18–20
Franklin and Marshall College: 74, 75
Fredericksburg, Texas: German speakers in, 109; German folklore in, 162; teaching of Standard German in, 178
Free Thinkers: and the American German press, 111
Freindschaft: in Pennsylvania, 154; in Nova Scotia, 159
Freistadt Lutherans. SEE Lutherans, Freistadt
French immigrants: German immigrants among, in North America, 109
French language: in high schools, 118, 122; in the Soviet Union, 123; in Virginia, 124; at Massachusetts Institute of Technology, 125; and bilingual education, 125, 126, 165, 166, 167, 168; social disadvantages of speaking, 174
Frenchville, Maine: bilingual schooling in, 125
Frey, J. William: and dialectology, 9; and structural descriptions of American German, 9–10; and the study of Pennsylvania German, 14, 75; and Pennsylvania German folksong research, 75, 87
Frisian: and Low German Mennonite, 8
front-rounded vowels: in Virginia German, 63–68
Fuderzettel: and the *Versammlinge*, 92
Fulda, Indiana: German folklore traditions in, 162

Gaardner, Bruce: on bilingual schools, 177
Gallup, George Horace: and informant selection, 132
Gehman, Ernest G.: and dialectology, 9
Gehman, Henry Snyder: and Pennsylvania German, 154
Gehring, Conrad: and Pennsylvania German folklore, 99

generative analysis: and the study of German dialects, 11
German Americans. SEE American Germans
German Baptist Brethren: 151
German Baptist Church: 91
"German Coast": and German in Louisiana, 109
German folklore. SEE folklore, German
Germania (Milwaukee, Wisconsin): and German in Wisconsin, 49
German immigrants: in Wisconsin, 49; geographic distribution of, 108–110; German language literature by, 115; and German in education, 121–122
German language: and English, 7, 56–57; and bilingualism, 8, 55, 125–126, 144; and German settlement in Wisconsin, 45–49; as a written language in the United States, 56, 115–118; of Pennsylvania German folksongs, 89; as an immigrant language, 107–112; as an indigenous American language, 112–118; distribution of, in the United States, 113–114; and education, 117, 118–126, 139, 162; students of, 118, 122; as a medium of instruction, 122–123. SEE ALSO Alemannic; Amana German; American German; American German press; Bible German; Eastphalian dialect; Hanoverian Low German; High German; Holstein dialect; Hutterite German; Iowa German; Low German; Mennonite German; Mennonite Low German; Palatine dialect, northern; Pennsylvania German; Pomeranian German; Standard German; Swabian; Swiss German (American); Virginia German; Wisconsin German
German langauge press. SEE American German press
German Linguistic Atlas: 141
Germans: settlement of Pennsylvania by, 15–18; migrations of, from Pennsylvania to Virginia, 59. SEE ALSO Americans, German; Franconian Germans; Wisconsin Germans
Germantown, Illinois: German folklore in, 162
Germantown, Pennsylvania: and the Ger-

man settlement of Pennsylvania, 15; and the origins of Pennsylvania Germans, 35

Germany: and dialect studies, 4–5, 6; immigration to the United States from, 7, 17–18, 46–47, 62, 107–110 *passim*; and the origins of Pennsylvania German folklore, 98–99, 100; and American German literature, 111; and German language in education, 119, 121, 140, 168, 173; study of American German in, 134, 135, 139, 140, 144

Gezwitscher: and Pennsylvania German, 82

Gibbons, Phebe Earle: and Pennsylvania Germans, 70

Gilbert, Glenn G.: on Texas German, 3; on dialect differentiations, 7; and structural descriptions of American German, 9–10; and *Atlas of Texas German*, 114; on designing teaching materials, 172

Gilbert, Russell W.: and Pennsylvania German language and culture, 76

Gillespie County, Texas: 109, 157

Gilliéron, Jules: and training of fieldworkers, 133

Gladfelder, Millard E.: 154

Glassie, Henry: 86

Görzen, Jakob W.: and dialectology, 9

Goschenhoppen area: folksong research in, 87

Goschenhoppen Historians: 85, 87

The Goschenhoppen Region: 86

Graebner, August L.: 117

Green County, Wisconsin: Swiss German in, 52

Green Lake County, Wisconsin: percentage of Germans in, 49

Grimm, Alfred: 117

Grimm's law: 4

Grundsow Lodges: and Pennsylvania German folklore, 91, 92–93, 98.

A Guide for Collectors of Oral Traditions and Folk Cultural Material in Pennsylvania: 86

Gumperz, John J.: 9–10

Haldeman, Samuel Stehman: and Pennsylvania German, 3, 14, 72; and dialectology, 9

Halifax, Nova Scotia: German immigration to, 158

Halle, Morris: 11

Hamburg Township, Wisconsin: German language in, 50

Hanover, Province of: immigrants to Wisconsin from, 51

Hanoverian Low German: English influence on, in Wisconsin, 53; studies of, 56

"Hansjörg": 99

Harbaugh, Henry: 74, 81

Haugen, Einar: and Norwegian in the United States, 43; and German in Wisconsin, 54; and bilingualism, 131; and American German linguistic data, 143, 152

Hausman, Ruth L.: 87

Hays, H. M.: 9

Haysville, Indiana: German language in, 162

Heavenly Recruit Association: and Pennsylvania German folksong research, 89

Hegins Valley. SEE Lylens Valley

Heidelberg, Pennsylvania: 148

Helffrich, William A.: and American German literature, 116

Heller, Otto: and German in education, 120

HemisFair (1968): and the Institute of Texan Cultures, 141

Henry Harbaugh, Pennsylvania Dutchman: 81

Herold (Milwaukee, Wisconsin): 49

Der Herold der Wahrheit: 157–158

Hershey, Pennsylvania: and Pennsylvania German folklore, 92

Hesse: emigration from, to Pennsylvania, 18

High German: and Standard German in Wisconsin, 53; and the breakdown of Pennsylvania German folk culture, 97; written, in the United States, 115–116, 118, 157; and informant interviews, 132; and the value of recording religious services, 150

Historical Linguistics: 5

Historic Scharfferstown: 85

Hoffman, Walter J.: 14, 84

Holland, Michigan: bilingual education in, 166

Holstein: immigrants to Wisconsin from, 51
Holstein dialect: preservation of, in Wisconsin, 52
Holtzman, Jerome: 9
Horne, A. R.: and dialectology, 9; and the study of Pennsylvania German, 14, 154
Hostetler, John A.: 87, 97
Hufford, David S.: 86
Hughes, Everett Cherington: and German in education, 119
Hutterite German: 10
Hutterites: and bilingual education, 126; and linguistic atlases, 127; value of studying the religious services of, 151
"The Hymns of the Amish Ausbund in Philological and Literary Perspective": 88

ideological literature: American German, 111
Illinois: spread of Pennsylvania Germans into, 16; German concentrations in, 17; number of studies of German in, 43; number of German immigrants in, 45
immigration. SEE migrations
Indiana: Swiss German in, 10; spread of Pennsylvania Germans into, 16; German concentrations in, 17; Pennsylvania German speech islands in, 60; folklore in, 162
Indian languages: and education, 126, 165; and recording of language data, 138; Mexican government policy toward, 171. SEE ALSO Navajo language
Indians: and bilingual education, 172
Industry, Austin County, Texas: 110
informant selection: importance of, 131–132, 133, 161
Die Inshurans Bissnes: and dialect plays, 93
Institute of Texan Cultures: 141–142
Institut für Deutsche Sprache: 144
Iobst, Clarence F.: 82
Iowa: German dialect differentiation in, 7; Low Saxon German in, 10; spread of Pennsylvania Germans into, 16; German concentrations in, 17; studies

of German in, 43. SEE ALSO Amana German
Ira, Alfred (pseudonym). SEE Grimm, Alfred
Ireland: bilingualism in, 175
Israel: bilingualism in, 175
Italian language: 108

Jackson, George Pullen: 88
Jamaica: 130
John, Vera: and bilingual education, 164

Kaerricheleit: 89
Kaerriche-Weise: 90
Kansas: studies of German in, 43; German language in, 63, 129; settlements of Pennsylvania Germans in, 71; German-speaking Russian immigrants to, 108; German language education in, 123; linguistic informants in, 152
Kanzeldeutsch: 151
Kauffman, Henry J.: 76, 82
Kehlenbeck, Alfred P.: 9–10, 67
Kenkel, Frederick Philip: 117
Die Kerenzer Mundart des Kantons Glarus: 3–4
Kernlieder: 94–95
Keyser, Alan G.: and Pennsylvania German folksong research, 87
Keyser, Samuel J.: and generative grammar, 11; and linguistic geography, 131
Kieffer, Elizabeth Clarke: 81
Kirchenleute. SEE Kaerricheleit
Kirchliche Volkskunde: 97–98
Kishacoquillas Valley, Mifflin County, Pennsylvania: 88
Kitchener, Ontario: as area of resettlement, 7
Kloss, Heinz: and the study of Pennsylvania German language and culture, 14, 85; and Pennsylvania German radio, 94; atlas of German speech islands by, 113, 128; on written German in Texas, 157
Knortz, Karl: 85
Kohl, Johann Georg: 70, 158
Korson, George: 81, 86–87, 88, 91
Kranzmeyer, Eberhard: 6
Kratz, Henry: and structural descriptions of American German, 9–10
Kriebel, Howard Wiegner: 80

Kulp, Clarence, Jr.: 87, 90
Kurath, Hans: and generative grammar,
11; and linguistic geography, 130, 131;
and the training of fieldworkers, 133;
and securing the life histories of informants, 152
Kutztown, Pennsylvania: and Pennsylvania German folklore, 92; local place
names near, 148; *The Pennsylvania
German Manual* published in, 154
Kyger, M. Ellsworth: 82

Labov, William: and sociolinguistics, 6,
131; and informant interviews, 132;
and sampling, 132; and theoretical
linguistics, 133
LaCrosse, Wisconsin: German-language
press in, 49
Lambert, Marcus Bachman: 14, 19, 80
Lancaster, Pennsylvania: dialect radio
programs from, 93
Lancaster County, Pennsylvania: as a
boundary of German concentration, 17;
linguistic geography of, 21–23, 25–26,
28–29, 31; and complex distributions
of lexical differences, 32, 33, 34, 35;
and the origins of Pennsylvania German, 36; dialect of, 60–64; migrations
to Virginia from, 62; study of German
language and culture in, 85; and the
breakdown of Pennsylvania German
folk culture, 97; place name pronunciations, 148–149
Lancaster Rifle Accessories: 82
Landis, George Diller: 82
Landis, Henry Kinzer: 80, 82
langsame Weisen: 88
Later Poems (John Birmelin): 82
Latin America: students from, 125; and
bilingual education, 167, 174, 175
Lattwaerrick. SEE Applebutter Boilings
*Lautbibliothek der Europäischen Sprach-
en und Mundarten*: 56
Laval University: study of bilingualism
at, 131
Leach, MacEdward: 86
Learned, Marion Dexter: and dialectol-
ogy, 9; and Pennsylvania German, 14,
72–73, 74
Lebanon: foreign language instruction
in, 123

Lebanon, Pennsylvania: dialect radio programs from, 93; and eradication of
Pennsylvania German, 155
Lebanon County, Pennsylvania: linguistic
geography of, 21–23, 26, 29, 31; study
of German culture in, 85; population
of, 155
Lee County, Texas: Germans in, 174
Lehigh County, Pennsylvania: linguistic
geography of, 21–32; and complex dis-
tributions of lexical differences, 32–
33, 34; and origins of Pennsylvania
German, 35–36; dialect of, compared
with Virginia German, 60–62; and
place name pronunciations, 148
Lehmann, Winfred: 5
Lehn, Walter: 9–10
Levi, Kate Everest: 51–52
*Lewis Miller, Pennsylvania German Folk
Artist*: 82
*Lexical Differences between Four Penn-
sylvania German Regions*: 82
lexicography: dialect, 130; limited na-
ture of, 145
liars' contests: 91, 94
Library of Congress: 86
Lick, David E.: 80
Die Lieder der Wiedertäufer: 88
Liegner Matche. SEE liars' contests
linguistic atlases. SEE atlases, linguistic
Linguistic Atlas of New England: 133,
152
*Linguistic Atlas of Pennsylvania Ger-
man*: 60–64
Linguistic Atlas of Rumania: 131
Linguistic Atlas of the United States: 5
"Linguistic Atlas of the United States
and Canada": 135, 136, 141
linguistic change: and Virginia German,
69. SEE ALSO sound change
linguistic geography: and Georg Wenker,
4; and linguistic laws, 4; place of, in
the humanities, 4; and Neogrammarian
doctrine, 4; confusion of, with dialectology, 5; and study of German, 130,
131–132; and sampling, 132; limita-
tions of, 145
linguistics: and Neogrammarian doctrine,
4; and dialect studies, 6; and folklore,
142, 148, 160–161; and the recording
of local place names, 148–149

Linguistic Variants in the Pennsylvania German Region: 82
Lippe-Detmold: immigrants to Wisconsin from, 51, 52
literarische Umschrift: 137
literature. SEE American German Press; English-language press; ideological literature; newspapers; nonfiction; periodicals; plays, dialect; poetry
Livingston, John H.: 112
Lochemes, Michael J.: as an American German author, 117
Lorraine: emigration from, to Pennsylvania, 18
Louisiana: and the "German Coast" 109; and bilingual education, 165, 166
Louw, Stephanus Andreas: 134
Low German: and Standard German in Wisconsin, 51, 53, 54; and Wisconsin German Questionnaire, 55–56; and English in Wisconsin, 56; front-rounded vowels in, 67; and informant/interviewer relations, 161; and folklore traditions, 162. SEE ALSO Hanoverian Low German; Mennonite Low German; Pomeranian German; Sauk County Low German
Low German Mennonites. SEE Mennonites, Low German
Low Germans: in Brenham, Texas, 162
Low Saxon German. SEE American Low Saxon German
Lunenburg County, Nova Scotia: bilingualism in, and dialectology, 7; German immigration to, 158
Lutheran Church: and Germans in Wisconsin, 51; and Pennsylvania German language and culture, 74, 97; *Kaerriche-Weise* of, 90; dialect services in, 94, 150; and Germans in New Amsterdam, 109; and higher education, 112; and the survival of German as a spoken language, 113; in Brenham, Texas, 162; in Haysville, Indiana, 162
Lutherans: and the preservation of German in Wisconsin, 50; Freistadt, 56; Old, 111, 127; Missouri Synod, 113, 122; American German authors among, 117
Luxemburg: immigrants to Wisconsin

from, 51–52; foreign language instruction in, 123
Lykens Valley: bilingual folksingers in, 100–101

McDavid, Raven I., Jr.: and sociolinguistics, 6, 131; and generative grammar, 11; and linguistic geography, 130, 131
Mackey, William: and bilingualism, 131
Madison, Wisconsin: 137
Maeddedischt-Weise: 90
magazines. SEE periodicals
Mahantongo Valley: folksongs of, 87; bilingualism in, 100–101
Maine: German immigrants in, 109; bilingual education in, 125, 165–166
Main River: 18
Mang, Lawrence H.: and dialectology, 9
Manheim, Pennsylvania: 148–149
Manitowoc, Wisconsin: German-American culture in, 50, 51; Standard German in, 51; the influence of German on English around, 56
Mannhardt-Festschrift (1958): 114
Mannhein, Germany: 148–149
Marathon County, Wisconsin: 50
Marburg, West Germany: dialectology collections at, 130; and lack of funds for linguistic studies, 139; as possible depository of American German data, 139; and German Linguistic Atlas, 141; and *Institut für Deutsche Sprache*, 144
Mariah Hill, Indiana: German folklore in, 162
Maryland: Pennsylvania Germans in, 15, 71; smaller German concentrations in, 17; German language and culture in, 86; religious sectarianism in, 89; changes of German surnames in, 149
Massachusetts Institute of Technology: and bilingual education, 125, 167
Mecklenburg, Germany: immigrants to Wisconsin from, 51
Mennischte-Weise: 90
Mennonite German: dialect differentiations of, 7
Mennonite, Low German: European loan words in, 8; state of the study of, 10;

article on, 143; and teaching materials, 172–173

Mennonites: Prussian, 6, 7; and Pennsylvania German, 16, 36, 37, 60; secondary settlements of, 60, 62, 63; and Pennsylvania German folksong research, 88, 90; United, 89
—, Old Order: and Pennsylvania German folksong research, 90; and the breakdown of Pennsylvania German culture, 97, 98; and spoken German, 114, 151; church schools among, 123; and linguistic atlases, 127

Mercer, Henry C.: 84–85

Mercer Museum: 84

Methodists, German: folksong research among, 88; and dialect church services, 94; and American German religious publications, 111

Methodist Church: and Pennsylvania German religious sectarianism, 89; *Maeddedischt-Weise* of, 90. SEE ALSO United Methodist Church

Mexican Americans. SEE Latin Americans

Mexico: resettlement of Prussian Mennonites in, 7; early German settlement in, 110; and bilingualism, 125, 171

Meynen, Emil: 85

Michigan: and bilingual education, 126, 168

microfilm: and dissemination of linguistic data, 137

Midwest: and the comparison of American German dialects, 63; secondary settlements of Pennsylvania German in, 71; migrations to, 81–82; and Pennsylvania German folksong research, 91; German FLES in, 121–122; German religious services in, 151

Mierau, Eric: 9–10

Mifflin County, Pennsylvania: as a boundary of German concentration, 17; folksong research in, 88

migrations: 81–82

Miller, Cora: 9–10

Miller, Daniel: 14

Miller, Lewis. SEE *Lewis Miller, Pennsylvania German Folk Artist*

Millersville State College: 76

Milnes, Humphrey: 9–10

Milwaukee, Wisconsin: German-language press in, 49; and preservation of German in Wisconsin, 50, 51; American-German culture in, 51; study of German in, 55; German as a spoken language in, 113; German FLES in, 121–122

Minnesota: survival of German language in, 129

Mississippi: German immigrants in, 109

Moelleken, Wolfgang W.: on dialect differentiations, 7; and *Deutches Spracharchiv*, 138; on Mexican Mennonite Low German, 143

Moll, Lloyd A. L.: 82

Montgomery County, Pennsylvania: as part of the eastern region of Pennsylvania German, 21; and complex distributions of lexical differences of Pennsylvania German, 34; and the origins of Pennsylvania German, 35, 36; the study of German language and culture in, 85; dialect names for residents of areas of, 149

Of Months and Days: 82

Moravians: folklore of, 84; genealogies of, in America, 154

Morgantown, West Virginia: 124

Morning Call (Allentown, Penn.): 74–75

Most, Johannes: 111

Moulton, William: and lingustic theory, 6

Muhlenberg College: 74–75

Die Mundarten Bayerns: 3

Münster, Germany: dialectology collections at, 130; and *Deutsches Spracharchiv*, 137, 138, 140, 144

Nachklänge germanischen Glaubens und Brauchs in Amerika: Ein Beitrag zur Volkskunde: 85

Nassau Germans (Texas): 10

National Carl Schurz Association: and the study of American German, 139; and German teaching in the United States, 139, 176, 177; and bilingual schools, 178. SEE ALSO Carl Schurz Memorial Foundation

National Museum of Canada: 143

Navajo language: and bilingual education, 126, 165, 168

Nebraska: and Pennsylvania German folksong research, 90
Neogrammarian movement: 4
Netherlanders: 109
New Brunswick: and bilingual education, 165
Newell, William Wells: 71
New England: poetry from, 71; and bilingual education, 125, 166
New Guinea: and German/English contact, 130
New Mexico: immigrants in, 109
New Orleans: and bilingual schools, 165
newspapers, German-language: in Wisconsin, 49, 56; and the origins of Pennsylvania German folk culture, 99; and the distribution of German speakers, 109. SEE ALSO American German press
New Sweden: German as an official language of, 109
New York: German immigrants in, 45, 109; German language school in, 126; English dialects in, 133
New Zealand: teaching of German in, 117; and German/English contact, 130
Nitzsche, George E.: 82
nonfiction: by German Americans, 110–111
Northampton County, Pennsylvania: 17
North Dakota: 108. SEE ALSO Dakotas
Northumberland County, Pennsylvania: as a boundary of German concentration, 17; linguistic geography of, 21–26, 28–30; and complex distributions of lexical differences, 33; folksong research in, 87
Norwegian language: 43, 152
Nova Scotia: and folklore research, 101, 158–159; German immigration to, 158

Oheim, Georg: and American German literature, 116
Ohio: Swiss Germans in, 10; settlements of Pennsylvania Germans in, 16, 17, 60, 63, 71; German immigrants in, 45
Oklahoma: German in, 63
Old Lutherans. SEE Lutherans, Old
Old Order Amish. SEE Amish, Old Order
The Old Order Amish of Lancaster County: 80

Old Order Dunkards. SEE Dunkards, Old Order
Old Order Mennonites. SEE Mennonites, Old Order
Old Order River Brethren. SEE Brethren; River Brethren, Old Order
Old World. SEE Europe
Olson, May E.: 109, 110
O'Neil, Wayne A.: 11
Ontario, Canada: and German-English bilingualism, 8; settlements of Pennsylvania Germans in, 17, 71; and folklore research, 71; religious sectarianism in, 89
Örtel, Maximilian: 111
Oswald, Victor A., Jr.: 9–10
Owens, J. G.: 84
Ozaukee County, Wisconsin: preservation of German in, 50

Pacific Northwest: 138
PADS: 143
Palatinate: 17, 18, 149
Palatine German, American: in Canada, 8; study of, 10
Palatines: 36
Papa Gernet. SEE Brown, Willy
Paraguay: German language in, 110
parochial schools. SEE schools, parochial
Pattison-Delamater campaign: 87
'S Pennsylfawnisch Deitsch Eck: 74–75
Pennsylvania: German population of, late 1700's, 15; German settlement of, 15–18; peak use of German in, 16–17; area of German concentration in, 17; and secondary settlements of Pennsylvania German, 18, 58, 59, 71; number of German immigrants in, 45; dialect differences in, 55; as original locus of Pennsylvania German culture, 71; German poetry in, 71; folklore research in, 71, 158–159; religion in, 89, 150; foreign-language education in, 124, 126; survival of German language in, 129; local place names in, 148; family history in, 151–154
Pennsylvania, Commonwealth of: and the study of Pennsylvania German language and culture, 86
Pennsylvania Dutch. SEE Pennsylvania German

Pennsylvania Dutch: A Dialect of South German with an Infusion of English: 14, 72
"Pennsylvania Dutch," and Other Essays: 70
Pennsylvania Dutch Days: 92
Pennsylvania Dutch Dialect Writings and Their Writers: 80
Pennsylvania Dutch folk festivals: 92
Pennsylvania Dutch Folklore Center: 75. SEE ALSO Pennsylvania Folklife Society
Pennsylvania Dutch Folksongs: 86
The Pennsylvania Dutchman: 75. SEE ALSO *Pennsylvania Folklife*
Pennsylvania Folklife: 75, 154
Pennsylvania Folklife Society: 75, 85, 87. SEE ALSO Pennsylvania Dutch Folklore Center
Pennsylvania Folklore Society: 84
Pennsylvania German: Haldeman's treatment of, 3; and bilingualism, 7, 149, 154–155, 159, 173; and archaic English, 7–8; studies of, 10, 14, 43; peak use of, 16–17; secondary settlements of, 16–17, 59–60; development of, 18–20, 35–36; linguistic geography of, 19–32, 35–37; and complex distributions of lexical differences, 32–35; and a comprehensive description of German in the United States, 43–45; and linguistic atlases, 56, 114; compared to other American German areas, 60–64; no front-rounded vowels in, 64; *Buschdeutsch* as a name for, 70, 158; cultural areas of, 71; study of, by academic institutions, 72–76; and folk culture, 101; anthologies of, 118; problem of disseminating data about, 136; and the Wisconsin Historical Society, 141; and dialect names, 149; euphemisms in, 150; attitudes of speakers of, toward, 154–156; attempts to eradicate, 155–156; in family letters, 156–157, 158
Pennsylvania German Barns: 82
Pennsylvania German Bookplates: A Study: 80–81
Pennsylvania German Folk Art: An Interpretation: 82
Pennsylvania German Folk Festival: 91
Pennsylvania German Folklore: An Interpretation: 82
Pennsylvania German Folklore Society: 73, 75, 76, 81–82. SEE ALSO Pennsylvania German Society
Pennsylvania German Folk Tales, Legends, Once-upon-a-Time Stories, Maxims, and Sayings Spoken in the Dialect Popularly Known as Pennsylvania Dutch: 80
Pennsylvania German Illuminated Manuscripts: 80
The Pennsylvania German Manual: 154–155
"Pennsylvania German Riddles and Nursery Rhymes": 84
"Pennsylvania Germans" (J. G. Owens): 84
Pennsylvania Germans: and linguistic behavior, 6–7; dialect differentiation among, 7; origins of, 7, 17–18, 35; secondary settlements by, 15, 16, 59–60; early settlement by, 15–18; discovery of, in the nineteenth century, 70–71; breakdown of the folk culture of, 95–98, 161; and German language literature, 110, 115–116; the neglect of higher education by, 112; place-name pronunciation of, 149; genealogical myth of, 153; pronunciation of English by, 154–155; similarity of, to Nova Scotian Germans, 158; preservation of Catholic folklore traditions by, 163
The Pennsylvania Germans of the Shenandoah Valley: 82
Pennsylvania German Society: and the study of Pennsylvania German folk culture, 76–81, 84; and ethnic societies in America, 83–84. SEE ALSO Pennsylvania German Folklore Society
Pennsylvania German Tombstones: A Study in Folk Art: 82
Pennsylvania German Verse: 80
Pennsylvania High German: 101, 150
Pennsylvania Historical and Museum Commission: 86
Pennsylvania Songs and Legends: 86–87, 88
Pennsylvania Spirituals: 87
Pennsylvania State University: 76
Pequea Creek: Swiss settlement along, 36

periodicals: and German in Wisconsin, 49; and American German literature, 115. SEE ALSO newspapers
Peru: German language in, 110
Philadelphia, Pennsylvania: predominance of non-Germans in, in late 1700's, 15; and the origins of Pennsylvania German, 35, 36; and the discovery of the Pennsylvania Germans, 71; folksong research in the area of, 87; American Council on German Studies in, 126; and the teaching of German in the United States, 139
plain sectarians: folksong research among, 87
Plant Names and Plant Lore among the Pennsylvania Germans: 80
plays, dialect: and Pennsylvania German folklore, 91, 93
PMLA: 143
Pochmann, Henry A.: 85
poetry: of Pennsylvania Germans, 71
Polish language: 107, 126, 166
political literature. SEE ideological literature
Pomerania: immigrants to Wisconsin from, 51, 52
Pomeranian German: in Wisconsin, 50, 52, 56
Pop, Sever: on dialectology and dialect geography, 5; and the study of German language in the United States, 130; and informant selection, 131–132
Portuguese language: and bilingual education, 165
Posen: immigrants to Wisconsin from, 51, 52
Potomac River: German migrations across, 59
prairie states: German speaking Russian immigrants to, 108
Presbyterians. SEE Scotch-Irish Presbyterians
press. SEE American German press; English-language press
Price, Utah: German-language education in, 124
Princeton Theological Seminary: 154
"Problems of Linguistic Research Among Scandinavian Immigrants in America": 54–57

Pronunciation of English in the Atlantic States: 11
Protestant churches: and German in Wisconsin, 52; and German as an indigenous American language, 113; and the preservation of folklore, 162–163
Protestantism, American: 97
Protestant literature: in German in the United States, 111
Proverbs of the Pennsylvania Germans: 73
Prussia: immigrants to Wisconsin from, 51, 52
Prussian Mennonites. SEE Mennonites, Prussian
psycholinguistics: 131
Puerto Rico: 108, 125
Pumpernickle Bill. SEE Troxell, William S.

Quebec, Canada: and bilingualism, 125, 131, 165, 166

radio programs, dialect: 91, 93–94
Rauch, Edward H.: 14
Raunick, Selma Metzenthin: 116
Reading, Pennsylvania: and the origins of Pennsylvania German, 36; dialect radio at, 93–94; American German literature in, 116
The Red Hills: A Record of Good Old Days Outdoors and In, With Things Pennsylvania Dutch: 73–74
Reed, Carroll E.: and structural descriptions of American German, 9–10; and the study of Pennsylvania German, 14, 19, 20, 60–64, 114; German speech islands, 129; questionnaire of, 161
Reed, David: 136
Reformed Church: and American German folk culture, 74, 90, 94, 97, 150
Regina, Saskatchewan: 8
Reichard, Harry Hess: 74, 80, 93
Reinert, Guy F.: 82
religion: and German immigration to Wisconsin, 52; and spoken German in Virginia, 59; and Pennsylvania German folk culture, 74, 95–96, 97–98; and the Pennsylvania German Society, 80; studies of, among the Pennsylvania Germans, 82; and the "Atlas of

Nineteenth-Century German Settlements in the United States," 128. SEE ALSO churches; songs, religious
religiöse Volkskunde: 97–98
religious groups: and German in the United States, 43–45; and the breakdown of Pennsylvania German culture, 98; literature of, 111; services of, in German, 150
reunions: among Pennsylvania Germans, 153–154
revivalism. *See* Anglo-American revivalism
Reyes, Clara: as an American German author, 116
Rhenish Palatinate. *See* Palatinate, Rhenish
Rhenish Prussia: immigrants to Wisconsin from, 51–52
Rhine area: immigration to Nova Scotia from, 158
Rhineland: emigration from, to Pennsylvania, 17, 18; disappearance of the dialect of, in Wisconsin, 52
Rice University: securing life histories of German Americans at, 152
River Brethren: value of studying the German religious singing of, 151
River Brethren, Old Order: folksong research among, 87
Rockingham County, Virginia: as an area of resettlement, 7; and the supposed extinction of Virginia German, 59
Roman Catholic Church: and the preservation of German in Wisconsin, 52; and American German religious publications, 111; and the neglect of German American higher education, 112; and the survival of spoken German, 113; and the preservation of folklore, 162–163
Roman Catholic Irish: and the Scotch-Irish Presbyterians, 83
Roman Catholics: and written American German, 117, 126
Romanticism: and the origins of dialectology, 3–4
" 'S Rote Gaisbort Schumacher": 93–94
Rothensteiner, Johannes: 117
Rumania: and informant selection, 132;

and non-English languages in the United States, 171
Rummel, Clara: 116
Rupp, William J.: 80
rural areas: predominance of Germans in, in Pennsylvania, 15; and German dialects in Wisconsin, 51, 113, 114, 119, 129; and German in education, 119
Rush, Benjamin: 15, 72
Russian language: loan words from, in American German, 8; and bilingual education, 177
Russian-German brotherhoods: 90
Russian immigrants: 108, 109

St. Agatha, Maine: bilingual schooling in, 125
St. Louis, Missouri: German as a spoken language in, 113; "South Side Dutch" of, 114; German FLES in, 121–122
San Antonio, Texas: 141, 178
Sapon, Stanley: 132
Saporta, Sol: 131
Saskatchewan, Canada: 10
Sauk County, Wisconsin: Eastphalian dialect in, 52
Sauk County Low German: English influence on, 53
Saxony: immigrants to Wisconsin from, 51–52
Schach, Paul: 14
Schantz, "Parre": 74, 78
Schleswig: 168
Schleswig-Holstein: 174
Schmeller, Johannes: 3
schools: and Pennsylvania German, 72–76; bilingualism in, 127, 164–178. SEE ALSO education
—, parochial: Lutheran, 51, 52; and bilingual education, 125; Amish, 159–160
Schreiber, William I.: 88
Schteddelrutsch: and dialect plays, 93
Schultz, Arthur R.: 85
Schuylkill County: linguistic geography of, 21, 23–26, 28–31; and complex distributions of lexical differences, 33, 34; folksong research in, 87; and dialect names, 149
Schuylkill River: and the regions of

Pennsylvania German, 21, 23, 26; founding of Reading, Pennsylvania on, 36
The Schwenkfelders in Pennsylvania: 80
Scotch-Irish: 15–16, 59, 100
Scotch-Irish Presbyterians: 83
Seebote (Milwaukee, Wisconsin): 49
Seidensticker, Oswald: 72, 73–74
Seifert, Lester W. J.: and structural descriptions of American German, 9–10; and Pennsylvania German, 14, 19, 20, 60–64, 82, 114; and German in Wisconsin, 55, 56, 114; atlases of, 114, 129; and problem of disseminating linguistic data, 136; and Wisconsin Historical Society, 141; questionnaire of, 161
Selzer, Barbara: 9–10
sermon German: 150
Sheboygan, Wisconsin: 49, 51
Shelley, Donald A.: 82
Shenandoah County, Virginia: 59
Shenandoah Valley: secondary settlements of Pennsylvania Germans in, 15, 60, 71; persistence of German in, 58–59; and folklore research, 71
Shoemaker, Alfred L.: and dialectology, 9; and the study of Pennsylvania German folk culture, 74, 75, 87, 110; dialect radio program of, 93–94
Short Bill (California): and bilingual education, 167
Shuffler, Henderson: 141
Siebenbürger Sachsen immigrants: 114
Simmel, Georg: 119
Sing and Dance with the Pennsylvania Dutch: 87
Slavic churches: 91
Smith, Elmer Lewis: 82
Snyder, G. Gilbert: 93
Snyder County, Pennsylvania: linguistic geography of, 21, 23–25, 28–29; and complex distributions of lexical differences, 33
social dialectology. SEE sociolinguistics
social structures: and dialectology, 5–6
sociolinguistics: study of, recommended, 131; and bilingualism, 131, 144
"Some Pennsylvania German Lore": 84
songs, religious: Pennsylvania German, research in, 87, 88–91, effect of, on

Pennsylvania German folksongs, 89; value of studying, 151. SEE ALSO folksongs, Pennsylvania German
Songs Along the Mahantongo: 87, 99
sound change: in Virginia German, 64–69
South Dakota. SEE Dakotas, the
Soviet Union. SEE Russia
Spanish Americans. SEE Latin Americans
Spanish language: and bilingualism in Texas, 55, 143–144; as an immigrant language compared to German, 108; students of, 118, 122; in Virginia, 124; and Elbert Covell College, 124–125; and bilingual education, 125, 126, 165, 166, 167, 168, 178; as a challenge to English in the United States, 171; and minority group assimilation, 172; social disadvantages of speakers of, 174; and bilingualism in Dade County, Florida, 177
speech islands: value of the study of, 7
spelling bees, dialect: 91, 94
spirituals. SEE songs, religious
Springer, Nelson P.: 88
Springer, Otto: 14, 72
Standard English. SEE English, Standard
Standard German: and Pennsylvania German, 18, 29, 36–37, 89; and German in Wisconsin, 50–51, 53–54; in Virginia, 59; and front-rounded vowels, 67; in Texas, 67, 178; and Pennsylvania German folksongs, 89; orthography of, 137; and bilingual education, 173, 177; the teaching of, in Texas, 173, 178
Starr, Frederick: 84
Staunton, Virginia: 59
Stewart, John G.: 82
Stiefel, Otto A.: 112
Stine, Clyde: 76
Stoudt, John Baer: 80, 84
Stoudt, John Joseph: 71, 82
"The Strange Music of the Old Order Amish": 88
Strasburg Township, Lancaster County, Pennsylvania: 73
Strubberg, Friedrich: 158
structural analysis: and dialectology, 5
structural linguistics. SEE linguistics, structural

Sugar Grove, Pendleton County, West Virginia: American German in, 59, 60–62, 63
Sunbury, Pennsylvania: and dialect radio, 93
Susquehanna River: 15–16, 28
Susquehanna University: 76
Swabian German: in Michigan, 10; and development of Pennsylvania German, 18–20
Swedes: 109
Swiss German (American): state of the study of, 10; preservation of, in Wisconsin, 52; studies of, 56
Swiss immigrants: and the origins of Pennsylvania German, 36, 37; and front-rounded vowels, 64, 65; in the Dayton, Virginia, German community, 64–65
Switzerland: German dialects of, 6; German-speaking immigrants from, 18, 47, 52, 62, 108; and origins of Pennsylvania German folklore, 99; non-German-speaking immigrants from, 108

Tanzania: and German/English contact, 130
tape recorder: and linguistic interviews, 134; and dissemination of linguistic data, 136–137, 138; and folklore material, 142
Temple University: 154
Texas: and bilingualism, 55, 143–144; front-rounded vowels in, 67; early German immigrants in, 109; German descent in, 122; and bilingual education, 122, 126, 167–168, 175, 178; survival of German language in, 129; and the Institute of Texan Cultures, 141–142; German religious services in, 151; linguistic informants in, 152; written German in, 157
Texas German: Glenn Gilbert's treatment of, 3; dialect differentiation of, 7; study of, 10, 43; and a comprehensive description of American German, 43–45; and linguistic atlases, 56, 114; attempts to eradicate, 156; German novels as a source for data on, 158;

bilingual influence on, 159; and German teaching, 172–173, 178
Texas Germans: and German-language literature, 115, 116; genealogical myth of, 152; and the demand for bilingual schools, 174; social position of, 174. SEE ALSO Nassau Germans (Texas)
Transcriptions of Items from the Bethlehem Diary Relating to Early Celebrations of Christmas in Bethlehem, Pennsylvania: 82
Trexler, Benjamin F.: 116
trilingualism: in Wisconsin, 50–51; among the Amish, 101; and bilingual education, 177, 178
Troxell, William S.: 80, 86, 87, 91
Trubetzkoy, N. S.: 5
Tulpehocken Creek: 36
Twelvetide: 82

Ukraine: and Low German Mennonite, 8
Unfehlbare Wetterverse: 116
Unger, Claude W.: 80
Union churches: 150
Union County, Pennsylvania: 17
United Brethren. SEE Brethren, United
United Christians: 89
United Church. SEE Reformed Church
United Evangelicals: 89
United Mennonites. SEE Mennonites, United
United Methodist Church. SEE Evangelical United Brethren
United States: study of American German in, 43–45, 135; immigration from Germany to, 107–110; attitude toward family history in, 153; folklore study in, 160; bilingual education in, 168
United States Office of Education: 126, 164–165, 172
United Zion's Children: 89
University Microfilms: 137
urban areas: study of German in, 10, 55; predominance of non-Germans in, in Pennsylvania, 15, 16; Standard German in Wisconsin, 51; and the Versammlinge, 92; and the origins of Pennsylvania German folklore, 99; German as a spoken language in, 113, 114; German education in, 120

Van Buren, Maine: and bilingual education, 165–166
Venezuela: German language in, 110
Vermont: German immigrants in, 109
Verner, Karl: 4
Versammlinge: 76, 91, 92–93, 94, 98
Viereck, Wolfgang: 43
Vildomec, V.: 131
Virginia: migrations of Pennsylvania Germans into, 15, 59, 62; as the location of smaller German concentrations, 17; study of German language and culture in, 86; bilingual education in, 124, 166–167
Virginia Department of Education, Division of Research: 166–167
Virginia German: supposed extinction of, 59–60; and secondary settlements by Pennsylvania Germans, 59–60; compared to Pennsylvania German, 60–64; front-rounded vowels in, 63–68. SEE ALSO Dayton German
Volkswagenstiftung: 176
vowels, front-rounded: in Virginia German, 63–68

Walther, Hilde: 116
Washington County, Wisconsin: preservation of German in, 50
Watertown, Wisconsin: 50, 51
Wausau, Wisconsin: 50
Wayland, John Walter: 58–59
Waynesboro, Virginia: 59
Weber, Max: 119
Weinreich, Uriel: 5, 131
Weiser, Conrad: 36
Wenker, Georg: 4, 5, 139
Wenker's forty sentences: 5, 11
Westmorland County, England: 100
Westphalia: immigrants to Wisconsin from, 51
West Virginia: persistence of German in, 58–59; study of German language and culture in, 86
Weygandt, Cornelius: 73–74

Wiese, Herbert F.: 9–10
Wilson, H. Rex: 7
Winteler, Jost: 3–4
Wisconsin: German immigration to, 17, 45–49, 51–52, 108; German studies in, 43–45; German-language press in, 49; German language in, 49–54, 129; trilingualism in, 50–51; German FLES in, 121–122; and bilingual schools, 126; methods of questioning linguistic informants in, 153
Wisconsin German: development of, 51, 52–53, 57; atlas of, 114
Wisconsin Historical Society: 140, 141
Wiskonsin Banner: and German in Wisconsin, 49
Wolkan, Rudolf: 88
Womelsdorf, Pennsylvania: 36
Wood, Ralph C.: and Pennsylvania German language and culture, 74; and spoken German in the United States, 114; translations into Pennsylvania German by, 115
"Wordatlas of Pennsylvania German": 20, 22, 24, 25, 28, 32
A Working Bibliography for the Study of the Pennsylvania German Language and Its Sources: 72
Wörter und Sachen: 75
"Die Wunnernaas": and Pennsylvania German radio, 93
Württenberg: emigration from, to Pennsylvania, 18, 36

Yiddish: and structural dialectology, 5
Yoder, Don: and Pennsylvania German folk culture, 75, 87, 99, 100–101; and Pennsylvania German bilingualism, 100–101
Yoder, Joseph W.: 88
Yoder, Paul M.: 88
York County, Pennsylvania: 15, 17

Zagel, Hermann: 117
Ziegler, Charles Calvin: 82